AFRICA
in Modern Literature

MARTIN TUCKER is co-editor of *Modern British Literature* in the "Library of Literary Criticism" series, and editor of a new revised four-volume edition of *Moulton's Library of Literary Criticism of British and American Authors,* published in 1966. Now Associate Professor of English, Long Island University, he has contributed reviews and literary criticism to many leading publications.

AFRICA
in Modern Literature

A Survey of
Contemporary Writing in English

Martin Tucker

Frederick Ungar Publishing Co.
New York

The author is grateful for the cooperation of the following
in allowing the use of copyrighted material:
A Burnt-Out Case, The Viking Press, Inc.; *Aissa Saved,* Curtis
Brown Ltd.; *Allan's Wife,* A. P. Watt & Son; *A Wreath for Udomo,*
Alfred A. Knopf, Inc.; *Black Power,* Harper & Row, Publishers;
Britain and West Africa, Her Majesty's Stationery Office; *In a
Province,* William Morrow & Co., Inc.; *Journey Without Maps,*
William Heinemann Ltd., Laurence Pollinger Ltd., The Viking
Press, Inc.; *Red Strangers,* Chatto & Windus Ltd.; *The Crescent
Moon,* E. P. Dutton & Co., Inc.; *The Measure of My Days,*
Mrs. S. G. Millin, Abelard-Schuman Limited; *The People of South
Africa,* Mrs. S. G. Millin, Constable & Co. Ltd., Alfred A. Knopf, Inc.;
The Story of an African Farm, Hutchinson Publishing Group, Ltd.;
They Were Still Dancing, Holt, Rinehart & Winston, Inc.; *Things
Fall Apart,* William Heinemann Ltd., Ivan Obolensky, Inc.; *Turbott
Wolfe,* William Morrow & Co., Inc., The Hogarth Press, Ltd.

Printed in the United States of America

Library of Congress Catalog Card Number: 66-19472

To My Mother and Father

Foreword

This book was begun several years ago. At that time no work of criticism on literature by Africans writing in English had been published. Since then a few such works have appeared. I am indebted to these for the stimulation and encouragement they have given me in my own studies, although my opinions may at times be at variance with the views expressed by their distinguished authors. This study differs in scope from other works of literary criticism on African writing in that it is an attempt to survey literature about Africa written in English in the twentieth century, and thus treats American and English writers, as well as Africans, as an integral part of "African literature" as a whole. In this sense it is an international and comparative literature study.

I justify my approach, at least in part, by the fact that division by nationality and national group is only one way of understanding and abstracting the essence of a literature. In many cases the black and the white African are influenced by the same literary models and prone to the same social pressures. Peter Abrahams, the Cape Colored writer from South Africa, for example, is as much influenced by the English and American literary traditions as by a Pan-Africanism that stretches from Ghana to England to the United States.

Because so much of this literature is concerned with thematic material—and with the "image" of Africa—great emphasis has been given to prose writings, particularly the novel, in which social realism and commentary play an outstanding part. I have not treated poetry and drama as fully as the novel, since the novel offers a richer field for discussion. Indeed, creative fiction relating to Africa has been so prolific that some prose writings have had to be treated somewhat briefly, while others have had to be passed over in the interests of "immediate" relevance.

In an age where color, and nationalism attending on color, play such a major and often explosive role, certain selective terms are necessary. Some Africans object to the word "Kaffir," pointing out that Kaffir means "unbeliever" and thus is a pejorative label. Others object to the word "Bantu" because of its associations with the South African government's policies of *apartheid*. Few writers today use the term "Kaffir," yet Rider Haggard in the nineteenth century employed it indiscriminately in his idyllic descriptions of Zulu warriors. For the sake of clarity, the words "black," "white," and "Colored" have been utilized to pinpoint the authors of and characters in the works under discussion; the word "African" is also used to describe a black native of Africa, but not a white native of South Africa. The term "Colored," or "Cape Colored," is here depictive of only those people in South Africa descended from the marriage of Hottentot and European/Asian parents. Ultimately, when the color question is resolved, or becomes irrelevant, verbal distinctions of color also will become unnecessary, and a clearer distinction—by moral and political ethic—will emerge.

In the revision and expansion of my original manuscript, I have been aided by many people. It is impossible to thank each of them individually; I should, however, like to express my gratitude to a few. Ezekiel Mphahlele in his pioneer work of literary criticism, *The African Image,* was an early influence. Professor David H. Greene of New York University originally encouraged me to begin this work. Collin Gonze, formerly editor of *Africa Today,* accepted some of the material in different form for a series of essay-articles in that publication. Nancy Jeanne Schmidt kindly sent me a copy of her dissertation, "An Anthropological Analysis of Nigerian Fiction," whose text, while differing in scope from my own study, I was able to use for comparison with my own findings. My editor, Michael Levien, provided the eye of an eagle in matters of style and consistency of form, and the needle of an objective reader who required substantive "proof" for every generalization. I would also like to thank my sister, Mrs. Shirley Helfman, for her assistance in the typing and preparation of the manuscript for publication. Finally, I would like to express my appreciation to Long Island University for its concrete encouragement of this project.

M. T.

New York, 1967

Contents

ONE

Definitions and Difficulties

Consideration of African literature and literature about Africa by Western critics is a relatively new area of literary criticism. Fifty years ago no African literature was discussed in world literature encyclopedias, and certainly no courses in African literature were offered at Western universities. Today the situation has altogether changed. The new world literature encyclopedia now being prepared under the general editorship of W. Bernard Fleischmann [1] will afford coverage of African literature in native and adopted languages; furthermore, studies of African literature in English, French, German, and African languages may now be embarked upon in schools in the United States, Europe, and on the African continent. African literature is recognized as an essential element of world literature, and the African writer who feels culturally alienated from either the Western or Eastern world is now the exception rather than the rule.

---

[1] *Encyclopedia of World Literature in the 20th Century,* to be published in three volumes by Frederick Ungar Publishing Co., New York (Vol. I in 1967; Vols. II and III, 1968). The relevant entries will be: *Afrikaans Literature; Neo-African Literature;* and *South African Literature in English.*

Still it must be admitted—or at least the present writer will admit it—that African literature is a new and strange territory to many Americans. Because of its novelty and its unique qualities, African literature is much as Africa itself must have been to the white explorer and adventurer in the nineteenth century: a land full of discovery and charm, rich in native resources, and ready (depending on one's point of view) for modern exploitation. The Englishman today is more inclined to be familiar with African literature than the American, for a number of reasons. Africa has played an important role in English history, and many of the free nations of Africa, having once been British colonies, are now members of the Commonwealth; probably because of this affiliation, more Africans go to England to study than to the United States. The *Times Literary Supplement* of London publishes a Commonwealth Literature issue at least once a year, in which African literature, both in English and other languages, is prominently discussed. Not subject to a similar exposure, the average American, even among those who regularly read the literary journals, is by comparison an innocent about Africa.

It is natural, then, for an American to ask: "What is African literature." The search for a definition of African literature unearths other questions. Is African literature that body of work written by Africans or by writers of African descent? Or is it the literature created by writers throughout the world about the milieu, essence, and the thematic and psychic particularities of the African continent? Is African literature restricted to works written in a language native to the African continent, or can certain works of an Englishman like Joyce Cary and an American like Ernest Hemingway be considered a part of African literature, at least in a broad view? Questions such as these were raised at a conference of African writers held at Makerere University College, Kampala, Uganda, in 1962. The conclusions were certainly debatable (and in subsequent conferences are still being debated), but the general consensus was that "the essential elements of African literature were the African viewpoint . . . the moral values, the philosophy, and customs of African Society."[2]

If African literature is that literature that breathes the spirit of Africa and carries in its textbag the feel of the African continent, it follows that writers not born in Africa may be considered a part of that literature. Shakespeare writing on the Moor in *Othello* and *Titus Andronicus* may even be said to be a part of this vast African literature in its broadest sense. Naturally most critics will be aware that a sense of proportion determines all categories and classifications: African literature is distinguished by spiritual and psychic qualities as well as by mere geographic content and biography. African writers can probably best be characterized by four broad divisions:

1. The Westerner or other non-African writer who utilizes the subject matter of Africa in a language not native to the African continent.
2. The African writer, black or white, who utilizes the subject matter of Africa in a language native to the African continent.
3. The African writer who utilizes subject matter other than Africa, but who writes in a language native to the African continent.
4. The African writer who utilizes the subject matter of Africa, but who writes in a Western language that has, by custom, become part of the African means of communication.

Using this convenient outline it may be said that African literature "exists" in several languages: in English (Chinua Achebe, Joyce Cary, Cyprian Ekwensi, Graham Greene, Ernest Hemingway, Langston Hughes, Wole Soyinka, to name a few); in French (Bernard Dadié, Birago Diop, David Diop, André Gide, Joseph Kessel, Jean Lartéguy, Jean Malonga,

---

[2] Bloke Modisane, "Literary Scramble for Africa," in *West Africa*, No. 2352 (June 30, 1962), 716.

Ferdinand Oyono, Jean-Joseph Rabéarivelo); in German (Kurt Heuser, Janheinz Jahn); in Danish (Johannes Buchholtz); in native African languages (David Cranmer Theko Bereng, Thomas Mofolo, Samuel Yosia Ntara); in the English of South Africans (Nadine Gordimer, Sarah Gertrude Millin, Alan Paton); and in Afrikaans (Nuthall Fula, Ernst van Heerden).

Each of these "literatures" has its special characteristics, and within the overall context of creative literature issuing out of Africa each falls into a general pattern. For example, it can be said that four traditions are reflected in the modern novel in English about Africa. These traditions are dominantly romantic, psychological, satiric, and sociological. The writers who have played the greatest part in extending these influences are H. Rider Haggard, Joseph Conrad, Evelyn Waugh, Joyce Cary, William Plomer, and Alan Paton. A special case may be made for Olive Schreiner, whose work has influenced all later South African literature, but whose own novels are a development of the post-Victorian bleak humanism as represented in Thomas Hardy and Herbert Spencer. And these traditions are not so much exclusive as preeminent, and although they are not restricted to any one period, their dominance is found in certain specific decades.

The romantic, idealized portrait of the Noble Savage, which Rider Haggard and his literary descendants presented, enjoyed its greatest vogue at the end of the nineteenth and at the beginning of the twentieth century, but the vogue is still observable today in the fascination of Africa for the romantic, and what many black Africans call the neocolonialist, imagination of Westerners. These labels are applicable to those readers who hold that the blacks are charming, mysterious, wayward children of nature, an attitude that has resulted in such diverse fare as books and stories about Tarzan, Sheena (Queen of the Jungle), and even Othello, who is seen as an innocent black man trapped by the wily cunning of a white Renaissance plotter. The attitude is intimately connected with the spirit of primitivism, a spirit that has often animated anthropologists and historians as well as literary men in their love for the undefiled Noble Savage. Such primitivists hark back to the past for their ideal, and find their lost Garden of Eden in some historic moment centuries ago. These men may be termed "chronological primitivists." Other men find and have found their primitive ideal not in the prime moments of history but in the prime of contemporary life, in the jungles and forests of a timeless dream universe of their own making. This second kind of primitivist—often called a "cultural primitivist"—seeks a civilization that has not been infested with any of the mixed blessings of the modern industrialized world.

African historians also often divide their literature into such broad categories as "classical" and "contemporary," applying the term "classical" to literature embracing the folklore and history of a group of people, and the label "contemporary" to works depicting modern events and personalities. In practice, the "classical" tales often become hymns to the "pure" times of an African tribe before contact with European or Western man, while "contemporary" fiction devolves into a critical examination of the social, religious, and political forces dividing (or uniting) modern Africa. A recent example of "chronological primitivism" is the first novel of Hjalmar Thesen, a South African of Norwegian descent whose *The Echoing Cliffs* (New York, 1964) presents an idyllic state of primitive people destroyed by the more technologically advanced Bush people. Whatever the historical and literary merits of Hjalmar Thesen's tale, the milieu is that of a man yearning for the gloriously impossible past. Dreams of Eden, whether in Africa or elsewhere, do not recede, much less die away; they are the eternal, idealistic flickerings of mankind.

Africa, seen as an exotic and primitive land inhabited by Noble Savages, fascinated the English mind at least as early as the Elizabethan era. Thomas Underdowne's *The Ethiopian* (1587), based on Heliodorus, was perhaps the first full-length

English work in which an African had the leading role. Shakespeare's *Othello* represents in part the fascination with Africa that filled the court of Elizabeth I. The "philosophy" of the Noble Savage also had its adherents in Columbus, in his descriptions of the *beaux yeux* of the Caribbean Indians, and in Rousseau. If English decorum in the eighteenth century, under the rational guidance of neoclassic writers, tended to downgrade the Noble Savage, the romantic writers who followed them more than made up for any slights. Yet not all romantic writers saw in the savage the embodiment of a noble species. Hoxie Fairchild, an eminent scholar in the field, says that even among the romantic partisans of the savage, few were "at any time ready to swallow him whole." [3]

In the Victorian age the African became a stock figure in literature; undoubtedly part of his popularity was the result of interest created by David Livingstone in his works on South and Central Africa, by H. M. Stanley in his accounts of his Congo travels, and by Richard Burton in his re-creations of his journeys down the Nile and into Tanganyika and East Africa. Unfortunately, almost until the end of the nineteenth century, the bulk of novels in which Africans appear were written by second- and third-rate authors; it was not until the last twenty years of the century that novelists of stature like Rider Haggard, Joseph Conrad, and Olive Schreiner came into their own. The most popular subject with the minor novelists was the slave trade, and although most of them excoriated its evils, at the same time they tended to exploit this theme—for an ever-eager public—by recourse to sensationalism. In general, however, Victorian novelists were more realistic in describing the African than were earlier English writers, and most of them used the African scene as a theme for humanitarian social protest. Ironically, the only Victorian novelist of stature who

---

[3] Hoxie N. Fairchild, *The Noble Savage: A Study in Romantic Naturalism* (New York, 1928), p. 499.

wrote on Africa was a romanticist; and he, H. Rider Haggard, was to tip the literary scales back to an exotic primitivism. As early as 1896, he was bemoaning the Western invasion of Africa: "That country of which Allan tells his tales is now, for the most part, as well known and explored as the fields of Norfolk. All is changed." [4]

Rider Haggard's enormous popularity was achieved with the publication of his fifth novel, *King Solomon's Mines*, in 1885. All his later novels—and especially *She* (1887), *Jess* (1887), *Allan Quatermain* (1887), *Allan's Wife* (1889), and *Nada the Lily* (1892)—were read by a wide public. With the exception of his novels about Iceland and Egypt, the bulk of his fiction has for its theme the mysterious heart of black Africa, within whose setting the author used a familiar structural device: the quest. A white hunter seeks a lost, fascinating kingdom and civilization. In *King Solomon's Mines* Allan Quatermain, Sir Henry Curtis, and Captain John Good go in quest of the fabled Ophir, the storehouse of Solomon's treasures. In *She* these three explorers discover a kingdom in which the queen never grows old. In *Heu-Heu: or The Monster* (1924) Allan Quatermain seeks the worshippers of the devil-god Heu-Heu in the remotest part of Africa. In *Maiwa's Revenge* (1888) Allan discovers the evil kingdom of Wambi, and in *The Ancient Allan* (1920) Allan Quatermain, Sir Henry Curtis, and Captain Good set forth on an expedition into the interior of Africa in an attempt to discover what hitherto no other man has found. In their travels they discover a strange, beautiful land ruled by Sorais, Lady of the Night, and her elder sister Nyleptha.

Rider Haggard's tales are steeped in a primitive Africa, a country remote from the mundane progress of white, Western

---

[4] From a letter written in 1896 and later used in *Allan's Wife*. It is quoted by Lilian R. Haggard in *The Cloak That I Left* (London, 1951).

civilization. Although, as Susanne Howe says, his understanding of the mind of the primitive African was limited,[5]
Haggard was sympathetic and respectful of African, particularly Zulu, civilization. Umslopagaas, in *The Ancient Allan*,
is an idealized portrait of a primitive warrior who is graceful
even when he swings an axe to kill his enemies.

Rider Haggard's fascination with Africa stemmed from his
belief that the African, in his intuitive state, possesses some
secret which the rational white man has lost. In *Allan's Wife*
the Zulu, Indaba-Zimi, is blessed with a psychic, magic sense
which informs him with an understanding superior to that of
the three white hunters around him. Yet it is a curious fact
that Haggard's heroes, after they have found the lost Garden
of Eden in Africa, after they have tasted the joys of unspoilt
nature, find some reason to return to their own civilized world.
Like Melville's hero in *Typee*, they find or invent an excuse
to return to the less pleasurable world from which they have
wandered. Haggard kept sending his heroes—Allan Quatermain, Good, and Curtis—back to undiscovered, joyful kingdoms, but invariably they left the natural state of grace after
only a brief immersion in it. Of course the exigencies of plot
may well be the key to these withdrawals; the explanation
could well be that Haggard had to rescue his heroes from joy
in order to allow them another trek through the next volume
of his Quatermain series. But Haggard's implicit attitude
toward pleasure suggests another explanation. Here Haggard
reveals a consistent ambiguity. In all his novels the quest for
beauty is what idealizes the character; the indulgence in
beauty is brief and ridden with guilt and self-justification.

This conflict between pleasure and guilt can be seen clearly
in Haggard's depiction of a minor character in *Allan's Wife*.
A man has gone into the interior of Africa to escape the travails
of worldly life, but he cannot escape the sense of guilt which

---

[5] In *Novels of Empire* (New York, 1949), pp. 120-122.

pursues him in reference to his daughter. These are his words:

"I thank Heaven for it," said the old man. "Listen, my children, many years ago a great shame and sorrow fell upon me, so great a sorrow that, as I sometimes think, it affected my brain. At any rate, I determined to do what most men would have considered the act of a madman, to go far away into the wilderness with my only child, there to live remote from civilization and its evils. I did so; I found this place, and here we have lived for many years, happily enough, and perhaps not without doing good in our generation, but still in a way unnatural to our race and status. At first I thought that I would let my daughter grow up in a state of complete ignorance, that she should be Nature's child. But as time went on, I saw the folly and the wickedness of my plan. I had no right to degrade her to the level of the savages round me, for if the fruit of the tree of knowledge is a bitter fruit, still it teaches good from evil. So I educated her as well as I was able, till in the end I knew that in mind, as in body, she was in no way inferior to her sisters, the children of the civilized world. She grew up and entered into womanhood, and then it came into my mind that I was doing her a bitter wrong, that I was separating her from her kind and keeping her in a wilderness where she could find neither mate nor companion. But though I knew this, I could not yet make up my mind to return to active life; I had grown to love this place. I dreaded to return into the world I had abjured. Again and again I put my resolutions aside."   (pp. 709-10)

Haggard brought world-wide attention to the exotic novel about Africa. His influence was vast, and a whole stream of novels imitating the more sensational qualities of his fiction followed in the wake of *King Solomon's Mines*. While in his hands the Noble Savages were representatives of a demanding civilization, his followers, in their eagerness to satisfy the public demand for romantic illusion, were to corrupt and sentimentalize Haggard's image of Africa.

These streams, Africa as an exotic forest and as a path for an often misguided humanitarian expedition, were to run into the twentieth century, though the emphasis later shifted to the depiction of the political evolution of Africa as a self-governing land. In addition, Africa in the early twentieth century came to represent a psychological journey, a descent into the Central Station of one's existence, a look at one's own heart of darkness.

The Conradian tradition regarding Africa—that is, seeing Africa as a journey by way of experience to painful maturity—was most popular in the 1930's and 1940's when, in popular banter, it was often said that one went either to a psychoanalyst or to Africa. Today Conrad's influence may be seen in Robert Shaw's *The Sun Doctor* (London, 1961), Frederick Prokosch's *Storm and Echo* (New York, 1948), Graham Greene's *A Burnt-Out Case* (London, 1961), Saul Bellow's *Henderson the Rain King* (New York, 1959), Thomas Hinde's recent novels *A Place Like Home* (London, 1962) and *The Cage* (London, 1963), Philip Diolé's *L'Okapi* (Paris, 1963),[6] and David Caute's *The Decline of the West* (London, 1966).

Although as a literary mode the satirizing of the struggles in Africa seems to be frowned upon by many contemporary critics, the tradition of spoofing introduced by Evelyn Waugh and Joyce Cary in the 1930's continues with such books as *Jimmy Riddle* (London, 1961), by Ian Brook, *Devil of a State* (London, 1961), by Anthony Burgess, and *The Confessions of Jotham Simiyu* (London, 1965), by Harold Beaver. The most dominant influence in the past decade in the English novel about Africa has been sociology; in their attempts to portray the new African milieu with its problems of independence, nationalism, and displacement of the white settler class, both African and non-African novelists have tended to resort to the artless cudgel of fervent propaganda.

Today that stage is passed, and a new literature dealing

---

[6] *Okapi Fever*, tr. by Peter Green (New York, 1965).

more with individual development of character than with the depiction of political scenes is in evidence. Wole Soyinka's *The Interpreters* (London, 1965), Chinua Achebe's *Arrow of God* (London, 1964) and *A Man of the People* (London, 1966), and Onuora Nzekwu's *Highlife for Lizards* (London, 1965) are all instances of a tremendous surge of creative literature that is true to the realities of the African milieu but is not a servant to its nationalistic demands. Perhaps ironically, a book by a Frenchman—*L'état sauvage* (Paris, 1957),[7] by Georges Conchon—is one of the few examples in the past decade of a novel depending for its motif on racism and the inevitable clash between black and white prejudice—ironic because the French have claimed theirs to be a rational and enlightened attitude that overrides color and racial prejudice.

It was after the novel *Heart of Darkness* (London, 1903), by Joseph Conrad, that English fiction about Africa changed its direction. Hitherto, both English and foreign novelists had utilized Africa as a school for moral instruction; the Germans, particularly, saw Africa as a testing-ground for their superior moral qualities. Conrad, to the contrary, introduced Africa from a psychological standpoint; his "exploration" of the continent signified a state of compulsion. Conrad's influence has extended outside the English language—André Gide, driven by the same compulsion as Conrad, journeyed to the center of the African continent, an account of which he rendered in his *Voyage au Congo* (Paris, 1927). Gide, who dedicated his book to Conrad, wanted, like the latter, to hear the message within the overpowering silence of the African terrain. He uses imagery similar to that of Conrad: "What we want is precisely to leave the beaten track, to see what one does not see ordinarily, to enter profoundly, intimately, into the heart of the country."[8] Again like Conrad, Gide did not regard

---

[7] *The Savage State,* tr. by Peter Fryer (New York and London, 1965).
[8] *Travels in the Congo,* tr. by Dorothy Bussy (New York and London, 1929), p. 61.

Africa as a mere biographical incident. It was not his personal experience at Matadi and Kinchassa on the Congo River in 1890 that gave Conrad the major impetus to write *Heart of Darkness*; as recorded in his diary [9] Conrad had decided to visit the strange land of Africa when he was only nine years old. In a striking literary parallel Gide says in his book, "I was barely twenty when I first made up my mind to make this journey to the Congo—thirty-six years ago." It is this obsessive belief that the deep hinterland of Africa will open the door to the illumination of self that characterizes the writing of Conrad, Gide, Graham Greene, the German writer Kurt Heuser, Thomas Hinde, and a host of other novelists. Africa becomes for these writers not a geographic center but a psychoanalytic tool. In describing his reaction to the blackness of Africa in his early travel book *Journey Without Maps* (London, 1936) Graham Greene explained the attraction Africa has held for a vast number of writers since Conrad:

> But there are times of impatience, when one is less content to rest at the urban stage, when one is willing to suffer some discomfort for the chance of finding—there are a thousand names for it, King Solomon's Mines, the "heart of darkness" if one is romantically inclined, or more simply, as Herr Heuser puts it in his African novel, *The Inner Journey*, one's place in time, based on a knowledge not only of one's present but of the past from which one has emerged. There are others, of course, who prefer to look a stage ahead, for whom Intourist provides cheap tickets into a plausible future, but my journey represented a distrust of any future based on what we are.
>
> The motive of a journey deserves a little attention. It is not the fully conscious mind which chooses West Africa in preference to Switzerland. The psycho-analyst, who takes the images of a dream one by one: "You dreamed you were asleep in a forest.

---

[9] See *Joseph Conrad's Diary of His Journey Up to the Valley of the Congo in 1890,* with an Introduction and Notes by Richard Curle (London, 1926).

What is your first association to forest?" finds that some images
have immediate associations; to others the patient can bring out
nothing at all . . . and when I say that Africa has always
seemed an important image, I suppose that is what I mean, that
it has represented more than I can say. "You dreamed you were
in Africa. Of what do you think first when I say the word,
Africa?" and a crowd of words, witches and death, unhappiness
and the Gare St. Lazare, the huge smoky viaduct over a Paris
slum, crowd together and block the way to full consciousness.

But to the words "South Africa" my reaction, I find, is immediate: Rhodes and the British Empire and an ugly building in
Oxford and Trafalgar Square. After "Kenya" there is no hesita-
tion: "gentlemen farmers, the seedy aristocracy and gossip
columns." Rhodesia produces: "failure, Empire tobacco and
failure again."

It is not then *any* part of Africa which acts so strongly on
this unconscious mind; certainly no part where the white settler
has been most successful in reproducing the conditions of his
country, of the inexplicable. This Africa may take the form of
an unexplained brutality as when Conrad noted in his Congo
diary . . . or a sense of despair.   (pp. 9-10)

To some extent Conrad's psychosymbolic use of Africa is an
extension of Haggard's quest theme. Haggard's characters
traveled to distant territories, into the interior of the past,
and they also discovered secrets which enabled them to return
to Western civilization wiser men than when they had left it,
but they were not driven by a psychological compulsion. Their
interest in the quest was intellectual, romantic, and perhaps a
wish-fulfillment for the lotus of oblivion; they were not, however, looking consciously or subconsciously for a faith to fill
the emptiness within themselves.

Conrad's influence is most apparent in Graham Greene, who
reveals his debt to Conrad through references in *Journey Without Maps* and *In Search of a Character: Two African Journals*
(London, 1961). It is also apparent in other writers, in two
such diverse novels as *The African Queen* (London, 1935),

by C. S. Forester, and *Mamba* (Boston, 1956), by Stuart
Cloete, in the use of the motif of the journey down the real
river to the metaphysical destination of personal development.
In *Journey Inward*,[10] by Kurt Heuser, the Conradian theme
of self-development through confrontation with one's hidden
desires is conveyed within the plot of a land surveyor who
travels into unexplored and uncharted regions. Among the
many novels patterned after this mold are: Robin Maugham's
Behind the Mirror (New York and London, 1955); Gerald
Hanley's *Drinkers of Darkness* (New York and London, 1955);
Frederick Prokosch's *Storm and Echo* (New York, 1948);
David Mathew's *Mango on the Mango Tree* (New York,
1951); Johanna Moosdorf's *Flight to Africa*;[11] Elspeth Huxley's *The Red Rock Wilderness* (New York and London,
1957); Robert Shaw's *The Sun Doctor*; and Saul Bellow's
Henderson the Rain King. Robin Maugham's *Behind the Mirror* reads like an updated version of *Heart of Darkness*: a
British screenwriter travels to Africa to interview an ex-diplo-
mat and writer who is there living in seclusion; the identities
of the subject and the object, the narrator and the famous
writer, become increasingly interfused.

The Conradian theme, the necessity of traveling to the dark
places of the earth in order to bring light on one's self, does
not necessarily equate man's journeying with success. In *Heart
of Darkness* the man who plunges deepest is the one who
drowns, while Marlow, the narrator who observes but does not
participate in evil, travels back to the safety of Western civilization. In Conrad's only other piece of fiction about Africa,
a short story entitled "An Outpost of Progress," the harmful
effects of Africa—its heat, its drudgery, its sloth—lead to the
suicide and murder of the two white heroes at an isolated

---

[10] Tr. from the German by Willa and Edwin Muir (New York, 1932).
[11] Tr. from the German by Richard and Clara Winston (New York,
1954).

African trading station. Conrad does not idealize Africa as the romantic and adventure novelists do; he presents Africa and the consciousness of Africa in terms of a psychological compulsion which ends always in pain, and sometimes in death.

This obsession of the white man with black Africa as a psychological, spiritual, or moral road to salvation is not confined purely to fictional literature. Its expression has been so pervasive that a reaction has set in among African and American Negro novelists, who see in it another expression of the white man's condescension to Negro and African civilization. Richard Wright in *Black Power* (New York, 1954) attacked this white man's psychic need of Africa, calling it a millstone around the African's neck: "Those few Europeans who do manage to become serious about Africa are more often prompted by psychological reasons than anything else. The greatest millstone about the neck of Africa for the past three hundred years has been the psychologically crippled white seeking his own perverse personal salvation" (p. 343).

Possibly in reaction to the proliferation of novels using Africa as a psychological determinant or crutch, a new kind of novel in English about Africa has appeared. In this type of novel—common in England and the United States in the past decade—Africans are viewed as entrants into the new drama of independent social and political forces. Unfortunately many of these novels are tracts which are not detached enough from their social protest to meet an essential function of literature: the delineation of human character. Their prototypes are Sir Harry Johnston's *The Man Who Did the Right Thing* (London, 1921), William Plomer's *Turbott Wolfe* (London, 1926)— though those two novels were to some extent successful in portraying complex human beings.

The most popular kind of novel in English about Africa from 1940 to 1960 was distinguished more for its sociological commentary than for its artistic realization; it suffered from an abundance of evangelical enthusiasm, whether that evangelism viewed Africa as missionaries' or romantics' or politicians' or anthropologists' territory. Fortunately, African writers from both sides of the continent have already begun to accomplish the fusion necessary for literature—the heat of ideas distilled by the cold purity of form, the commingling of two elements, art and sociopolitics, in which each is servant to and in harmony with the other. Today the most important and hopeful development in the African novel and drama lies in the emergence of a group of African writers, living mainly on the East or West coast and writing in English or French. These are the writers who have begun to play the major role in the new African literature. These are the writers who have passed through—and some of whom have stayed with—the inspiring breeze of *Négritude*.

The concepts of *Négritude*, and the writings they have inspired, afford another example of the diversity of African literature within a larger unity. *Négritude* is undoubtedly the most widely known of all African literary movements and concepts. It is a term coined by the Martinique poet Aimé Césaire in his long poem *Cahiers d'un retour au pays Natal*. Césaire's poem was neglected when it was first published in 1939, but it rallied a movement in support of its ideas when it was reissued in 1947 in Paris with an introduction by the surrealist poet and artist, André Breton.

A spiritual and nationalistic concept, Négritude has come to mean for both Africans and New World Negroes (it is important to remember that Césaire is a West Indian and that his poem is about the rebirth of his spiritual vitality through immersion in African "waters") the acceptance of one's "Negroness" and all that that acceptance brings with it in the sphere of comparative culture. Léopold Senghor, perhaps the most famous contemporary African poet (part of his fame springs from his twofold role as poet and as president of the Senegal Republic), calls Négritude an emotion, and claims that emotion is Negro, a special characteristic of the Negro people. Senghor also claims that the African spirit is healthier than the American or European one because it does not analyze or rationalize or categorize feelings. For Senghor, Négritude is the immediate emotional response to nature, and the nature of things, or, in his own words, it is the "sum total of all the cultural values of Africa." Négritude is the "African personality," the "being-in-the-world of the Negro" (Jean-Paul Sartre's definition), the "Africanity" or indestructible roots of the "African soul."

Négritude may be considered a parallel to "American-ness" in American literature (surely another debatable subject: everyone knows what is truly American, but each has his own opinion on the matter; yet all are agreed that something uniquely American exists). It is both an attitude and a style: the assumption of an African personality. Its subject matter roots itself in the history of Africa—in colonial injustice, in slavery and in the slave trade, in exile and in alienation, in the forced assimilation into a dominant European culture. Its personality and style reflect the "essential" elements of the African people—whether in Africa, the West Indies, the United States, or France, or in students at Moscow University; in short, the black people all over the world—their joys and sufferings, their nostalgia for and dreams of the return to a glorious past, their conflicts between traditional life in village and forest and the opportunities and responsibilities of a modern urban social fabric.

Négritude, especially in poetry where the concept has led to the creation of shibboleths and revolutionary slogans, is an expression of the Negro rhythm, tone, and color. In this sense it is both a reactionary and a progressive movement. The poets under its influence have placed African models—mythic, historic, quasi-literary—before them as they write. A white European caught in the romantic toils of Négritude was D. H. Lawrence, who in his mystical emphasis on the sexual fertility

of Africans, as exemplified in their black statuary, was revealing one kind of primitivism. More than a return to the past,
however, is taking place: a declaration of independence of and
equality with other cultures is now voicing itself. It is just this
cry of individualism—of "Africanity" or "African-ness"—that has
occasioned the many paradoxes of Négritude.

The Négritude movement reached its height of passion in
the forties and fifties when African colonies were beginning to
reclaim their national independence. *Présence Africaine* was
founded in 1948 in Paris with the express purpose of speaking
for the Negro intellectual, and through him for the Negro race
and its achievements. Alioune Diop, the founder and editor
of this French-language journal, asked for "contributions" to
help "define African originality." At first a purely literary magazine, *Présence Africaine* increasingly became a forum for politics and politico-cultural matters, and among its contributors
have been Kwame Nkrumah of Ghana (in translation into
French), Sekou Touré of Guinea, and Mamadou Dia (later
the Prime Minister of Senegal and the author of *The African
Nations and World Solidarity* [Paris, 1960; London, 1962]).
Présence Africaine was largely instrumental in the formation
of the Société Africaine de Culture (SAC), which with its two
international conferences brought world-wide attention to the
meaning and force of Négritude. The American Society of
African Culture (AMSAC) also grew out of this movement.

Thus in its early phases Négritude served as the cultural
arm of the nationalist movement; it provided another justification for the right of African nations and people to their individuality and racial distinctiveness. Négritude also knit the
French-speaking writers of Africa into a Pan-African movement; all Africans shared in their own uniqueness, and therefore were a part of the same cultural ferment. When political
independence came to most former African colonies, the Négritude movement lost much of its force, for the spirit of Pan-

Africanism dwindled before the individual problems of each nation.

Today a further withdrawal into smaller units of allegiance, in some cases back to the tribal authority, is in evidence, and only Senghor and a few French-speaking African writers are among the celebrants of Négritude. A host of African critics either vocally hostile to or silently critical of the concept have denied the validity of its power except as a historical fact within the context of sociology. James Baldwin, the American Negro writer, and Ezekiel Mphahlele, the South African Mosotho critic and novelist, both admit that emotion may be Negro, but that emotion may also be white. Baldwin sees in the American Negro writer Richard Wright the same qualities that Senghor sees in him, but Baldwin attributes those qualities not to an innate African heritage but to a number of other factors that have only partially to do with Africa. Mphahlele, along with a large number of Nigerian writers who use English as their literary language, objects to what he feels is the cultural insularity of Négritude. The wheel in the past generation has come full circle. Mphahlele believes that Négritude isolates the African from his brother writers and other people in a multiracial world by painting his "blackness" in terms other than the color of his skin; he believes that an African can only express the African-ness in him when he does not consciously or self-consciously exclude his world heritage. Whereas Senghor has claimed that Négritude gives to the Negro his sense of individuality and thus reestablishes his equality with other peoples, Baldwin, Mphahlele, and most Nigerian writers express the view that Négritude squeezes the African writer between a vise of shrill cultural nationalism and quaint folk culture.

Baldwin's remarks on Négritude sound like his remarks on the Black Muslim movement in America: that it is a separatist movement which has distorted its legitimate goals of

Negro recognition and self-awareness by blinding itself to everything but the color of skin. Baldwin, as well as many African writers, is thus calling for an end to racial and national flames of feeling; the black racism of Négritude is as abhorrent to them as the white racism of South Africa. Aimé Césaire, on the other hand, still lives in the belief that the Negro gains his identity "because of Europe," even though he bows to the inescapable admission that culture is not "a racial product." On the final day of the first Congress of Negro-African Writers and Artists, held in Paris in September, 1956, Césaire stated: "What unites all Negroes is the injustices they have suffered at European hands." This kind of historic resentment is to many critics another piece of evidence confirming the stagnant, separatist bias of Négritude.[12]

Part of this hostility to Négritude may also be due to the ironic division of modern African writing into different foreign languages. Generally speaking, the writers expressing themselves in French have proclaimed and supported the concepts attending Négritude, while those poets, novelists, dramatists, and essayists writing in English have denounced the movement. Négritude is largely a French-African concept: Césaire, Senghor, Diop, all write in French. *Présence Africaine*, the most influential African journal in French-speaking Africa, was and continues to remain the propagandist outlet for Négritude.

---

[12] The power of Négritude has lost little of its controversial force. The first World Festival of Negro Arts, sponsored by UNESCO and supported by the governments of France and Senegal, was held in Dakar in April, 1966. At the festival Léopold Senghor again declared Négritude the most important cultural and inspirational force and rallying cry for African artists in the twentieth century. Several writers and painters engaged in colloquiums on the elements that constituted their art: African or European. Perhaps the most memorable remark came from Tchicaya U'Tamsi, who won the Festival Prize for poetry in French. U'Tamsi said: "The fruits of négritude should not be picked by black hands alone but also by the hands of men of goodwill everywhere." See John Povey, "Dakar: An African Rendez-vous," in *Africa Today*, XIII, No. 5 (May, 1966), 4-6.

Césaire's poem, which initiated the word (though the concept was long known if dormant in the spirit of West Indians), spread from the bookstalls of Paris to the savannas of West and Central Africa. André Breton created his own clique and claque for the concept among French dadaists and artists. And perhaps most vocally, Jean-Paul Sartre, in his preface ("Orphée Noire") to Senghor's *Anthologie de la nouvelle poésie nègre et malgache*, published in 1948, gave the word a chic and panache African intellectuals neither expected nor ultimately found beneficial. It would be ironic if the English-speaking Africans really base their objection to Négritude on its French-ified approach: the question of African personality and culture would again become a matter of Western spheres of influence. Certainly the objection to Négritude on the part of Africans using the English language is to some extent due to envy of and petty hostility to the brilliance of the abstract theorizing of the French-influenced movement. More profoundly, however, the English-language critics have another objection: Négritude has more and more confined itself to French-African culture and thus, while claiming African universality—which by its very nature can merely exist as an abstraction—represents only one part of African culture.

Négritude has been outlined in these pages because all literary movements, like all social movements, are the results of previous revolutions. Négritude has spawned a host of opponents in Nigeria and Ghana, who, partly as a result of discrediting the movement, have created their own rubric. Thus, African literature, like comparative European literature, has made and is still making its imprint through diversity. A study of modern African literature, and modern literature about Africa, which may at first glance seem parochial, provides the African continent with another perspective: its literary history personifies the history of the important revolutions in Africa during the past several hundred years.

Some commentators object to discussing Africa or literature

about Africa as a homogeneous unit, pointing out that Africa
does not consist of a single, indivisible phenomenon, but of
many tribes, countries, religions, and histories. While it is true
that for an understanding of things African, individual distinctions must be taken into account, nevertheless it is not in-
valid to treat Africa as a whole, or literature about Africa by
Africans and non-Africans in a general scheme. Recent books
attest to the need for an overall view as well as for a detailed
analysis. In *The African Image*, Ezekiel Mphahlele, a young
black South African literary critic, has taken all the fiction
about Africa written by English, American, and by African
authors and attempted to reconstruct the dominant image of
the black man as seen by white writers. Once again a parallel
may be drawn with American letters. No one is any longer
afraid to talk of the special qualities of American literature,
qualities that contain inconsistencies as well as peculiarly dis-
tinct local traits. The literary highway through America has
of course often been taken; the pathways into African literature are now open, and enough maps have been charted to
provide the traveler with proper guidelines.

TWO

West Africa in
an English Light

1

The surging renaissance of Nigerian novelists that includes among others Chinua Achebe, Wole Soyinka, John Pepper Clark, Onuora Nzweku, Cyprian Ekwensi, and Gabriel Okara, and the creation of African publishing companies, African printing presses, and African literary journals are providing the base of an entire new body of West African literature in English. Before its sparks lit the terrain in the 1950's, however, fewer novels and plays and volumes of poetry were written in English by West Africans or about West Africa than respective works in which the setting was the exotic lands of the Congo or the cool waters and mountains of East Africa. Except in the work of Joyce Cary and of some American writers influenced by Cary, this area, comprising Nigeria, Ghana, Liberia, the Cameroons, Sierra Leone, the Ivory Coast, and Portuguese Guinea, was sparsely represented in creative English literature until 1950; even today in Ghana, while literary activity has manifested itself in a vital outpouring of drama and poetry, a

23

novel of stature—much less a full-length novel—has yet to be written. And while the action of Graham Greene's *The Heart of the Matter* is set in Sierra Leone, Africa is for Greene not one particular place but a gigantic condition. Part of the explanation for this curious neglect may lie in the fact that West Africa has been dominated by French culture; and the vast number of books—poetry, drama, and short stories in French—testify to this dominance. Nigeria, now the most important source of indigenous literature in Africa, was already past the stage of primitivism and thus less attractive to white writers looking for the "proper" setting for exoticism and savagery than the fabled jungles of the Congo. But another reason may be the paradox that Nigeria has consistently called on her writers for public service. Illustrative of this paradox is the fact that even as late as 1962 the most prolific and popular writer in Nigeria, Cyprian Ekwensi, tried to combine his post as Director of Information for his government with the full-time job of writing novels. Ekwensi's experience represents the problem confronting a writer who has achieved recognition on the world stage. For the writer in Nigeria is acknowledged as a significant contributor to society and daily culture; paradoxically he is as a result so honored with administrative responsibilities that he is left with less and less time to write.

Before the current Nigerian renaissance five major themes dominated the novel in English about West Africa: the slave trade; the tragicomedy of administration by the British (exemplified by Joyce Cary and his followers); politics of violence and sadism (as in John Wyllie's *Riot*); despair and moral crisis (the supreme example of which is Graham Greene's *The Heart of the Matter*); and the confrontation of African and European civilization at the beginning of the twentieth century. One early novel, *The Uncounted Cost* by Mary Gaunt, utilizes the old-fashioned humanitarian approach, but in its undertones of guilt and anxiety it reflects the modern British literary approach to West Africa.

Until 1932, when Joyce Cary published the first of his Nigerian novels, most of the novels written about West Africa were romantic thrillers, a genre which has its vogue in every age. If they lacked verisimilitude, they were nevertheless able to exert a strong hold on the popular imagination. Until the late 1940's, Africa still seemed to many a land of remoteness and mystery, a land with an aura of fantasy which they felt no need to test against reality. But if Africa cast an image of fantasy in the minds of many writers and readers, it was also a mirror that reflected basic conditions of man, and the writers who saw these conditions were unanimous in their protest against them. Conrad's attack on the imperialist ventures in Central Africa is well known. Not so well known is a woman who cried out just as passionately, though not so magnificently.

In her autobiographical narrative, *Alone in West Africa* (London, 1924), Mary Gaunt states that, when her husband died, she might have gone to live with her parents in a comfortable small Australian town; but she preferred the dangers of independence as a free-lance writer in London. After reading tales of traders and adventurers in West Africa, Mary Gaunt fell in love with the region, and much like the nine-year-old Conrad, who placed a pin on a map of the Congo, saying that that was the place he was going to see some day, she vowed she would get to the land of gold dust, crumbling forts, ivory, and palm oil. In London, she wrote stories and novels, most of them about West Africa. While all of these early writings were mediocre, after years of effort and research she produced salable fiction. In 1904, she published her West African novel, *The Uncounted Cost*, which became a bestseller, visited the land of her dreams, and wrote an autobiographical report of her trip up the River Volta. Like Mary Kingsley, another white lady who came to Africa at the end of the nineteenth century, she startled the provincial English administrators and the tribal chiefs when she entered African bush villages as a respectful visitor eager to learn their customs.

Although Mary Gaunt wrote *The Uncounted Cost* before visiting Africa, this novel is no less revealing of the West African milieu than her accounts drawn from first-hand experience. The novel clearly reveals her Conradian attitude to the African. She is full of sympathy for his plight; she is aghast at his black magic and savage methods of punishment (she describes in some detail the execution of a native by his being tied against an ant-heap). She senses the attraction of the vastness and anonymity of Africa, and she feels the great pull of "primitive" beliefs and theories. Ultimately, like Conrad, she rejects Africa. It is a place to go through, a challenge, but it is not a place to remain in. And if she has sympathy for the African's enslavement, she cannot conceive of his equality with the Englishman in social and political spheres. She believes in the African's potential as a cultured human being, but she sees no place for him in an ordered society, no means by which his humanity could be utilized. Africa, where his ancient traditions once worked, has been wrested from him, and he is not equipped to go elsewhere.

The plot of *The Uncounted Cost* reads like one of Kipling's adventure stories, and in its sympathy-without-commitment for the wrongs experienced by the African it has a Kiplingesque atmosphere. The heroine, Anne Lovant, is a novelist who has written many tales about Africa though she has never visited the continent. For the past two years she has been living a trial marriage (Anne is an advanced thinker) with Dicky Bullen, a British naval officer. The test period has ended with Dick's decision that Anne and marriage are not right for him. As the novel opens, Anne's close friend Kitty Pearce is having a surreptitious flirtation with naval commander Joe Cunningham. Kitty's husband, a doctor, is stationed in West Africa and regularly sends an allowance to his "faithful" wife. Anne tells

Kitty that her flirtation is immoral: in her affair with Dicky Bullen, Anne was at least committed.

Since this is an early post-Victorian novel, sex is not mentioned, but its innuendoes are mightily exploited. For his weekend of fun with Kitty, Joe Cunningham misses his ship, which sails away without him, and the following day he is tricked into threatening his superior officer. The result is his court-martial and dismissal from the service. Bitterly Cunningham prepares for a new career, a career which takes him as an administrative officer to West Africa, to the very station where Kitty's husband is practicing medicine. Because he likes Fred Pearce, Cunningham tells him the story of his downfall but keeps Kitty's identity a secret. Dicky Bullen also comes to the station, to work for his old friend. And finally—and inevitably in such an earnest novel where moral questions must be neatly answered—Kitty arrives to visit her husband, bringing her friend Anne Lovant with her. The five are now together in Africa, where the niceties of convention are to be stripped away, and truth is to be faced under the blazing sun.

What makes Miss Gaunt's novel more than a conventional romance is its subplot, its African note. The task which Joe Cunningham, as an officer of the British Crown, must meet is the extermination of fetish worship in his district. To insure the spread of Christian and Western supremacy, under the guise of bringing civilization to the blacks, all fetish cults have been outlawed. Since West African religion, in almost all cases, encompasses fetishism,[1] this decision is tantamount to denouncing centuries of African culture. Miss Gaunt does not investigate the ramifications of this conflict, but in the figure of Kudo Mensa she presents a sympathetic portrait of a

---

[1] Dr. Geoffrey Parrinder, in *Religion in West Africa* (New York, 1961), schematizes African religion into four basic components, one of which is the juju or fetish.

wronged man. Kudo Mensa is an educated African prince, a
black man who has been to Oxford and studied divinity at
Balliol College. Ordained a priest of the Church of England,
the Reverend John Trotter has returned to West Africa to help
his country. But after several months he renounces his Anglican
priesthood; instead, he becomes a priest of the ancient fetish
cult *Rewah* and is known to his followers as Kudo Mensa.
Kudo tells Anne that he is a "man before his time" who must
revert to primitivism. Educated beyond the needs of Africa—
and not accepted by the British—he can only find a place for
himself by steps that are retrogressive. Kudo is fighting a lost
cause; he is trying to lead his people back into the mysteries
of an ancient cult. He is not a new character in English literature: he is a Kurtz in reverse, a man who has surrendered to
white culture in the heart of England and come back to Africa
to find no place reserved for him. He fights a losing battle,
because a battle, a cause, even if doomed, fulfills a desperate
longing in man.

In her description of Kudo, Miss Gaunt shows concern for
his rootlessness, and sympathy for the conflicts which have
damned him to the wrong path. When Kudo is captured by
Dicky Bullen, her lover, Anne feels compassion for the help-
less, underfed, weak African in the grasp of the muscular,
physically superior and cruel white man. She pleads with
Dicky not to flog Kudo, but Dicky eagerly snaps the whip. It
is this constant humiliation by the white man that, by the end
of the novel, turns Kudo into a monster. Bent only on killing,
Kudo attempts to wipe out the compound where Anne, Kitty,
Joe Cunningham, and Fred Pearce have taken refuge. Fortunately British troops arrive at the propitiously glorious moment. As Miss Gaunt puts it, these four British citizens had
"held Dalaga against heavy odds. The British flag still flew!
One more step had been taken in the clearing of the dark
places of the earth!" (p. 288).

Mary Gaunt, like Joseph Conrad, represents the end of one

tradition and the beginning of another. Just as Conrad brought a psychological awareness to the fascination of Africa for the white man, Mary Gaunt brought an understanding of the intelligent African whose education under contemporary conditions inevitably destroyed all his roots without giving him new ones. Both writers were humanitarian in their attitude to the sufferings of oppressed natives; but this attitude, while always a part of them, was not what truly motivated them. Conrad was fascinated by the "abomination" of Africa; Mary Gaunt was held by its promise of nobility. In the Reverend John Trotter-Kudo Mensa, she showed that nobility-gone-wrong. The Noble Savage now became the modern rootless intellectual who can act only in the most violent, senseless manner. He was to be the prototype of a host of African heroes who are compelled to commit violence against the white men they both love and hate.

Before 1950, when the problems of independence were discussed in many novels about Africa, the most popular subject for white writers using the West African locale was the slave trade. Undoubtedly this subject is the most dramatic in the history of West Africa, for it represents the crossing of tribal loyalties, family betrayal, and civil allegiances—one tribe turned against another tribe, selling its former friends into the white man's or Arab's slave camp. It is important at this point to distinguish between slavery and the slave trade, although the novelists writing on this subject often fail to make the distinction. Slavery has been in existence since the early history of man and in some ways represents an "advance in civilization," [2] since the early warriors killed their enemies rather than accept the administrative burden of enslaving them. Evil as slavery is, it has had some distinguished ad-

---

[2] See the discussion by Joyce Cary, *Britain and West Africa* (London, 1946), pp. 7-36.

herents. Joyce Cary wrote: "Slavery has often been so mild that slaves refuse freedom, and domestic slavery has sometimes been benevolent. As lately as 1919, when I offered freedom to some African slaves, they refused it. They preferred to stay in their master's family."[3] Less than ten years ago, Robin Maugham bought a slave in a North African market in order to free him, but earned no gratitude for his act. In *The Slaves of Timbuktu* (New York, 1961) Maugham tells of his experience and also of the economic slavery still in practice in Nigeria and North Africa, where the children of poor parents are sold to wealthier families and work for them as servants until their adulthood.

The slave trade, however, has never been justified. It is "dirty work," and "the less-said-about-it-the-better" is the attitude of those who have worked in it. The Arabs, who were the great masters of the slave trade for centuries, had markets in Timbuktu, Tunis, and other North African ports. Cruel and despotic, the traders marched periodically into villages in the interior of Africa, killed what children and old men they could not employ, burned whole villages, and then with the African men and women and children yoked together like cattle, they marched off.[4] So bad was Arab pillage and the raiding of the Ashanti war lords of the Gold Coast (now Ghana) that Joyce Cary observed:

The partition of Africa, whatever the complex of motives behind it, was a blessing to the African masses. Its worst evils, even of the Congo under Leopold's concession, were not so bad as the perverse and ruinous cruelty of slave raiders and despots like

---

[3] *Ibid.,* p. 21.
[4] The history of the slave trade is documented in Basil Davidson's *Black Mother, The Years of the African Slave Trade* (Boston, 1961), and in Sean O'Callaghan's *Slave Trade in Africa and Arabia Today* (New York, 1962). In fiction, C. S. Forester gives a revealing picture in *The Sky and the Forest* (Boston, 1948).

the Ashanti kings. I rode once through a city gate in a mud
wall. Half an hour later, I reached another gate and passed out
from the wall. There was nothing between but grass. That whole
great city had been wiped out, not many years before, by the
Emir of Kontagora, whom I knew—a tall, grave man, handsome,
and of most distinguished bearing. To him, a Moslem aristocrat,
as to the Early Dutch of South Africa, Christian patriarchs, the
pagans were animals designed by God only to be hunted and
enslaved.[5]

Slave trading on the West African coast did not begin until
the seventeenth century, the great era of trade competition
whose contestants were England, France, Holland, Portugal,
and Spain. There were no demands for slaves by Western
countries until that time, but from 1620, when a Dutch ship
landed at Virginia to sell the first Negro slaves in America
to tobacco planters, slave trading became a valuable economic
factor. England did not join the slave trade till the Restora-
tion because of her internal Civil War problems, and her
engagement in it was brief, ending in 1767 when Granville
Sharp, an evangelist, brought a suit against a slave owner who
had "imported" a slave into England. The ruling in favor of
Sharp ordained that no man could be a slave in England, and
thus any slave, as soon as he reached English soil, was a free
man. England continued her abolition policy by serving notice in 1807 that any Englishman engaging on the high seas
in the transport of slaves would be held guilty of a criminal
offense. During this same year the United States of America
forbade the importation of slaves. Legally, the slave trade
ended by 1830. It did not end in fact, however, for Europeans
continued to supply Caribbean markets with slaves. Portuguese traders especially engaged in this traffic, employing
Ashanti war chiefs as their suppliers. The fierce Ashantis of

---

[5] *Britain and West Africa,* p. 48.

what is now Ghana warred on weaker tribes in the interior of
Africa and brought back enough human booty to satisfy the
Europeans' and their own greed.

It is this last phase of the slave trade that has fascinated so
many English and American writers. Jean Kenyon Mackenzie,
a missionary for fourteen years in the Cameroons, published
several works of nonfiction before writing her first novel, *The
Trader's Wife* (New York, 1930). In this work Lucy, a girl
full of romantic illusions who grew up in abolitionist Newport,
Rhode Island, in the early nineteenth century, is the trader's
wife. In Africa, Lucy, who had thought herself removed from
the issue of slavery, who had found the talk of abolitionists
dull, realizes she cannot be indifferent to the existence of
slavery. This realization of her commitment leads her to ignore
her serious illness and walk out into the cold night to unlock
the corral where the slaves are kept prisoners. Yet when Lucy
and her personal slave Atemba open the corral, at first the
slaves are so astounded by their mistress's act that they cannot run away; they do not know what they are supposed to do.
At last, when they realize the meaning of Lucy's act, they flee.
The physical and spiritual exertion of Lucy's act has weakened
her to the point that her slave Atemba is forced to leave her
at a native hut, where he puts her gently on a wooden bed
and then rushes out for his own safety into the darkness. Thus
Lucy, who had sought to be in neither world—that of the
abolitionist or of the slave trader—is in the end rejected by her
African slave and by her white compatriots. When she is discovered the next morning, her husband realizes he did not even
know she was missing. Nor does he know why she is in the
hut—her ways are incomprehensible to him, and he attributes
his lack of insight to the strangeness of all women. His final
act of ignorance is to kick away the corral keys, which had
fallen there the night before; Harcourt neither knows nor cares
what secrets they may unlock.

Miss Mackenzie's short novel is written in a starkly simple

tone, and she avoids all abstract discussion of the question of slavery. Her eye focuses on several symbolic tableaux: the barracoon (the corral in which Africans are penned while waiting for the ships that will take them into slavery); the humid, stifling heat; the vast emptiness of an African beach. Her ear is trained on the splashing of the waves, the teasing waves of monotony and imprisonment, and on the wailing in the corral. It is this wailing that finally penetrates Lucy's consciousness; it becomes her dirge. Yet though she dies soon after her act of freeing the slaves, she has found a way out of the prison of her self. Her death, unlike her life, is meaningful. She has found that the question of slavery is not merely an abolitionist or even a Christian problem; it is a matter of humanity.

The slave trade probably made its greatest impact on English and American readers of comparatively recent years in two very popular novels by Marguerite Steen, *The Sun Is My Undoing* (London, 1941) and *Twilight on the Floods* (London, 1949). The locale of these novels is the Gold Coast and the English port of Bristol. *The Sun Is My Undoing* deals directly with the trade, while *Twilight on the Floods* probes the life of John Flood, great-grandson of the hero of *The Sun Is My Undoing*. John, one of the few men in the Flood family concerned about human values, loses his life in the Ashanti War.

The novel which gives the best picture of slave traffic in West Africa is probably *Barracoon* by H. C. Hervey. Published in New York in 1950, it received scant critical attention. Hervey is a popular writer whose prolific output and occasional descents into sensationalism have tended to obscure his true talent. Besides *Barracoon,* he has published one other novel about West Africa, *The Iron Widow* (New York, 1931), an adventure story with a message. The "iron widow" is the guillotine in a Senegambia prison known as The Red Hotel, run by a cruel commandant and his half-caste mistress. All the pris-

oners in The Red Hotel are deserters from the French Foreign
Legion, and so brutal and inhuman is treatment meted out to
them that some wish devoutly for the "iron widow" death.
Hervey's books, however, even when they deal with the sordid,
do not merely exploit sensationalism. In *The Iron Widow* the
sadism is a valid part of the scene. *Barracoon* has its fill of
murder, lust, and torture, but again Hervey uses these aspects
of life as a means of presenting a viewpoint. Maria Tristau da
Castra, the seventeen-year-old heroine, first sees the barracoon
shortly after her arrival in Portuguese Guinea in the 1850's
as the wife of a middle-aged Portuguese slave trader. She is
unaware of its significance, but after the first load of slaves
has arrived she soon learns her husband's business. What she
also learns is that the ship on which she and her husband,
Dom Arsenio da Castro, spent their honeymoon and which
brought them to Portuguese Guinea was a slave ship. It is the
first, but not the most bitter, moment in her war with her
husband.

The personal tragedy of Maria is tied in the web that includes slavery, the slave trade, and Maria's outrage at her
husband's sexual relations with African and half-caste women.
In time Maria learns to accept her husband's sexual philander-
ing, even to understand it, for as she herself matures she feels
a loving sympathy toward an African slave. But the barracoon
and the waves of the ocean beating against the African shore
never let Maria forget her disgust with slave trading. Dom
Arsenio, a sadist by nature, forces Maria to sit through a slave
auction. When the British, who have proclaimed slave trading
illegal and are inspecting all suspicious craft, try to intercept
one of Dom Arsenio's boats, that illustrious gentleman has all
the slaves murdered to destroy proof of his guilt.

The final blow for Maria is the torture of the African whom
Arsenio has given her as a personal slave (the gift is part of
Arsenio's sadism, a way of forcing her to accept her role as a
slave trader's wife). When she attempts to free the slave from

the barracoon her husband intercepts and mocks her. En-
raged, Maria kills her husband.

Although Hervey may have read Jean Mackenzie's *The
Trader's Wife*, it is more likely that both writers chose the
essential symbols of slave trading and exploited them. In both
books the climax comes when, after being unable to bear the
sound of the wailing in the barracoon and the beating of the
ocean waves, the heroine makes her decision to unlock the corral. And in freeing the slaves, both heroines pay a heavy price.
Lucy dies, and Maria will—the book implies—have to serve a
prison sentence. Freedom has its price.

Both these novels romanticize the African. Whenever he
appears as an individual, he is chivalric, gentle, and without
rancor. Atembu, in *The Trader's Wife,* yearns for freedom
but expresses no violent words. Amadu, the slave whose torture brings the action of *Barracoon* to a climax, is also a
tender, gentle creature. Both Africans are of royal lineage,
and each treats his white mistress like a princess. Both, then,
are Noble Savages, in the long line of idyllic heroes who have
been wronged without reason but who do not resort to violence. Atembu escapes into the forest to begin an old life, the
life of the happy primitive, while Amadu runs to the port city
to get the help of an English administrative officer.

Both novels also bear the tension of repressed sexuality.
In *The Trader's Wife* that sexuality is so covert that its presence is felt only by implication, but the sexual connotation
of the African prince's arm on the swooning Lucy in the dark
corral cannot be obscured. Nor can his tender placement of
her in bed, before he leaves her forever, be so innocent as Miss
Mackenzie wishes it on the surface. Before he leaves the
cabin Atembu rustles Lucy's dress so that it will look fluffy.
The aura of sex which no book about white women and black
men has yet avoided is even more rampant in *Barracoon*:
with a young woman, not out of her teens and barely yet
awakened; with the dark, ebony images of masculinity all

about her; with a sadistic, older husband prone to sexual
jealousy—the atmosphere is rife with sexual innuendo. Arsenio,
so confident on the surface, is afraid of his wife's youth. He
throws her into contact with an English naval lieutenant, making it impossible for her to avoid a night together with him.
Arsenio spreads the rumor of his wife's infidelity with her
princely African slave, yet as soon as he suspects the rumor
may be true—when he sees the look of happiness pass between
Maria and Amadu—he is mad with rage. Not even Iago
burned with more hate. And Maria, whose love for the African
has been without conscious desire, incurs the wrath of the
English lieutenant she loves when she tells him her dream:
"Why do you turn your eyes from me, Jan Kerth? What is in
them that you do not want me to see? I had a dream, a *dream*:
and in it my slave came to me and took the fear from my
heart; is that wrong?" (p. 248). Maria is caught between a
virtuous English lieutenant who cannot understand her casual
acceptance of black people as equals, in fact her preference
for things primitive, and a husband who has no moral prejudice against Negroes but cannot conceive of them other than
as chattels. Maria tries to explain her love of the primitive
in nature—"I hoped they [the lilies] would die. But they
didn't; touched with the gift for growing things that primitive
fingers have, they flourished" (p. 247)—but neither the lieutenant nor her husband understands.

The four major characters of *Barracoon*, like the major
figures of *The Trader's Wife*, are isolated from each other.
The hell of their private lives is intensified by the barriers of
racial prejudices. It is only by their taking the forbidden step,
associating with black men (and thus arousing all the sexual
fears of a white society), that the two women are able to feel
free in their reactions and actions. In this sense both novels
present the sexual context as an integral part of the color
problem. No miscegenation occurs, but its unheard music
reverberates throughout the novels.

2

During the 1920's and 1930's several novels dealing with the contemporary social, moral, religious and personal problems of South Africa were published in Great Britain and the United States. A few novels exploited the exotic locale of the Congo, and one mid-African chief wrote a fictionalized autobiography of his childhood in Africa and of his adult experience in the United States and England, where he had studied. The contemporary milieu of West Africa was handled by only one English writer. Fortunately that writer was a major figure in English literature, and his books explored the universal conditions of a man under a particular setting.

Joyce Cary wrote five African novels between 1932 and 1939. They were the first novels he published. The action of four of these novels was set entirely in Nigeria where Cary had fought in the British Army during World War I and where he had served as a magistrate and executive officer in the British Civil Service. Cary came to Nigeria in 1913 after an education that included a full curriculum at Oxford, art courses in Paris and Edinburgh, and a special program of Irish Cooperation under Sir Horace Plunkett. His experience in Borgu, Nigeria, gave him access to first-hand information about native life, and he used this material in his first novel, *Aissa Saved* (1932). The novel is a picture of life in the Shibi Rest Camp about 1912. Its residents include the assistant administrative officer, Bradgate; the missionaries, Mr. and Mrs. Carr; and the natives. In this novel, as in all Cary's other African novels, the conflicts revolve around Christian and juju religions; native psychology and British bureaucratic customs; and Moslem-Christian-African antagonism.

Aissa Saved is an ironic title, for Aissa, a beautiful half-breed who keeps changing her mind about her religion, saves her spirit at the end of the novel, but her body is hacked apart and left to be eaten on an ant-heap. Aissa turns to Christianity because she finds it "beautiful," but she does not understand the missionaries' attitudes or even those of the overzealous Christian natives who castigate her for having indulged in love play with her lover Gajere. Aissa is the first of a long line of typical Cary heroines. She is neither Christian nor juju, but immense in spirit. And her religious beliefs are part of the larger problem of personality, as Cary sees it. She believes strongly in the principles of Christianity when she remembers and is moved by them, but when her lover Gajere shows up or when a native feast for the primitive god Oke is in progress, she quickly forgets them. This desire to please all gods causes a riot, which ends in the amputation of Aissa's foot.

Aissa returns to the fold of Christianity, but more riots occur when she sleeps with her lover Gajere and tells the Christians not to bother her any more because she has "done enuf for Christ." The conflict between religions is further compounded by the Moslem supporters of the Emir who are ambushed by the Christians. By the time order is restored, Aissa, her baby Abba, and her lover Gajere have been murdered, and Mrs. Carr, the missionary, has died. Besides the religious conflict, Cary also treats the problems of "progress." At a meeting of the Emir's Council, one of the Moslem officers says:

> Everything is getting worse, he would shout at them: "The clerks come, Yorubas, white men, these Christians now. All is being spoilt. You do nothing, you cowards. Soon the railway will come. Berua got it and look at Berua. The old judge said, make this railway, and all the Yoruba thieves and whores and soldiers' women, all the corrupt boys and Christians in the land came there and spoilt it. See Berua now. The young men push you into the drain, the girls laugh in your beard, the people are like shameless animals. No railway, I say, no bridge—no roads, these are very bad things. Children must not go to school to learn to

spit upon their mothers and fathers. We'll stop these Christians and their witchcraft." [6]

Four novels later Cary is treating the same conflict of "progress" versus "primitivism" in his depiction of the Waziri and the Emir in Fada (the setting of *Mister Johnson* [London, 1939]) who do not like the new road because they "say bring all kind of rascals to Fada—spoil dis bush people." The Waziri tells Mister Johnson, "I know what your road will do—I've seen it before—everything turned upside down, and all for nothing." [7] Significantly, both speeches against progress in the two novels are by Moslem rulers objecting to a change in African life, and imply Cary's awareness that progress or change was more threatening to the feudal Moslem overlords than to any other national or religious group.

Cary's second novel, *An American Visitor* (London, 1933),[8] continues the same investigation into the contradictions of freedom. In the Carfax edition, Cary stated that his novel was about an anarchist of the most extreme kind. Marie Hasluck is an amateur anthropologist and journalist who arrives in Birri having read Thoreau and Rousseau and having come to the conclusion that all natural states of man are superior to civilized ones. She is Cary's ideal of American naïveté, but she is not a simple nuisance or a dangerous fool. Cary, in his preface to the Carfax edition, admires her for her simple faith: "But the truth seems to lie deeper. It is that the faith which lies beneath anarchism is just as necessary to the world as the reason which creates systems of law. . . . The anarchist, in short, has a good case." Cary pits Marie, the anarchist, against Monkey Bewsher, the man of power. All his books are serious, but since at the same time they are comedies Cary

---

6 *Aissa Saved*, Carfax edn. (London, 1952), pp. 95-96.
7 Carfax edn. (London, 1952), p. 85.
8 Carfax edn. (London, 1952).

has his characters fall in love, marry and be happy. However, since each of them is decent but willful, no change occurs in their attitudes until it is too late to matter. Marie understands her own character as a result of Bewsher's death, but there is no indication that this self-knowledge will change her attitude to life. The anarchist streak in Marie—like the bohemian streak in Mister Johnson, Gulley Jimson, and Aissa, and like the drive for power in Bewsher, Elizabeth Aladai, and Chester Nimmo—is unquenchable.

Cary's second novel also deals with missionaries, and here Mr. and Mrs. Dobson are as antagonistic to the civil power (because, in their eyes, it is based on force) as are the Carrs in *Aissa Saved*. Like the Carrs, the Dobsons see their work wiped out by the conflicts between white and black civil strife, but a new and more political note enters this novel, a note which Cary was to develop further in *The African Witch*. Cary was beginning to pay attention to the opportunists in Africa—the natives who think of Marie as another "good-for-nothing" white to be used in their struggle, and the English opportunist, Cottee, who wants to open up Birri to get at its mineral wealth.

In his third novel, *The African Witch*, Cary again uses a Nigerian town as the focus of conflict between freedom and authority, but the novel has greater relevance than the problems of colonialism. Elizabeth Aladai is the Chester Nimmo of Africa, a human being driven by a lust for power. Lisbet, as she prefers to be called, is a juju priestess who reigns supreme at the end of the novel, having wrested control from the more moderate forces and having attained the undeserved gratitude of the British government. It is Cary's thesis of extremes in operation again: the extremes always win, because they offer shibboleth and enthusiasm.[9] Fortunately every ex-

---

[9] See Cary's comments on art and rhetoric in *Art and Reality* (New York, 1958), especially p. 148.

treme spreads itself so thin that it reaches the middle of the line, and another extreme takes over. This is the one hope that mars the triumph of the juju priestess at the end of the novel, when, in the expansiveness of her victory, she subjects her husband to the indignity of crawling on all fours like an animal into her house-temple.

The African Witch is Cary's most colonial novel, while at the same time it reveals his general principles on freedom, law, order, and anarchy. For this reason it is extremely important in the development of the colonial novel. Its cast, numbering at least thirty major characters, contains all the elements of the colonial world. The hero, Captain Rackham, an assistant police commissioner, seems suspiciously like Cary himself: he is an Irishman, but a product of British schools, and he likes to boast that he came to Rimi because it "was the first job that offered him the open air and some polo." In a situation reminiscent of E. M. Forster's *A Passage to India* Rackham becomes good friends with Louis Aladai, a young Rimi priest who has been educated at Oxford and is in line with thirty-nine other candidates for the emirship of Rimi. Louis' dream is to unite the Christian-European civilization with the African culture and achieve the best of all worlds. It is a dream doomed to failure, because men—Africans, Englishmen, and others—are not ready to give up their freedom, their willfulness, their separateness even for an ideal, especially when that ideal is a mythic simulacrum. Cary is sympathetic to Louis Aladai, but his novel presents Louis as a dreamer who asks too much of people at the present moment. The politician who succeeds is not the intelligent, cultured Louis, but his sister Lisbet, the juju priestess. Lisbet maps her campaign from her juju house, a hovel where children, denounced as witches, are tortured and left to die. She organizes the young Rimi women into a passive resistance army and is sure that whatever the army does, the British will not shoot down women.

Both Lisbet and Louis Aladai symbolize the transitional world of the African under British "progressive" leadership. Aladai has modern, European ideas but cannot realize them because his people do not trust such ideas. He is the intellectual African of the 1930's and 1940's—the man who does not feel at home either with his own people or with the English. His sister, on the other hand, can succeed where Louis fails. Wholly savage, she suffers no conflicts. She deals with white people without suffering any qualms of conscience. Elizabeth is the realist and survivor of the holocaust in Africa. Louis is the intellectual idealist betrayed on all sides.

In the preface to the Carfax edition, Cary wrote that *The African Witch* was not intended as a criticism of colonial policy: "My book was meant to show certain men and their problems in the tragic background of a continent still little advanced from the Stone Age, and therefore exposed, like no other, to the impact of modern turmoil. An overcrowded raft manned by children who had never seen the sea would have a better chance in a typhoon." The major location of Cary's novels, if he is to be taken at his word, is the human jungle and not the forests of Nigeria. Yet his novels are intimately tied to their setting, perhaps because Cary was mainly a visual artist and all his thinking was expressed in visual terms. A writer like Graham Greene can set his novel *The Heart of the Matter* in Freetown, Sierre Leone, and even state that he is after the essence of Africa, and yet be less bound to that continent than Cary. Greene's novel is about the backwaters of any colonial outpost. It would not seriously damage the novel to relocate it in East Africa or Malaya: the condition of the soul and the intense area of guilt would not be displaced. However, Cary's novels are too particularized in their depiction of the African milieu to be relocated elsewhere. The universal may spring from the particular, but the particulars never lose their African grounding in Cary's novels.

In *Castle Corner*, one of his five African novels, Cary surveyed England and Ireland as well as Africa in its panoramic spread of events and scenes: some ninety-three characters appear in the book. *Castle Corner* was probably the first attempt by Cary to break away from the African mold, by joining Africa to other areas of the globe, where his sensibilities might be refreshed and re-exploited.[10] *Castle Corner* was to be the first part of a trilogy, but this trilogy was abandoned when the materials proved too rich and unwieldy for Cary to handle. Interestingly enough, Cary, according to Molly M. Mahood, associated Ireland as well as Africa with latent treachery. That he should abandon a trilogy in which both areas of geographic and psychic content attracted and frightened him may be an instance of Cary's proclivity for reaching for the richest disorders of humanity and then, aware of the immensity of the task confronting him, withdrawing. In any case, Cary returned to his African material for only one more novel, the last and greatest of his African phase, *Mister Johnson.*

Simpler in style (it is written in the present tense throughout) and structure (a chronological development with few characters, it centers on one major character and only briefly gets him off the stage) than his other African books, *Mister Johnson* reveals again the persistent theme in Cary's fiction. Such themes, when stated baldly, lose much of the perceptiveness and emotional intensity with which Cary invested them, but they center on two major human failures (and near-successes): man's inability to understand his own actions, and his inability to understand the actions of others. Mister Johnson wants so much to be a European—preferably like Lieutenant Rudbeck. He wants to go beyond the tribal, African ways of

---

10 An unpublished novel, *Arabella,* written in the mid-1930's, also represented an early attempt to move away from the African milieu. *Arabella* was a political satire denouncing both Nazis and communists; its principal character, a learned, credulous professor said to be based on the character of Bertrand Russell, was the dupe of both totalitarian systems. See Andrew Wright, *Joyce Cary: A Preface to His Novels* (New York, 1958), pp. 50-52.

his Nigerian village. He wants to be a white-collar worker, a professional clerk, but such a clerk as the world has never seen. Cary says of him in the preface to the Carfax edition: "Mr. Johnson is a young clerk who turns his life into a romance, he is a poet who creates for himself a glorious destiny."

Every day that Johnson is on the road supervising a gang of road workers he has his boy servant carry a special chair. Although Johnson is too busy to use the chair, it must sit there in the sun all day indicating Johnson's status. The chair, like everything else that is European in Johnson's life, serves no practical purpose. Johnson's tragedy is that his aspirations are based on the symbolic values of European life, without these values having any real attachment to European customs. He is unlike other African characters in that he is not so much caught between two worlds as he is without roots in any world. He is the individual par excellence, the high-spirited, irrepressible, intelligent, charming bohemian who cannot fit in anywhere for any length of time because he does not wish a state of order.

Johnson is truly an early Gulley Jimson (the bohemian painter hero of *The Horse's Mouth*), an older Charley Browne (Cary's adolescent charmer in *Charley Is My Darling*)—a charmer who cheats, lies and loves his way into the affections of all who come his way. He has a dash, a wild lack of inhibition that lets him express compassion as if it were a community campfire. He expresses his love and warmth not in the conventional ways devised by an intelligent, alert, orderly minded society but in outbursts of spontaneous joy. The punishment for this spontaneity is restraint. Like Gulley Jimson and Charley Browne, Johnson is finally subdued by the society about him. Each of the three men is put out of the way: one in a reformatory, the other by pneumonia, and the last by execution. All the world loves a bohemian, but it has not yet found a home for him in Cary's novels except in a prison cell or an isolated hospital bed. The price of bohemianism in

Cary's novels is thus human punishment and spiritual freedom. Mister Johnson represents Cary's notion of African spontaneity, the corresponding notion of which is that art, like
life, is born every moment and that to hedge it in or crush
it by static forms is harmful to its reproduction. In view of
Cary's later fiction, it seems fair to state that Mister Johnson
is his favorite character type, the free spirit wailing and
wallowing his way through life.

Mister Johnson is young and eager and very willing to learn
from his European superiors, especially Rudbeck, the English
lieutenant he reveres. Rudbeck, however, is not so keen to
understand the African mind. He wants to get on with his
road-building and is not concerned with spanning the human
bridge. Rudbeck, like Mister Johnson, represents one of the
many-faceted sides of Cary. Cary also enjoyed road-building
when he served as a magistrate in Kaiama, Nigeria, in 1919.
Molly M. Mahood makes the comparison between Rudbeck
and Cary in this way:

> . . . [Cary] admits, like any other artist, that he has lost interest
> in the road now that it is nearly finished. He was experiencing
> the lassitude he makes Rudbeck feel at the end of his road-
> making effort in *Mister Johnson*. And like Rudbeck, he was
> finding that the authorities took little interest in his achieve-
> ments.[11]

When Mister Johnson, in the succeeding waves of misfortune that overtake him, grasps the last meaningful act in
his life, to be shot by his friend, Rudbeck is shocked into the
recognition that Johnson's fate is part of his doing. He asks
Johnson, "So you don't think this trouble of yours is partly my
fault, perhaps" (p. 246). And Johnson answers that the inspiration of Rudbeck's friendship has saved him from becoming a scoundrel. The answer, though Johnson means it sin-
cerely, does not satisfy Rudbeck, for he knows now he has

---

[11] *Joyce Cary's Africa* (Boston, 1965), pp. 56-57.

failed. Not wishing to be bothered with human complexities, he has avoided involvement with Africa. He dislikes the imperialists because they are meddlers with evil intentions, and he dislikes the missionaries as well, because they, though with the best of intentions, also meddle with people's affairs. And yet, at the end of the novel, Rudbeck is aware that his refusal to commit himself to Johnson's foolish attempts at friendship has resulted in an unnecessary tragedy. Johnson's death might have been avoided.

Mister Johnson is thus, on at least one level, a novel very like E. M. Forster's *A Passage to India*. In both these novels the author explores the futility of the attempts by two members of different racial groups to live and work with one another. The last scene in *A Passage to India* shows an Englishman and an Indian riding together but on separate ways. Johnson's and Rudbeck's fate was more tragic, but the essence of their loneliness is the same as in Forster's novel. This sense of despair may help to explain why Cary stopped writing about Nigeria. He had said all he wanted and had to say about it.

Although Cary left the African scene after *Mister Johnson*, he carried with him his interest in that thin line dividing presumption and sharing. This concern is especially reflected in Cary's last novel, *The Captive and the Free*, in which an evangelical missionary changes the course of many people's lives through the force of his personality. In Cary's early, African novels the missionaries who try to help (and who sometimes do help) are never fully accepted and never fully condemned for their intrusion into the lives of Africans.[12]

---

[12] Cf. Cary's comment in "My First Novel," in *The Listener*, XLIX, No. 1259 (April 16, 1953), 637: "I did not intend to attack the missions, which have done magnificent work in Africa—which by themselves, apart altogether from the opening up of the country, justified our conquest. When I was in Africa, the missions were still doing all the elementary education. Many people say that missions are interfering in Africa. The book [*Aissa Saved*] is really a study of the actual pressures on both sides."

When they are praised, it is for their uninhibited sharing of their gifts. This quality, the quality of being strong enough to be oneself in the company of others, is what moves Cary most. The quality appears in Mister Johnson, the African witch Elizabeth Aladai, the monkey-faced District Commissioner of *An American Visitor*, and in the lusty Aissa who thought of Jesus in amorous terms: "Jesus, you do plenty good thing for me I always do good for you, pray you every day, Jesus. You good frien to me Jesus, I know that."

Cary's first five novels represent a further development of the colonial or imperialist novel. His contribution was to deal with universal conditions in the complex sphere of imperialistic activity, Christian proselytizing, tribal warfare, and human inconsistencies. His African novels led to the development of certain types of men and women in his later masterpieces— the bohemian, the power-seeker, the confirmed optimist—but, just as significantly, they changed the course of the African novel. Africa had already been a Victorian morality drama; a psychological journey; a popular safari; a quest after the romantic unattainable. Now it became a seriocomic interlude in the eternal war between theoretic, personal anarchism and the power of order.

3

After a long period when West Africa as a theme and setting dropped out of English literature, in 1948 two further important novels about West Africa appeared. One, *The Walled City* by Elspeth Huxley, dealt with African affairs and their effect on a group of British civil servants, and shifted its scenes from northern Nigeria to London to a gray English seaside resort. Its emphasis was on the toll Africa extracts from its devoted servants; the result of loving Africa, at least for the Englishman, is tragedy and pain. Only the casual acquaintance, the uncaring observer, receives more from Africa than he has put into it. The other novel, *The Heart of the Matter* by Graham Greene, also dealt with psychological awareness through confrontation with the African mystique. Greene's Africa, however, was an impenetrable forest of darkness with just enough light around the edges to beckon the weary pilgrim, while Africa for Elspeth Huxley was a secular place with more worldly problems.

The Walled City is written in a kaleidoscope of time sequence—1942-1929-1919-1913-1933—through which is presented the development of an unnamed West African colony into an angry, nationalistic land. There is no chronological order of flashback or revelation: Elspeth Huxley's book is written in the manner of a person recalling significant past experiences which matured his view. Words or images give way to recollection; one recollection leads farther back, then forward, then back again. But the overall theme persists: the growth of a land from its slave-trading days through its colonial subjection and "enlightenment" up to the eve of its new independence. Robert, the hero, prefers the Africa of 1919—"You were your own master then" (p. 97)—to the Africa of 1929: "You're a puppet jerked on the end of a string by bosses" (p. 97). Robert's attitude is the key to the theme. The mythical West African colony in the early twentieth century was, whatever its faults, manageable (or so it seems, on reflection, to Robert). The new ferment is too complex, too painful. Robert is defeated by it at the end of the novel and goes off with a caravan to Mecca, in an endeavor to regain his spirit of participation in life.

Africa defeats Robert because it attacks him on two sides. He can understand, he believes, the imperialists and the officious administrators. When he arrives in 1913, he is a hopeful civil servant, with a new bride and a vision of fulfillment. He knows he can never rise far in the civil hierarchy because he won't "play the game," but he is not disturbed by his external lack of success. Nor does he believe his wife Priscilla cares about external recognition.

Through 1929, Robert and Priscilla find fulfillment in Africa. Though Freddy Begg, a pedant and a fool, rises "to the top," they are not discouraged. What destroys Robert and Priscilla is the spirit of the new Africa. The native Benjamin, who at first adored Robert and Priscilla, the British way of life, and the Mission teachings, rejects enlightened Europeanism. Benjamin, the sweet, pliant boy, becomes a vicious journalist not above lying in print to get the Africans to hate and destroy the British. Ultimately Benjamin destroys Robert's plan for making the colony financially independent of British capital; he does so in the name of nationalism.

Elspeth Huxley yearns for a return to the humane and intelligent colonial administrators of the past. But she is too aware to believe such a backward step can be taken. Her book is really a protest against the destruction of faith in rational behavior and compromise. The new African will not wait; he does not want to work with the whites, he wants the whites out of Africa. Ironically, to achieve this end he uses the methods of the Europeans he so despises—corruption, bribery, violence, and force. And the white man, who wants to stay in Africa, is equally at a loss. He cannot understand the hate the black man feels for him. When Robert leaves on his camel caravan to Mecca, he has symbolically rejected Christian and Western policy as a means of solving the African crisis.

In the closing scene Elspeth Huxley underscores the irony. The white man reverts to foot and camel over the long, hard African road to Marrakesh, Fezzan and Tripoli. In the final scene of her first novel, *Red Strangers* (London, 1939), an African boards an airplane and goes forward to take his place in the wider Western world. He has progressed from the tribal ways to a world role. While the black man flies to a new destiny, the white man has retreated on foot, hurt and isolated in his soul.

Major Scobie, the hero of Graham Greene's *The Heart of the Matter*, is much like Robert: always overlooked whenever an opportunity for promotion arises; indifferent to worldly success. But since Scobie is a compassionate man, he has empathy for his wife's disappointment in him. In the end Scobie gets the promotion his wife has so desperately wanted for her self-esteem, but neither of them enjoys the benefits of that promotion. Scobie, in despair at his inability to resolve an extramarital affair with a pretty young English girl ship-wrecked off the coast of Sierra Leone, commits suicide.

Greene's novel, like all his work, poses moral and religious questions cast in an urgent psychosymbolic imagery. It is this symbolic quality that has led one African novelist to have his hero call *The Heart of the Matter* the best novel yet written about Africa.[13] Certainly Greene's picture of the symbiotic conditions of his tight little colony has a harrowing reality: the drinking, the gossiping, the whoring, the spying, the blackmailing, the Moslem-Christian antagonisms, the despair, the impotence; nothing is left out. Yet these pictures are but part of a larger image, the image of seediness.[14] It is this quality which fascinates Greene wherever he goes; it is this quality which, once witnessed by him in Africa, made of that continent not a land in ferment but the shape of a human heart.[15] Even more, it is a state of psychic illumination:

---

[13] Obi, the British-educated intellectual of *No Longer at Ease* (New York, 1960), by Chinua Achebe, returns to Nigeria shorn of his nationalistic ideals and fervor. Undergoing a spiritual paralysis, he turns to Greene's novel as the best book by anyone on West Africa, except for the "happy ending"; Obi considers Scobie's suicide so convenient a solution as to make everyone happy.

[14] See Marie B. Mesnet, *Graham Greene and "The Heart of the Matter": An Essay* (London, 1954). Miss Mesnet discusses in detail Greene's attraction to squalor and corruption.

[15] See *Journey Without Maps* (p. 31): "I thought for some reason even then of Africa, not a particular place, but a shape, a strangeness, a wanting to know. The unconscious mind is often sentimental; I have written 'a shape,' and the shape, of course, is roughly that of the human heart."

It isn't that one wants to stay in Africa: I have no yearning for a mindless sensuality, even if it were to be found there: it is only that when one has appreciated such a beginning, its terrors as well as its placidity, the power as well as the gentleness, the pity for what we have done with ourselves is driven more forcibly home. . . . The only loot I had brought with me, as far back as one needed to go, was Africa: the innocence, the virginity, the graves not opened for gold, the mines not broken with sledges.[16]

Greene's approach to the Dark Continent is seen in many of the novels that followed his first novel about Africa. That approach represents a continuation of the Conradian attitude, a fascination with the dark places of the soul. But it also represents an exploitation of a continent as a symbol in a moral crisis, a crisis which ends in a spiritual victory through worldly defeat.

The general theme and attitude of *The Walled City* and *The Heart of the Matter*—Africa as a challenge that ends in defeat—pervaded the English literary scene for the next ten years. The *weltschmerz* did not end till after the first West African writings appeared in the mid-1950's, and then the optimism and vitality of this new African literature reinvigorated English writing and attitudes. A reader has only to compare Elspeth Huxley's novels about East Africa, where pain, violence, and corruption also occur, with her one novel about West Africa. In her novels about East Africa, the attitude is one of "Look, we've come through." In *The Walled City* the attitude is closer to "How did we make it?" and "Why do we continue to try?" Evident in the novel about West Africa in English in the late 1940's and 1950's was a nervous crisis.

Such a crisis has its effect on style as well as attitude, and no novel published by an Englishman between 1948 and 1958

---

[16] *Ibid.*, p. 10.

goes beyond hopelessness and despair and outraged sensibility. It is as if English writers were tired and waiting for a fresh current, a "wand of noble wood" that would clear the air.

Among those novels which show the debilitating effect of West Africa on the sensitive and compassionate white man is Ann Mary Fielding's *Ashanti Blood* (New York, 1952). Set in an isolated mining area, the action concentrates on the greed for gold which affects the entire cast of characters. Robert Haddon, the hero, is a man who has come to Africa with high ideals; he finds himself attacked on all sides, by inefficiency and corruption among the white settlers, by betrayal and hate among the Africans. Haddon's marriage also seems in danger of failing, and he blames the crisis on Africa: "It's this place. We should get away" (p. 175). The corruption of Africa is so strong that Haddon is prepared to shoot an old friend. He walks twenty miles through the bush, but at the climactic moment regains his sense of moral values.

Though Robert and his wife are saved from moral degeneration, they nonetheless fail in one fundamental endeavor. They are unable to uphold British standards. At the end of the novel they sail away from Africa. As in so many books, the arrival of a ship in Africa means hope and optimism and a determination to regain the lost Eden, while the departure of a ship, the return to England, signifies defeat. Like most colonials, Robert and Philippa, though they constantly talk about the benefits and comforts of English life, do not want to return to their homeland. Such a return dashes all their illusions against the harsher, narrower English realities.

The title of the novel derives from the name of a creeping plant with scarlet flowers that grows wild in the forests of Ashanti and the Gold Coast. Its petals look like blood. This *blood* is always in the background of Miss Fielding's novel: it is an image of hopelessness, a hopelessness which is underscored by the African saying she quotes in her foreword:

"Only when the flowers of Ashanti Blood turn white will there be no more bloodshed in Ashanti."

A better written novel, and one in which the attempt is to view the complex of activities in an entire area, "the dry colony of Hill Station" on the West African coast, is *The Loved Enemy* (London, 1952) by Stephen Coulter. In this novel, Africa affects its European residents in subtle degrees of difference, but its general effect is a derangement of moral fiber. People do not become immoral in Hill Station; they become bereft. The climate, the petty squabbles, the lack of intellectual and sophisticated activity—above all, the sense of isolation, of a narcissistic feeding on oneself—put *The Loved Enemy* squarely in the camp of the colonial novel. As an example of its genre, it meets most of the demands required of it. The missionary quarrels with the district commissioner; the junior officers and their wives drink too much; the psychological outcast who comes to Africa to forget his failure and discovers he has found a worse hell, a tighter prison (Hassett seems a direct descendant from Greene's Major Scobie)—all these people are here. And the forests, the lonely station where Edith Humble, a new arrival, goes to meet her husband, is appropriately and symbolically hidden in the bush—it needs two days by train from Lagos, then a day and a half by boat, and three more by lorry to reach it. And only four isolated whites live in this vast region.

Coulter's novel bears a strong affinity to Greene's obsession with the squalor of Africa. The plot centers on Hassett and his wife Paule, and Paule's stepfather, Old Man Bernard, who owns the big, profitable store in Hill Station. Paule will not leave Africa because she will not give up the opportunity of inheriting her stepfather's money. When it appears that she has lost all chance of securing it—her stepfather has decided to marry a young Syrian nurse—Paule murders her stepfather and arranges the evidence to implicate her husband in the old man's death. Ironically, Hassett himself had once thought of murdering Bernard, without making any plans to evade the consequences; his motive, too, had been to get the money his wife had always wanted, but the futility of it had decided him against it. Paule's deception is anyway unnecessary, since Hassett, who is willing to die or go to jail, slips in the yard and accidentally kills himself. The novel ends with Paule getting what she wants, but hers is a cold victory. The district commissioner, sure of her guilt, is also sure he cannot convict her before a jury, and he presses no charges.

Like Conrad, Coulter is fascinated by the "abomination." But for Coulter the "abomination" is the same as Greene's: it is represented in the relationship between whites and whites; the African element is only a background. The seediness, the despair are streets within the soul, and the rot, which is everywhere, does not stem from man's adventure with primitive black beliefs. The rot is a condition of modern man, and it overpowers Africa and primitivism. Conrad's story was the reverse, with black primitivism confronting the morality of white civilization. The new Africa in Coulter's novel is the Africa made seedy and corrupt by modern man's paralysis, and it finally overcomes Hassett, one of the few men still fighting a losing battle against despair. At the end, the district commissioner quietly carries on, but Paule, the force representing the European corruption, has triumphed.

Perhaps the oddest novel about West Africa in English, one surely out of its time, is Jonas Lamptey's *The Village in the Trees* (London, 1955), from which the following extract is taken:

Life here in Nyankwa was what he wanted to know. He had wanted to probe to the bottom of it, to know what really went on behind the façade of black skins, crumbling houses and silent forest. He had been fascinated, and this was where the mystery had led him, to the pit of hell itself. It was the revelation of an inconceivable evil which struck away the basis, faith in Nyankwa, on which his own life here had rested. Now he knew. He had *seen*. All he had so far done in Nyankwa, his friendship with Davis, his meeting with the Progressive Youth Association, his sympathies expressed on numerous occasions, appeared to him as the merest superficialities. Here, close at hand in the undergrowth where he did not dare to shine his torch a second time, was the truth, the product of a strange and terrible belief that reached back to the very beginnings of time. He was an eyewitness of evil as yet unfathomed. . . . He knew them all now. He had plunged into the depths. (p. 231)

Lamptey's book is important, not because it can be taken seriously (though it apparently was meant to be), but because it is part of a major trend of its decade. If Lamptey is more critical of Africa than others, he is still part of the English literary rejection of the scene. Others leave West Africa in despair; Lamptey's hero left it in anger and foolish self-righteousness.

Still another novel representing the British crisis in West Africa is *No Joy of Africa* (London, 1955) by W. R. Loader. Loader's title symbolizes his theme: Africa is not the romantic place that some English men and women conceive in their daydreams. It is a backwash and a hole of corruption. The hero Hardy is a strict, rigid, self-centered head of a British construction company erecting a new building to house the Legislative Assembly in the capital of an unnamed West African territory. The novel traces Hardy's descent from clean-living sobriety to drunkenness. While certainly there are flaws in Hardy's character, it is the impact of Africa upon him which impels the crisis of personality. Hardy, a disciplinarian, warns his fellow technicians about the dangers of African sloth— native women, prostitution, drink. Yet he himself succumbs to Africa's environmental blandishments. He loses his wife through his infatuation for a vapid, pretty girl, who leaves him to marry someone else. Hardy also loses his job, because his harsh measures have caused a strike by African workers. The double loss breaks his spirit and, at the end of the novel, as he prepares to do business with the local prostitute, an ugly mulatto, he sinks into an alcoholic stupor.

Other characters in Loader's novel also fail to adjust to Africa. Helen, from a poor, uneducated family in England, decides to be sophisticated. She experiments with an African lover, but her choice proves lamentable, for Joseph Sackey, a fierce nationalist, exploits whites unscrupulously. When Helen becomes pregnant and asks for his help, he laughs in her face.

Derek, an engineer from an undemanding home in England, cannot face the conflict which Africa thrusts on him. Effeminate and afraid of sex, Derek succumbs to the prostitute Effie. It is only when his fiancée writes to say she is coming to Africa that Derek realizes he is unable to cope with the sexual responsibilities of his manhood. He commits suicide.

Each of these whites has flaws in character. Africa becomes the place where man's identity can no longer be stored away. Loader's novel is pessimistic because self-revelation in the English leads not to tragedy or understanding but to suicide and defeat. Only the Africans benefit from their actions, while the English, unaccustomed to their new surroundings, flounder. The impact of Africa, in this novel of decadence, is fatal; and in the character of Derek, the novel about Africa shows its first signs of dealing with the new literary vogue of treating homosexuality. *No Joy of Africa* makes decadence look grim.

Loader's second novel *The Guinea Stamp* (London, 1956) is even more pessimistic. William Ofori returns from an education at Oxford to take a post at University College in West Africa. He soon forsakes his early attempts at synthesizing European ideas and techniques with the traditions of Africa. Ofori's enthusiasm and good will are destroyed by what he considers color prejudice by the British who run the college. As a result, he lends himself to the cause to make the college an independent university, managed and staffed by Africans. This project ends inevitably, as do most projects in Africa in the novels of the 1940's and 1950's, in a riot. Ofori kills his best friend, a white policeman, and is himself killed by African policemen loyal to the British. What makes this novel so despairing is that the education of the major characters in no way equips them to deal with the volatile problems of race prejudice. Indeed, the professors and their wives seem less able than the uneducated, nonintellectual characters of *No Joy of Africa* to work side by side with the African. Their humanity has been sapped by academic rivalry and petty ambition, and their honesty is always in danger of turning to rationalization, at which they are so adept.

At Fever Pitch (London, 1959) by David Caute is an African novel which tackles the problem of homosexuality openly, though less than adequately. Its central character, Michael Glyn, has joined the British Army in an attempt to run from his conflict, but in Bada, the capital of an African territory on the verge of self-government, Glyn finds he must assuage the force of his desires. The hero's obsession with his homosexuality prevents him from coming to grips with himself; his sexual proclivities bring little but mental suffering to him. He is virginal and hysterical, and his hysteria causes him to murder twenty-five Africans and be the first white man to stand trial in the new African country. Such a situation has enormous promise, for the trial and the courtroom could well have been the focus of the display of repressed bitterness on both sides. Yet Caute's novel ends without a trial scene. Instead, the author substitutes a curious last scene in which Glyn sleepily fondles a coin on which the African prime minister's image has been imprinted.

Three more novels dealing with the frustrations of the British Civil Service and African nationalism appeared in 1958. *Picnic at Porokorro* has as its central theme the familiar mine company plot; racial violence occurs as the greed of diggers urges them onto forbidden personal property belonging to the British Minerals Trust Company. The violence was at least partly caused by an irresponsible, self-styled liberal journalist.

Geoffrey Horne, in *Land of No Escape* (London, 1958), sends his hero Cleaver to a distant post, where he and his superior are the only two white men in five thousand square miles. A white mission teacher appears, but she is in despair at her failure to lead the natives to Christian morality and progress. Horne denies even the physical splendor of Africa: "Where was the bright sun of the tropics? This might have been an autumn day in England, the rain still heavy, a diaphanous mist over the forest, a chill striking at the bones" (p. 12).

Netta Muskett, in *Flame of the Forest*, followed the lead of others in exploiting native riots, this time in Sierra Leone, for the pivotal scene in her novel; in using for her hero a young police officer thrown into conflict between duty and humanitarianism; and in taking her title from a scarlet West African plant.

What all these novels reveal is the inability of Europeans to adjust to the African milieu. The impact of Africa has been too great for them. Yet the issue is not so simple. Each of these heroes, even the best of them, has flaws, and, when they are pitted against the demands created by the African milieu, it is their shortcomings that cause their defeat. This is the stuff of tragedy, man in battle with the elements, with the gods. It is modern man's tragedy in particular, man in battle with the forces of politics. That so many of these novels fail to attain the level of tragedy is due not to the choice of subject but in the refusal of the authors to imbue their protagonists with the quality of heroism. Only Greene and Elspeth Huxley present their heroes with some degree of respect and admiration. Scobie and Robert, for instance, are seen to be good men of their kind, who, through fortuitous circumstances, have to live out their lives at the wrong place and at the wrong time. But no such good men exist in the other novels that have been discussed. The men and women in those novels fail in Africa because of their intrinsic inadequacies as human beings.

A few novels of the 1940's and 1950's fall outside this tradition of despair. Two of these are about mission schools and teachers. One, *Swelling of Jordan* (London, 1950) by Ellen Thorp, is a historical novel based on the founding of the Christian Mission Society—the Yoruba Mission at Ibadan, Nigeria. Miss Thorp collected most of her material from *Seventeen Years in Yoruba Country* by Anna Hinderer, the wife of the first Christian Mission Society volunteer in Ibadan.[17] In *The Silk-Cotton Tree* (London, 1958), the locale of which is Liberia, Esther S. Warner uses familiar characters but invests them with a freshness of attitude and language. Her book is a pleasant antidote to the many West African novels of despair, though she also sees tragedy and pain as a necessary part of the transition of Africa—in the case of her story, into a Christian community. Since her interest is religious and personal, she does not deal with political events. Her natives are simple-minded though not unintelligent, likeable, and wanting to please, yet confused and, above all else, half-Christian and half-juju. They are much like the natives of Joyce Cary. Miss Warner's missionaries are also Cary-like. Huldamah (the name given to the Danish woman Miss Larson, who reads *Beowulf* to her African students) represents the ideal spinster teacher, a devoted, selfless woman who made a mistake in her youth (the traditional love affair and illegitimate child). Huldamah is an anarchist of the stripe of Mrs. Carr in *Aissa Saved*, and of Marie Hasluk in *An American Visitor*. She hates authority of any kind and fights against the narrow teachings of her superior, the Reverend Reed. Her attentions focus on a black

---

[17] See John Harris, *Books about Nigeria: A Select Reading List* (Ibadan, Nigeria, 1959).

girl—Hagar—who, like Aissa, is Christian with lapses. Hagar
has been impregnated by her African lover Isaac, who warns
her that Mrs. Reed, the minister's wife, will dismiss her as
soon as the truth is known. The use of Christian names is amus-
ingly symbolic, for Hagar goes off to a small bush village
where she helps Huldamah organize a mission church and
school. The novel traces Hagar's development from an immature young girl to a woman who experiences the loss of her
child, has an affair with a young American minister, and
comes to realize that Christians are not all of a kind. The
author's gentle criticism of missionaries continues throughout
the book. The minister and his wife and the Christianized
African Issac are self-centered and parochial. Symbolically
they remain in the comparatively big city while the purer
Christians, Huldamah, Hagar, and the young American missionary all go into the country. Huldamah, Hagar and the
American missionary "sin" but purge themselves through
their trek into the wilderness.

Like Hagar, the novel itself achieves part of its vitality from
the rhythms and word patterns of pidgin English. Yet the most
salient feature of *The Silk-Cotton Tree* lies in the fact that it
is in the Joyce Cary tradition of African novels. It is a comic
tribute to missionaries, a tribute which has its share of pejorative criticism. Its two heroines are anarchistic—that is, they are
strong champions of personal freedom without physical or
spiritual restraint. In the foreword to *Seven Days to Lomaland*
(Boston, 1954),[18] an earlier, nonfiction work about her mission instruction of three Liberians and their kinsmen, Esther
S. Warner gave the key to her philosophy: "It [this book] is
not scholarly, except that the kind of wisdom Emerson and
Thoreau gave us can be heard in the folklore of the deep
forests of Africa." It is significant that Marie Hasluck, the
anarchist of Cary's *An American Visitor,* also read Emerson

---

18 British edn.: *Trial by Sasswood* (London, 1955).

and Thoreau and saw these American "primitives" as the guiding spirits in her humanitarian philosophy.

4

R^{iot} (London, 1954), by John Wyllie, is the best political
novel on West Africa written by an Englishman. It differs
from other novels written by Englishmen during the same
period in its hopefulness of tone. Although in this book Wyllie
sees violence as payment by demand for the colonial past, he
conveys also a note of optimism—that a new, peaceful era
will emerge in Africa.

Riot is an episodic novel, with constant shifts of point of
view. The aim of its technique is to convey a sense of flux,
of moments that slip beyond rational control. Certainly the
reader is thrown into a whirlpool of events and character-
izations. In its approach it bears a strong resemblance to the
best novel about racial violence in South Africa, Episode by
Harry Bloom. Both novels make the point that so much bitterness exists beneath the forced smile, the polite snicker, that
any event can set off an explosion of human force. Bloom sees
that an apparently trivial circumstance—that the mere fact that
a collar is missing from a bundle of shirts which a Zulu washerwoman has delivered to a white South African lady—may well
initiate a riot ending in the slaughter of hundreds. Where the
atmosphere is charged with discontent, any excuse to explode
it will do. Wyllie, on the other hand, recounts a more sys-
tematic, more logical sequence of events—the riot starts because political extremists, exploited by Communists and fanatic
African nationalists, force it. Once the riot starts, however,
Wyllie presents a subtle and perceptive picture of the wide
range of forces involved in a West African country's struggle
for independence. On one side are ranged the white extremists,
on the other the black extremists, and in the middle stand

those who want to avoid the clash. The middle group is by far the largest in number, but as mediators they do not stand a chance; it is their tragic duty to sacrifice their lives until the principle of peaceful compromise gains men's allegiance again.

The black extremists of *Riot* include Mr. Browning, Mr. Zimmerman, and a vicious newspaper columnist who spreads his lies under the byline "Marcus Aurelius." The special target of their bitterness is the British-owned stores of the Combined African Traders Corporation, known familiarly to them as CATCORP. Because of the stores' high prices, and the profits which pass to absentee English hands, the extremists have a valid, exploitable issue. Zimmerman urges first a boycott; he tells a mob who have gathered to hear him speak that they must learn to hate the white man: "For then and only then shall we drive him out of the government of this country." When the boycott erupts into a riot, led by Browning and Zimmerman, it is temporarily halted by a white police officer, Rankin, who personally fires the shots that wound one African leader and kill another. Yet Rankin, like the police officers in many African novels—Alan Paton, Graham Greene, Stephen Coulter, and Joyce Cary, all have drawn police officers as sympathetic leaders—desires peace. It is his duty that forces him to kill.

Wyllie's *Riot* seems based on an event in Ghana (then the Gold Coast). Richard Wright has described the circumstances leading up to the riot, which broke out on February 23, 1948, following the nationwide boycott of imported goods that was put into effect in order to force foreign firms to reduce prices. When the boycott started, the British government and foreign merchants pledged to African leaders that prices would be reduced. The pledge was not kept, and rioting, looting of foreign stores, and bloodshed ensued. Twenty-nine people were killed, and 237 were injured.[19] The fictional riot, how-

---

[19] Richard Wright, *Black Power*, p. 93.

ever, is only a *modus operandi* for the author's exploration
into the attitude of various Africans, black and white. Two of
these whites are devoted visitors who attempt to efface the
injustices of the past through love. One, a Welsh girl named
Blodwell, marries an African. The other, an American missionary, Dortweiler, tries to make of Christian love an overwhelming force such that resentment for past wrongs, or hate
of any nature unworthy of man, has to turn its cheek and flee.
Both Blodwell's love and Dortweiler's Christianity are defeated, however, by the wrath of Africa. Blodwell, going to
meet her husband in town, is dragged down a deserted alley
and raped by an African. Naked and ashamed, she slinks away;
now she too has borne the African tragedy. Furthermore she,
who had demanded that she be a part of Africa, has truly become a part.

Yet Blodwell forgives the man who raped her, for she believes in the role she must play, the role of the white who must
accept black wrongs as a necessary transition from bitterness.
When she marries Sam Johnson, she begins to keep a diary
because she realizes that by marrying a black man she has
put herself in the position of "the covered wagoners." Yet her
marriage is not due to her wishing to prove something, but the
result of her inability to disprove her passion. Still, Blodwell
realizes that her love for an African is "abnormal. But, having
followed her journalist friend's observation to its conclusion,
she had realised that tastes in behaviour and therefore norms
in behaviour, change and evolve. What was abnormal today
might become the standard of tomorrow" (p. 119).

Blodwell, then, is one solution to the African problem:
through love one can transcend the fears induced by the color
bar. *Riot*, like several earlier English novels—most notably,
William Plomer's *Turbott Wolfe*—suggests interracial marriage
as a solution to the color question.[20]

---

[20] Carol Christian presents a much less idyllic view of intermarriage in
West Africa in her novel *Into Strange Country* (London, 1958).

Another middle way is offered by the American missionary Dortweiler and his wife, who want a blend of Christian and African culture:

> Primitive Africa knows and accepts as commonplace what western science is just beginning to apprehend, that through a person's mind it is possible for them to develop the physiological symptoms you were looking for so eagerly. . . . One day our knowledge and the knowledge that these people have will come together and be a science. When that happens there will be a new force in the world.   (pp. 83-84)

But Dortweiler also suffers brutal treatment at the hands of Africans.

Standing outside the riot is a South African Jewish painter, Benson, who is planning to leave Africa because he cannot live amid the changing conditions. He does not like the black man, and besides he is too old to change his views. He is one of the white homeless, a refugee who has no place in the new Africa. Yet because he is an outcast—an outcast three times, as a Jew, as an artist, and as a white man in Africa—he is able to view the scene objectively. What Benson sees through his artist's sharp eyes is that the African is ready for independence, but that he is not ready to consider the white man expendable. And although he is against interracial marriage, he declares that the white man must be "assimilated" (p. 254).

Benson comes to his conclusions only after he has witnessed the riot. In the beginning of the novel, he believes in the swift killing of the African rioters. He remembers the rape and death of his first wife and the destruction of his whole family by the Nazis. It is only after witnessing further, senseless killing that he comes to accept the inevitability of compromise. The novel thus ends on this note of hope.

Wyllie is an Englishman; Harry Bloom, the author of *Episode*, is a white South African Jew; and Peter Abrahams, who has written a novel about violence in West Africa, *A Wreath for Udomo,* is a Cape Colored (a strain of Hottentot and European, Asian and/or African origins) from South Africa. In the novels of these three men a similar picture evolves. The similarity is not due to any influence of one writer on the other but to the spirit pervading all Africa which sensitive writers imbibe. Bloom, in a personal interview in London in 1962, said he had not read *Riot,* though he was aware that his and Wyllie's books had many elements in common. All three writers believe that in the transition to African independence, the liberals, the peaceful compromisers on both sides, will suffer death and little gratitude for their selfless acts. They are paying the price of their greater understanding, of their vision. In *Riot,* even such an intelligent and liberal African like Sam Johnson, the black husband of a Welsh girl, dons an African tribal costume to show his allegiance when the violence starts.

Black understanding, like white understanding, is limited. Nor is the problem merely black against white; it is black against brown, and black against black. Wyllie and Bloom are careful to show the antagonism of the Africans to the Syrian and Indian merchant class. In *Riot,* an African walks into a shop and tells the Indian owner, "One day de black man go kill you Indian man, all. You be tief man. All Indians be tief man. One day I go kill you myself, you blood Indian man" (p. 17). In *Episode* Indian merchants are warned that when the protection of the South African government is lifted, there will be wholesale slaughter of them by the blacks.

Overshadowing everything, smearing the entire canvas, is the splash of blood. The fiction writers who deal with the politics of Africa do not see any way out of the inevitable clash. The disease of past wrongs and oppressions calls for bloodletting. The one hope is that the cure will not kill off the patient, and that from this loss of blood will arise a healthier, less divided body politic.

THREE

West Africa by Africans

.

1

Together, Chinua Achebe, Cyprian Ekwensi, Onuora Nzekwu, Wole Soyinka, Thomas M. Aluko, Gabriel Okara, Christopher Okigbo, and William Conton comprise a new development in the West African literary scene. All Africans, they have been publishing novels, poetry, and plays in English since the early 1950's. With the exception of William Conton, a native of Sierra Leone educated in Ghana, these writers are Nigerian, and their novels and poetry are rooted either in the Christian-juju complex or in the political ferment attending national independence. While the Nigerian novelists read and criticize each other's work, and know each other personally,[1] it would be inaccurate to suggest that their work manifests a conscious literary movement. They are writers who, functioning in a mobile society, have no formal set of principles such as those of Aimé Césaire and Léopold Senghor and other Négritude writers; as their work shows, their standards are preeminently individualistic. Nor do they speak

---

[1] Ulli Beier, "First Fruits: A Literary Letter from Nigeria," in *The New York Times Book Review* (January 28, 1962), p. 34.

through a journal like *Présence Africaine,* a periodical actively involved in the propagation of French West African culture, although, again, they contribute to such journals as *Black Orpheus, Nigeria Magazine,* and *Ibadan.* While in principle these Nigerian writers are reluctant to discuss the "African soul," a favorite phrase of the Négritude writers and once so popular an idea throughout intellectual Africa, they are willing to examine particular African problems and the techniques and themes of African literature.

The level of achievement of these writers has focused world attention on African and in particular Nigerian literature. Such is the activity and the ferment in this literature, which is little older than a generation, that trends once noticeable and popular five years ago are now forgotten. A writer like Amos Tutuola, who spawned the first wave of excitement when his work crossed the ocean to England, France, and America, is rarely read and little imitated in Nigeria today.

In general these West African novelists have treated four thematic areas. One is the primitive and/or tribal African society, the way of life untouched by European hands. Novels in this category tend not so much to glorify as to show respect for an ordered way of life that has passed. The admiration is not "nativization" or a romanticization of a dead past, but a cultural nationalism—a literary salute to Africa's achievement before European influence.

Another theme is the "pure" Africa at its first point of contact with European customs. The defeat of African culture, particularly the tribal way of life, becomes the central issue in these novels.

A third theme is the defeat of Africa, not by Europe per se but by the self-Europeanization of Africans themselves. Novels of this kind accept the passing of the European as a *de facto* condition. They raise no lament for the displaced European, but they cry out in protest against the legacy of Europe—the corruption, the bureaucratic sloth, the greed; the lack of strong family ties and of a sense of purpose. These novels are essentially warnings against decadence.

Lastly, are the novels whose overall theme is an extension of the others. The writers in this group see the dangers inherent in the new Africa, but they also accept the ineradicable presence of Europeanization in Africa. The African, in the eyes of these writers and probably their readers, will lead the way in the new world because he will combine the technological knowledge of Europe (which no longer can be denied to him) with the spirit of human kindness and love, a spirit which has been killed off in Europe but not in Africa. Thus the African makes the machine work for him in contradistinction to the European who is working for the machine. The African has it in his power to bring peace to the world because of his inner triumphs.

The origins of the African novel spring from folk tales, anthropological accounts, missionaries' observations, traders' reports, and explorers' journals. Just as it is difficult to place a firm line of demarcation between creative fiction and nonfiction by Europeans on Africa (for example, J. F. Stuart-Young's narratives and Laurens van der Post's travel writings), it is equally difficult to determine the first modern novel in English by an African. Many memoirs, utilizing fictional and narrative techniques, display a literary skill as accomplished as the novel, and such memoirs, with an African ambience, have appeared sporadically since the nineteenth century. In West Africa one of the earlier works of this genre was a fictionalized autobiography, *Lobagola: An African Savage's Own Story* (New York, 1930), by Bata Kindai Amgoza Ibn Lo Bagola. Lo Bagola's theme is stated in one of his key sentences: "There is no excuse for a white man to be less civilized, in the proper sense of the word, than we savages." His book is especially significant in West African literary history because it foretells the major theme of West African novels: Lo Bagola is not an African who stays in a village with traditional customs but a man who comes in contact with a vastly different civilization. He must learn to adjust to the changing conditions, and in the process of that adjustment he comes close to neurosis. Lo Bagola, who grew up in a remote village near the Niger Bend, was miserable when he returned to his village after an education in a white man's school. He later went to New York where he lectured, traveled, and wrote articles on Africa. In his own words he learned to "lie like a white man," but this faculty did not bring him happiness. Like an intellectual hero in a novel, Lo Bagola yearned for a return to the illusory happy past of his village and at the same time for the state of fulfillment suggested by modern power, yet was able to achieve neither. His book closes in irresolution, with the conflict in abeyance.

That conflict between tribal beliefs and modern technology, between intuitive faith in the past and rational optimism engendered by prospects for the future, is found in all of the four books written by Amos Tutuola, the first Nigerian novelist to be celebrated abroad. It is one of the ironies of literature that Tutuola is probably the best-known West African fiction writer in Europe and the United States (with the possible exception today of Chinua Achebe), yet Nigerians think little of him. His work has sold well on both continents, and his original and translated works have been the literary sensation of Paris. The reason for his French success may be laid to his style: it is an amalgam of African rhythms and structure with pidgin-English locutions. But just as Nigerians generally frown on the Négritude movement, so do they look on Tutuola's work as an artificial product and a dead end.

Tutuola is more a mythologist than a novelist. All his work is cast in the guise of fiction, but his heroes and heroines are more dream-figures than people of flesh and blood. His first novel, *The Palm-Wine Drinkard* (London, 1952), tells the story of a man who journeys through several nightmare adventures in the African bush after his palm-wine tapster has died.

The hero, who has drunk 225 kegs of palm-wine a day since he was ten years old, cannot find anyone capable enough to replace his dead tapster (who fell from a tree while tapping wine for him). Consequently he travels to Deads Town to retrieve his tapster. On the way he meets a "female cream image"; a quarter-mile-long total stranger with no head, feet, or hands but one large eye sitting Cyclops-like at the top of his body; and cold, hairy animals that sound like church bells.

The same elements of mythology are found in Tutuola's second book, *My Life in the Bush of Ghosts* (London, 1954). Here a boy in a polygamous household braves the terrors of the Bush of Ghosts in order to discover the meaning of "good" and "bad." The boy travels through "Lost or Gain Valley," which has to be crossed without clothes; he meets "burglar-Ghosts"—children who, having died in infancy, come back to the mortal world to torment their parents; and he sees a group of witches getting ready to eat a member of their family.

My Life in the Bush of Ghosts is not a sequel to *The Palm-Wine Drinkard*, for although the imagery springs from the same source, a wonderful grab bag of Jungian, Freudian, totem, taboo, and industrial images, the worlds in the two books are different. Tutuola's first novel dealt with Deads Town; his second portrays a world of spirits. These spirits have never died because they have never been alive. They are ageless and everywhere. Yet the tone of the two books is very much the same: fear exists in both, the fear of the journey and the attraction to it; the thrill of fear in the forest; the almost pleasurable fear when the lost boy is threatened by the Golden-ghost, the Silverish-ghost, the Copperish-ghost, the Smelling-ghost, and the Homeless-ghost. And although the boy returns to earth, the fear and the ambivalence still remain, for the boy dreams hopefully of being able to attend the centenary of the Secret Society of Ghosts.

Tutuola's third book, *Simbi and the Satyr of the Dark Jungle* (London, 1955), continues the journey motif. Simbi wants to

taste "Poverty" and "Punishment." She leaves h[...]
mother and her secure household to enter the myster[...]
that leads to knowledge, danger, and fearful mysteries.
Simbi's journeys includes a river-ride of several days [...]
sealed coffin, at the end of which the coffin slides into a fis[...]
town, and Simbi is unsealed, whole and alive. This adventu[...]
is as fantastic and convincing, in its setting, as Hermione[...]
voyage in *The Winter's Tale*. Simbi, unlike the heroes of
Tutuola's first two books, soon achieves her quest, for after
her kidnapping by Dogo she is sold into slavery and learns
enough of "Poverty" and "Punishment" to change her mind
about adventuring outside the limits of her town.

In *The Brave African Huntress* (London, 1958), Tutuola's
fourth book, the four sons of an old man die in the Jungle of
Pygmies. The remaining child, a daughter, decides to avenge
their death by scourging the land of these Pygmies. She is the
"brave African huntress," and she carries with her a magic
"cudgel." When her leg is cut off by a giant, one of the "obstacles" of the jungle, she joins the two parts together and
experiences no further pain. Thereafter she slays the "ob-
stacle." But her quest leads her into captivity by the Pygmies.
Marked with an "X," she is placed in Bachelors' Town, where
all men want her "to Wife." Significantly, she chooses a very
old man. Finally, she goes on to kill all the Pygmies and free
their prisoners (those hunters who had journeyed before her
to rid the land of the evil sprites). The image of a woman
leading her country to glory and happiness, and thus sustaining
the matriarchal African society, is here explicitly verbalized.

The journey motif, or the end to innocence, seems at the
core of all Tutuola's work. What seems especially important
is the change of his heroes' attitude to their journey. In *My
Life in the Bush of Ghosts* and *The Palm-Wine Drinkard* the
heroes return to earth, but they yearn for the mysterious forces
of Deads Town and the world of spirits. In anticipation of
their return to these worlds they revel in the eternal fears of

the forest. In *Simbi* and *The Brave African Huntress* the heroines are content to have returned home from their journey. Home is dull, it lacks the throbbing passion of the forest, but it is secure. Indeed, the theme of Tutuola's third book is Simbi's foolish desire to venture into "Poverty" and "Punishment." The brave African huntress is driven at least as much by a positive social goal—destruction of the ugly Pygmies—as by a psychological one. Tutuola seems to have progressed from a need to explore evil and darkness, a need compounded by fear of punishment for possessing that compulsion, to a more rational social approach to the conquest and elimination of evil. Even the styles of the books reflect the change of attitude. The bouncing, tossing sentences of *The Palm-Wine Drinkard* almost disappear from *The Brave African Huntress*, which has a stately, more conventional sentence structure.

Tutuola has had little influence on Nigerian writers principally because he has relied on a personal mythology and because many Nigerians feel he has been playing the court jester to the European literary kingmakers. Perhaps, too, the fact that he had little formal education—he attended two religious schools, one run by the Salvation Army and the other by the Anglican Church—is a contributing factor to his relative lack of stature in his own country. Nigerians regard him as a primitive showing no desire to move from his "primitive habitat." Yet it is likely that in time he will be seen as a real talent, not merely as a phenomenon that introduced the exotic barbarities of an African jungle to a living-room world. Even today he is not without influence abroad: as has already been affirmed, his easeful, vital rhythmic style brought the first wave of European and American attention to West African writers. His preference for English over his native language of Yoruba has in itself been significant, and his books, in spite of their mythical primacy, reflect the ambivalence of an Africa rooted in the tribal past yet caught up in a modern power struggle.

Cyprian Ekwensi is the earliest and most prolific of the socially realistic Nigerian novelists. His first writings were mythological fragments and folk tales. From these African materials he turned to the city and its urban problems, which he now feels are the major issues confronting his people. Ekwensi's fiction follows the pattern of his professional and educational career. Born of Igbo parents in 1921, he grew up in Northern Nigeria where he became acquainted with Hausa and Fulani folk tales; he later worked in this region as a forest inspector. Subsequently he studied liberal arts, pharmacy, and journalism in Ibadan, England, and at Achimota College in Ghana. He has been a schoolteacher, practiced pharmacy, and served as a journalist and upper-grade civil servant in Lagos. As Nancy Jeanne Schmidt points out in her hitherto unpublished dissertation, "An Anthropological Analysis of Nigerian Fiction," [2] Ekwensi's

. . . earliest stories were about Hausa and Fulani cultures and forest work in Northern Nigeria; his first novel about Fulani life; and his first chapbook was a love story about two Nigerian students who were separated when the boy went to England to study. His later short stories are about students, government and other workers, and city life. Three of his novels take place in Lagos, and the leading male characters in two are a reporter and a pharmacist. The descriptions of Lagos and Nigerian feeling in his fiction are indistinguishable from those in factual articles he has written, and his portrayal of employment problems in fiction are identical with those he described to two Nigerian students who asked him for advice about getting a job upon their return to Nigeria.   (pp. 187-88)

Miss Schmidt's description suggests that Ekwensi is servile to his environment, though she herself later qualifies her remark to indicate that while Ekwensi is dependent on his realistic setting and a spirit of realism in his work, he is also

---

[2] Northweste n University, Evanston, Ill. (August 1965).

a creative artist fashioning human clay out of cement sidewalks. Certainly his realism is his predominant characteristic; his reliance on sociological material often mars his fiction with the superficial patina of a journalistic exposé, but at his best moments his vision of the animal vitality of human struggle is powerful and evocative. Even at his weakest, when he indulges in what his critics call a "true detective" or "modern romance" level, he still exhibits narrative agility and inventiveness.

Ekwensi's first novel, *Burning Grass*, was not published in England until 1962, long after he had achieved fame with *People of the City* and *Jagua Nana*. It, and *The Leopard's Claw*, originally a BBC radio story published as a novella in 1950, are seminal works in which appear the themes that were later to occupy him in his "city period" as well as his current work.

The action of *Burning Grass* takes place in the Fulani countryside of Northern Nigeria; it is concerned with a time which is passing, and a new age which is beckoning. The burning of the grass symbolizes this passage of time, the moment of moving on, the time of departure for new lands and new goals. The hero is an old man, Mai Sunsaye, who gets a mysterious "wandering" sickness. His faithful son Rikku tries to catch up with him, but suffers instead his own adventures. It is the separate adventures of the two men that provides the rather pacific, dry-heat atmosphere of the novel. During his adventures Rikku falls in love with a virtuous young maiden, is kidnapped by a beautiful princess who later sacrifices her own life so that he may go free, and, finally, Rikku sees his old father die. Distraught at this death Rikku is nevertheless prepared for a new life: "Rikku would work as apprentice to Ligu until she gave him some cattle to start off on his own. That was a good thing" (p. 149). This journey motif—that of the young man's initiation into an awareness of adult responsibilities and burdens, into a choice between the magical past (his father's mysterious "wandering") and a present time shorn of the gift and charm of potent superstition—is what impels all of Ekwensi's fiction, even his most urban book, *Jagua Nana,* in which Jagua goes back to the Eastern section to find a potency she has squandered in the modern city. *Burning Grass,* though entirely devoted in setting to the rural North, refers at many points to what has become the central thesis of Ekwensi's work: the ambivalent, destructive-invigorating city life of Lagos. In *Burning Grass* the townsman's role is given to Hodio, who is described by the old man Mai Sunsaye at the end of the book in this way:

> He was certain that Hodio would do well as a dweller in the new town of Chanka. For Hodio, that would be a good thing and he would mature as a man; his wild streak would sober down under the routine of sugar manufacturing and building the new town. (p. 148)

Burning Grass has also another favorite Ekwensi element: the beautiful woman, somewhat tarnished if not corrupt (but the more fascinating because of her worldly experience), who burns herself out or dies in some glorious sacrifice. From Kantuma, the royal courtesan who dies in the struggle to free the handsome boy Rikku she has come to love, to the wayward Beatrice in *People of the City,* to the magnificently vital whore of *Jagua Nana,* is but a natural progression for Ekwensi's provincial romanticism.

The Leopard's Claw, a less developed work and not intended for serious consumption like his novels, is perhaps by this fact the most revealing of Ekwensi's attitude. The novella tells of a seventeen-year-old Eastern Nigerian college student, Rikku, whose soul is caught in a war between the old and the new spirit of Nigeria. Before that war is over, Rikku must leave college and taste of the primitive, witch-doctor world which calls so ardently to one part of him. Rikku goes to work in the forest, where he meets representatives of the Leopard

Men, a fetish cult. He is put through a series of initiations
by them, part of which consists of being smeared with the
blood of a leopard and left alone in the middle of the forest to
find his way back to a camp site. Like a leopard crawling
stealthily in the night, the initiate must not be seen by any
man, or else he dies. The fear that is so much a part of African
life pervades Ekwensi's tale, and Rikku, who scorned the safe
world of college, is now confronted with the fearful blackness
of the jungle.

Yet Ekwensi's book is not a glorification of this animalistic
world of fetishes; it is a tranformation of it. Rikku accepts the
leopard's claw as a sign of passing his initiation, but he is no
longer infatuated with the teachings of the forest cult. He
disobeys its chief by leading Burutu, whom the Leopard Men
want to kill, to safety. "I'm no longer afraid of Ole Man Forest,
or anybody. I feel free. It's like being born again and I want
to go back into the world."

Ole Man Forest, the Leopard Men's chief, lives in the Ju-Ju
House. He is a dethroned king, for his kingdom of Eveh, like
his hegemony over the mind of man, has been taken from him.
Even his daughter Izeni renounces him. In the last scene
before he takes poison, he has become a pitiful old wretch
begging Rikku for aid. His death is laid by the Leopard Men
to an ancient curse, but a modern doctor who mysteriously
appears in the forest says the death has been caused by
arsenic. The two cultures are again thrown into opposition,
but Rikku, a compromiser, does not try to dissuade the Leopard
Men or Ole Man Forest's daughter from their juju beliefs.

After the death Rikku returns to college and to modern
Nigeria. His "contempt" for the world has passed, and he no
longer feels that the primitive forest is "the tonic necessary
to restore his courage" (p. 75). At school his teacher tells
him, "You look as if you've been through hell." The symbolism
is plain. In accepting the past, he is able to join the new

Nigeria. Ekwensi ends his tale with this sentence: "Rikku's life thus entered another and, we hope, happy chapter."

Fear is the dominant tone of the novella. Rikku's bag is stolen while he is on a train; such a commonplace occurrence takes on a foreboding air in Ekwensi's story. Ole Man Forest has a "black tongue licking the blacker lips" (p. 33). The Leopard Men hunt for sacrifices to Death. The sacred Ju-Ju House spreads its mysterious evil throughout the forest. Significantly, when Rikku leaves the forest, he is once more at peace.

The Leopard's Claw deals with the fusion of primitive and modern civilization, but within two years of its publication this had already become a historical rather than a contemporary issue for Ekwensi. The more difficult task which he was now to illuminate in his fiction lay in the battle between personal needs and public duties. However, in his presentation of this conflict Ekwensi is by no means a tract writer, urging total dedication to social and political tasks.

Ekwensi's first published novel, *People of the City* (London, 1954), has a newspaperman as its hero. Amusa Sango is the intelligent observer of night and city life in Lagos, and although by the end of the novel he becomes very much involved in love affairs, he appears initially as an objective, impartial viewer. His mother, who still lives in Eastern Greens (a symbolic name, perhaps, for the idyllic countryside, the green land still uncorrupted by progress and city life), worries that her son will be misled by wicked women. Her fears prove to be justified but short-lived, for, although Sango is exploited by two women, he is redeemed by a third.

The novel is divided into three parts, with the title of each part revealing the author's design. The title of Part One reads: "How the city must attract all types and how the unwary must suffer from ignorance of its ways." Ekwensi shows most concern for the physically beautiful types who sell themselves.

Lagos, to judge from his novel, is a hell of prostitution. One of these prostitutes is Bayo, "young, handsome, strong, idle and penniless: that was Bayo. You know him well. He's in your city, too. He's in every city in the world. Irresistible to women, an encyclopaedia of the private lives of all the eminent men" (p. 25). Bayo, kept by adoring middle-aged women, tries one noncommercial venture into romance, with disastrous results: as he tries to abduct his sweetheart so that they can marry, he is murdered. Another type in Ekwensi's city is the mature teen-age prostitute: "A girl like this was not found outside the city. She was born here and she belonged here. A primary education, perhaps; a few restless years in a secondary school, and she was on her own. A real danger to men's moral loyalties. She knew intimately all the amusements of the Western world" (p. 63). All the city types are interconnected symbolically with a minor character, a department store clerk who cannot meet the heavy price city life demands. Financially, he overreaches himself. To get money to pay his debts he is forced to join a secret juju society and, when he tries to leave it, he is murdered. Like many proletarian novels, *People of the City* views its residents as victims caught in the squeeze of competing forces.

Part One ends with Sango's return visit to Eastern Greens to cover a story for his newspaper. While there, he visits the fiancée who has been selected for him by his mother. As he looks at this girl, educated in a convent, sheltered from the dirt of life, Sango realizes he has nothing in common with her. He knows that he cannot return to his innocence and that the girl lacks the knowledge to accompany him on his necessary journeys. The stage is set for his crucial battle.

Part Two, which is titled "When all doors are closed," pictures the further deterioration of Sango's beliefs and illusions. Sango meets Beatrice the First, the beautiful African mistress of a British engineer in Lagos. The novel is as much concerned with the destruction of Beatrice the First as with the

redemption of Sango. For Beatrice the First represents the
greatest threat to Nigeria: she is the intelligent, beautiful
woman who sells herself for excitement, for diversion. Her life
is a waste, for she never builds on her talents or her relationships. She leaves the British civil engineer for a Nigerian
landlord; she leaves the landlord for a Syrian merchant; she
leaves the merchant for a Nigerian truckdriver; and she leaves
the truckdriver, to die in a pauper's grave. Her beauty has
been consumed in a passion without meaning. She has come
from a farm in the interior to the big city to find the "high
life," and it is this search for glamor that destroys her.

In Part Three, which is titled "One way out," Sango's
mother dies after learning of her son's illicit love affairs, and
Aina, the girl for whom Sango had once felt a tenderness,
tries to blackmail him. But the novel does not end with hell
triumphant. An African girl, young, pretty, and *of* the city,
leads Sango out of the decadence. Her love, her sense of
morality, plus her commitment to the new Africa, renew
Sango's faith, and together they leave for the Gold Coast to
start a new life. The name of this girl is also Beatrice; she is
Ekwensi's earthly equivalent of Dante's Beatrice.

Ekwensi's novel is an attack on the city but only insofar
as the city is the repository of vice. Personal decadence, not
urban decadence, is the theme. But personal decadence, because of the realities of the New Africa, takes place in the
city. The city cannot be avoided if the New Africa is to emerge.
Lagos is thus a hell that must be got through. Such a view
leads Ekwensi into Christian imagery. The use of two guiding
female spirits with the name of Beatrice is a symbolic device
—Beatrice the First is an ironic exploitation of Dante's lady,
but Beatrice the Second radiates light and love literally. Lagos,
the dead city, is a hell of several spheres; the novel is prefaced
by the West African proverb, "Wrong doing is a hell; everyone mounts his own and descries that of another."

In *The Leopard's Claw* the hero went through a "hell" in

the forest. In *People of the City,* "hell" is the city. In Ekwensi's next novel, *Jagua Nana* (London, 1961), the heroine leaves the dead city to start a fresh life in a less corrupt town. Sango's last words are that he will return to Lagos because he must return. Jagua Nana leaves Lagos in sorrow but not regret. She says: "Here in Ogabu . . . they were part of their surroundings, as natural as the wind. Whereas in Lagos MAN was always grappling to master an ENVIRONMENT he had created. It was money, money, yet more money. She did not find the same rush here, the desire to outstrip the other fellow" (pp. 180-81).

Jagua Nana is another version of Beatrice the First, an Eastern Nigerian whose search for the "high life" has led her to Lagos. At forty-five, she is still attractive and glittering. Jagua, the name given her because of her similarity to the sleek British car, fits her perfectly. Ekwensi's great sympathy for Jagua pervades the novel. Her love of life, her need to give love and receive it, each facet of her temperament and emotions is drawn with a compassionate hand. Yet Jagua is also the symbol of the city and its destructiveness. Jagua did not marry till she was thirty, a late age for African girls. She was waiting for the "right" man in her Ibo village in Eastern Nigeria, but he never appeared. In resignation she married a well-to-do merchant but, because she was unable to bear him children, he left her. This lack of fecundity is the central point in Jagua's life. Her search for frenetic activity, her need for diversion is part of her attempt to escape awareness of her sterility. Jagua is able to bear all insults except those that refer to her empty womb. When, toward the end of the novel, she has an affair with a young stranger and is bearing his child, she feels satisfied at last. The child who has been named Replacement dies, however, two days after its birth. But Jagua has achieved a maturity that no longer allows her to blind herself in frantic sexual activity. Her baby's death, instead of driving her back into a life of abandon, gives her the strength to accept tragedy and she realizes finally that she cannot build a future by riotously spending her talents. She has been imprisoned in Lagos, "unable to extricate herself from its clutches" (p. 165). Now at last she is free of the false dream; she is going to stay on "dis side" of the River Niger.

Since Jagua and Lagos are synonymous, the implication follows that Lagos—exemplifying the city—is a hell punished by sterility, and that its activity is a grim masquerade to hide its inability to rejuvenate. Ekwensi comes close to explicit verbalization of this view, in another use of Christian imagery to describe the city: "Standing in that wreckage like a messenger from Lucifer's flood" (p. 129).

In *Jagua Nana* the contrast between city and country life is shown in several new ways not exploited in *People of the City*. Political strife in the Eastern Nigerian region is settled personally by Jagua, who uses old-fashioned sexual intrigue to bring two rival factions of a family together. In contrast, the politics of Lagos can be described only as foul. Jagua tells her young ex-lover, "No, Freddie, I no wan' you to win. . . . Politics not for you, Freddie. You got education. You got culture. You're a gentleman an' proud. Politics be game for dog. And in dis Lagos, is a rough game. De roughest game in de whole worl'. Is smelly and dirty" (p. 137). The vagaries of an election spell the murder of a corrupt politician and cause Jagua's flight from the city.

The one place where city and country meet in both novels is the nightclub. In *People of the City* Sango leads a band in a nightclub. Here he meets the dissolute Beatrice the First, but here also he plays the native rhythms of his Ibo village. The "Tropicana" club serves as the focus of Jagua Nana's activities: here she meets men, is bought by them and feels the glamor of city life. Yet it is at the "Tropicana" that Jagua engages in the primitive masquerade dance uniting her in spirit with her country's past. Taiwo, the corrupt politician, finds the dance distasteful. He tells Jagua it "is bushman dancing." But Jagua, already on the road to self-recognition, replies: "You just heard real music. . . . Jus' like in me own country. We get nearly the same kind of dance" (p. 132). And earlier, when Jagua had gone home for a visit, she had traveled to Ogabu, Bagana, Krinameh, and Onitsha, "all homes of traditional dancing."

Ekwensi's latest novel, *Beautiful Feathers* (London, 1965), is in the tradition of *Jagua Nana*, though in the later book the hero is a politician and manager of a pharmacy. Wilson Iyari, the leader of a Nigerian movement for Pan-Africanism, must suffer the neurotic behavior of his beautiful wife, Yaniya, who cuckolds him at the moment he is achieving strength as a political leader. Yet in deserting him and returning to the tribal milieu of her childhood for a rebirth of spirit, Yaniya is cursed by an angry god. Her son Obi dies of fever. In penance Yaniya takes a job as an airline hostess and attempts to make a new life. In the climactic scene she saves her husband's life by receiving the blow a knife-wielding assassin has intended for the politician's body.

In this novel, Ekwensi's thematic symbols recur. The beautiful but errant woman sacrifices herself for the virtuous man; the life of the city is represented as another kind of hell: "Lagos was rapidly becoming Nigeria's divorce centre. It was the mark of its outward sophistication that nowhere did a happy marriage really exist" (p. 41); the inhabitants of the city are beautiful people turned bestial and captive.

Beautiful Feathers is a familiar story, and very familiar territory for Ekwensi. It is, however, Ekwensi's most economically written work; the journalistic and sociological conglomeration of details which marred his earlier urban novels have been carefully avoided. In its portrayal of urban realities and the secrets of men behind locked apartment doors, the novel is powerful, but it is also a quasi-fairy tale, with its solution to political problems lying in the hands of beautiful wives and mistresses sacrificing their lives for the cause of a virtuous man.

Chinua Achebe, born some ten years after Ekwensi, is an Ibo from Eastern Nigeria. His background is thus similar to and different from Ekwensi—both have a personal relationship to Ibo customs and philosophy, and to the Igbo language. Ekwensi, however, was raised in the Moslem-dominated north of Nigeria, while Achebe grew up in the British-influenced section of Eastern Nigeria. Both writers were educated at colleges in Nigeria (Achebe enrolled at a government college in Umuahia and received his B.A. degree from University College, Ibadan), and both have worked for broadcasting companies (Achebe is now First Director of External Broadcasting, while Ekwensi is Nigerian Minister of Information). Both writers have achieved enormous fame in their own country and abroad. Achebe's books, for example, are required reading for a school certificate in Australia, and are included for study in college courses in English, American, and African universities; they have sold in large numbers in paperback reprints; and they have been translated into German, Italian, and Spanish. Both Achebe and Ekwensi have written of tribal encounters. It is this aspect of Nigerian life that most interests Achebe, even though his second book, *No Longer at Ease*, centers on Lagos and its fetid air of corruption. More than Ekwensi, Achebe is critical of the Europeanizing of Africa, and of missionaries who fail to leaven their teachings with an understanding of Africanism.

Achebe's first novel, *Things Fall Apart* (London, 1958), derives its title from Yeats's poem, "The Second Coming," and conveys the dilemma of a man—an artist by virtue of his use of tradition as a fixed way of life—in conflict with the change that is revising his society. The action is placed in the Ibo village of Umuofia after the arrival of the white man at the beginning of the twentieth century. Written in three parts, the novel creates an idyllic picture of pre-Christian tribal life. As the story opens, Okonkwo, the hero, is rich and successful, "well-known throughout the nine villages and even beyond. His fame rested on solid personal achievements." Because his father was a failure, Okonkwo was ruled by one passion—to hate everything his father Unoka had loved. "One of those things was gentleness and another was idleness" (p. 11). A confident, self-made man, Okonkwo takes pride in his country, his religion, his social and personal life, and creates a culture out of his beliefs. Achebe is somewhat ambiguous in his portrait of Okonkwo, for his defeat comes not only at the hands of the technologically superior white man, but as a result of his offending three religious deities—his *chi* (the spirit within), his *ndichie* (ancestors), and *Chukwu*, the High God and Creator. Achebe's novel is a record of Okonkwo's downfall, as a result of the clash between him and the demands of those around him, and of Okonkwo's proud, stubborn nature.

Part One concerns itself with Okonkwo's contented life as a rich man with three wives and many children. He beats his third wife who, because she is having her hair plaited, fails to be home in time to serve him his lunch. But since the beating occurs during the Week of Peace—during that time between harvesting and planting when no strife is allowed by the Earth Goddess (*alusi*), whose blessing is necessary to make crops grow—Okonkwo is ordered by a tribal priest to make amends. Without protest Okonkwo donates a large sum of money to the religious elders, for although he feels no shame at having beaten a wife for failing in her duties, he believes in the necessity of a socioreligious fabric. His neighbors accuse him of pomposity, but his sin is a minor one and it is soon forgotten. Achebe also reveals another facet of Okonkwo's personality: his love and compassion for his second wife, nine of whose children died in childbirth or infancy.

Festivities, marriages, the daily order of a village life, these are the elements of Part One of the novel. Okonkwo's downfall—foreshadowed by his sin of pride in placing his personal wrath ahead of the Week of Peace observance—begins in that moment when he is unable to forsake the demands of his social and religious group for the claim of individual love and protection made by a young boy he has tended since he took him hostage. The boy, Ikemefuna, who was condemned as a sacrifice to the gods, had called Okonkwo "Father." When in the forest he flees from the matchets aimed at him and runs to Okonkwo for aid, Okonkwo, afraid of displaying any personal weakness, strikes him down with his own matchet.

Okonkwo's next "sin" is a strange and not conscious one. At the funeral of the revered eldest man of the village, Ezedeu—the same elder who had advised Okonkwo not to partake in the slaughter-sacrifice of the young hostage, Ikemefuna —the homemade gun Okonkwo is carrying accidentally explodes. The impact of the explosion kills Ezedeu's sixteen-year-old son. As a result of this mishap, adjudged a crime by the villagers, Okonkwo is banished for seven years from his home territory.

Part Two of the novel concerns itself with Okonkwo's seven years in exile. During this time he learns of a white man who came to the region and was killed by natives because he was a stranger. The story went that his automobile, of which the natives were frightened, was tied to a tree in order to keep its spirit a prisoner. Some months later, other white men arrived in search of their missing companion. These white men stayed, and two years later the missionaries arrived. Okonkwo sends messages to his town urging violence against the white man, but the tribesmen are fascinated by the new religion. Okonkwo's son Nwoye is converted to Christianity and adopts the name Isaac. (Achebe's choice of this name may be a symbolic referent to the guilt of a son for his father's bloody sacrifice of another Isaac—Ikemefuna—to the gods.) Nwoye-Isaac is despised by Okonkwo as effeminate; the son is likened to the gentle grandfather whom Okonkwo despises.

Okonkwo also calls his village people effeminate for accepting white rule and Christianity and continues to urge resistance to the new order; but his advice goes unheeded. The white men seem immune to the "Evil Forest" where they are building a church. Even when an *osu* (an untouchable because it is the spirit of a slave from a past age) turns Christian and kills the royal python—"the emanation of the gods of water"—violence is averted.

In Part Three, Okonkwo returns to Umuofia after his long exile. But the village has changed. The soldiers and explorers have gone, but the missionaries, the District Commissioner, the white petty bureaucracy and the traders have come to stay. The first missionary tries to effect an understanding between the Africans and the whites, but his work is aborted when he falls ill. The second missionary believes in stern measures, and in retaliation for these measures Okonkwo and six other village leaders burn down the Christian church. They are arrested and then freed, but at a mass meeting protesting their treatment Okonkwo kills a police officer. Because Okonkwo knows his village will not support him in a war of vengeance or honor against the mighty white man, he hangs himself from a tree. By destroying himself, Okonkwo breaks a taboo of his religion. Since by his act his body becomes an abomination, a suicide cannot be buried by his people, and thus, ironically, the villagers have to ask the white police to cut down Okonkwo and bury him.

Okonkwo's death is the result of the arrival of the white man. This is Achebe's comment, that one of the greatest men in Umuofia killed himself and had to be buried like a dog. And all the District Commissioner can think of is the new knowledge he has gained to put in his book:

> The Commissioner went away, taking three or four of the soldiers with him. In the many years in which he had toiled to bring civilization to different parts of Africa he had learnt a number of things. One of them was that a District Commissioner must never attend to such undignified details as cutting down a hanged man from the tree. Such attention would give the natives a poor opinion of him. In the book which he planned to write

he would stress that point. As he walked back to the court he thought about that book. Every day brought him some new material. The story of this man who had killed a messenger and hanged himself would make interesting reading. One could almost write a whole chapter on him. Perhaps not a whole chapter but a reasonable paragraph, at any rate. There was so much to include, and one must be firm in cutting out details. He had already chosen the title of the book, after much thought: *The Pacification of the Primitive Tribes of the Lower Niger.*
(p. 185)

Achebe's novel thus ends with a ringing denunciation of intellectual dilettantes who pick on a man's philosophy for digressive tidbits. Like Ekwensi, and many British writers, he is particularly antagonistic to the anthropologists and journalists who exploit the African habitat.

Achebe's novel is remarkable for its insights into traditional situations. The elements are familiar: a mythical village; the coming of the white men and Christianity; the admirable picture of African tribal life; and the inevitable racism when black and white meet. Although many other writers have portrayed men like Okonkwo, none has revealed the cast of his mind so skillfully. Okonkwo is not idealized but made real. What destroys him is his unyielding pride; he fails to adapt to any change. The tragedy is that Okonkwo is made of noble heritage that has somehow become cursed. Yet Okonkwo's tragedy is not merely personal: it is the end of the black individualist, the tribal chieftain, the traditional rule.

Achebe's second novel, *No Longer at Ease* (London, 1960), also takes its title from the work of a modern poet. The phrase comes from a line in T. S. Eliot's "The Journey of the Magi": "We returned to our places, these Kingdoms,/ But no longer at ease here, in the old dispensation,/ With an alien people clutching their gods." The locale of the novel is Lagos, a Lagos much like the corrupt city of Ekwensi's fiction, and the hero a "been-to" (a Nigerian who has been to England). The novel continues the story of the Okonkwo family, for the "been-to" hero is Okonkwo's grandson, Obi.

The phrase which recurs in *No Longer at Ease* and which can be heard behind the other music of its pages is "Our people have a long way to go." Lagos, in Achebe's book, is a city which must be cleansed, but Achebe's emphasis is on the machinations of Europeans as well as the failings of Africans. Obi is a man who has squandered his great potential. He is on trial, as the book opens, for accepting a bribe. The novel is a flashback, an illuminating descent, into Obi's fall.

Lagos gets its share of responsibility for Obi's tragedy, for Achebe shows the dangers of the big city: the pimps, the prostitutes, the extortionists, and especially the siren call, "I'll teach you to dance the high life." When Obi asks the President of the Umuofia Progressive Union, Lagos Branch, for a loan, he is told:

> "You are one of us, so we must bare our minds to you. I have lived in this Lagos for fifteen years. I came here on August the sixth, nineteen hundred and forty-one. Lagos is a bad place for a young man. If you follow its sweetness, you will perish. Perhaps you will ask why I am saying all this. I know what Government pays senior service people. What you get in one month is what some of your brothers here get in one year. I have already said that we will give you four months. We can even give you one year. But are we doing you any good?" (p. 82)

Obi's real tragedy is his inability to fit into either an African or a European mold, or to combine the best of the two worlds. Instead, Obi displays his superiority without purpose and speeds his own defeat. Many Nigerians, Achebe says in his compassionate way, share in this defeat: Obi's mother and father, for failing to understand their impatient son's desire to achieve all that Western life has to offer; the Umuofia Progressive Union, for demanding a pragmatic view of activity when Obi's nature cried for creative expression; the Nigerians who accepted corruption as a way of life and expected Obi to conform; and the Syrian merchants who tempted Obi with their wealth of goods. Ultimately Obi's tragedy is the end of a cycle for the family of Okonkwo, a cycle which began with the first sin of Okonkwo—his individualism. Obi is the degenerate result of a father (Nwoye-Isaac) whose father rejected him. The grandson of Okonkwo has Okonkwo's individualism, but this individualism issues in sordid, petty corruption; it does not end in Okonkwo's tragic fall. Again, Achebe is criticizing the modern white European for bringing Africa to the point of conversion and loss. In exchange for the dubious currency of a better material life, the young African has traded in the spirit of a traditional ethic.

Honey for Tomorrow (New York, 1961), by the British novelist, Robert Lait, deals with the same kind of character as Obi. Lait's hero is educated and arrogant, and his downfall is as swift as Obi's. The novels have the same opening: a brilliant young Christian African is on trial for bribery and extortion. Lait's novel is one of the finest studies of civil service life in East Africa; Achebe's is one of the most perceptive novels written about an educated black African's deterioration. It is pertinent to remark that Lait's sympathy for the African blurs his vision. He excuses his African from the human duty of decent behavior because of the wrongs done in the past to his people. Lait can excoriate his Englishmen, even accept their humiliation and torture as fitting ends to a colonial era, but he cannot criticize African indecency without rationalizing it. Achebe, less driven to be superficially understanding, less compelled to make amends for the white man's past, manages to imbue his African with a host of good and bad qualities. Although he finds fault with many particular white individuals, he does not cast blame on all of white society.

Achebe's third novel, *Arrow of God* (London, 1964), goes

back in time and setting to the Ibo villages of *Things Fall Apart,* and again pits a tribal chieftain against the changing realities of modern Africa. Ezeulu, the Chief Priest of Ulu and god of the six villages of Umuaro, plays the power game against his tribal rivals and against the British colonial system. Friendly to the British, Ezeulu finds that he must oppose them at the very moment they offer him more nominal power. The battle between them is symptomatic of the battle between tribal and modern life, between an independent and proud people and a colonial system that at best can only offer condescension, and between the old religions and the attractive economic assurance of Christianity (whose converts learn to read and write English and go on to the better and sometimes the only available jobs). Ezeulu, in anger at his own people, postpones the harvest of the yams and thus brings economic privation to them. Ironically, his decision to punish his people and strengthen their traditions destroys the fabric of the village life, for it turns many of the villagers to the more permissive Christian religion. And when Ezeulu hears of the death of his favorite son, he takes the news as a punishment by the gods for his willful acts. As the novel ends, Ezeulu and the tradition he represents are both broken by the "arrow of God." As in Achebe's other novels, it is the strong-willed man of tradition who cannot adapt, and who is crushed by his virtues in the war between the new, more worldly order, and the old, conservative values of an isolated society. Achebe tends to see the white man as culprit, though not the only one, while the black man who follows or resists is lost and wandering in a stormy passage. It is Achebe's remarkable classical simplicity of style—the almost heroic calmness of his accusatory statement—that provides the richest kind of tension for his profoundly ambivalent portrayals.

Achebe's most recent book, *A Man of the People* (New York and London, 1966), reveals a further development of his double-edged and scarred compassion. In his first three

novels Achebe clearly indicated a bias against the white
European settler who had brought with him the seeds of war
and corruption; whatever the faults of black tribalism, it had
at least a tradition that ennobled and unified the Ibo people.
In *A Man of the People* Achebe takes on the corruption of
Nigerians in high places in the central government, but he in
no way claims or deals with the white man's responsibility for
this corruption. In this latest novel, Achebe avoids practically
all mention of the white man: again the milieu is a black
man's society, only it is no longer a society in conflict, it is a
society in transition. The twentieth century has come now to
dominate Africa, and whoever's fault it is, Achebe does not
care to say. What Achebe achieves here for the first time is a
comic as well as critical treatment of the clever politician for
whom the trappings of power are everything; in other words,
Achebe is characterizing the pomposity and duplicity of modern African politicians.

Achebe could have gone another way. By indulging his
obvious critical spirit against the white man's corroding effect
on African tradition he could have become more and more
of a propagandist. He could have turned to journalism and
sensationalism (the ingredients of his plot—election riots and
an army take-over—furnish him with a ready-made opportunity) and written a novel in the style of Cyprian Ekwensi.
He has instead shifted his emphasis to the comic aspects of
human foibles in a threatening situation. Having had his say
about the cause of the Nigerian corruption (the white man's
decadence and the African's fall into temptation and submis-
sion to white power), evidently he now feels free to deal with
corruption from the uncluttered viewpoint of a sardonic rac-
onteur. Aware of the underlying contradictions of power politics and its very real power, he makes several telling thrusts.
The narrator, a teacher named Odili, is invited to visit Chief
Nanga, now a famous politician. Years before he entered
politics, Nanga was Odili's teacher and he is quick to notice

that the bright compliance he recognized in Odili in his student days has not left him. Nanga's invitation becomes the
means of Odili's journey into the big city from the small village where he is teaching; in this context A Man of the People
is in the tradition of the story of the yokel who visits the sinful
city and emerges from it scathed but victorious, while the so-
called "sophisticates" and "sinners" suffer their just deserts.

Odili's first tangle with Nanga comes about because of their
rivalry over a beautiful girl, Elsie. When Nanga succeeds in
sleeping with her, Odili angrily and jealously denounces him
and his politics. Odili's second brush with Nanga is also the
result of a female—in this case, it is the second-wife-to-be of
Nanga, a girl named Edna with whom Odili has fallen in
love. No doubt Achebe is satirizing the stew in which politics
and romance and every other socially competitive act is prone
to be embroiled. For even Odili, fine and upright as he is,
cannot admit that his political stand against the corrupt Nanga
has as much to do with petty romantic jealousy as it has with
politics. When Odili falls in love with Nanga's second wife
(-to-be), the reader cannot help suspecting that this is but
another step in the escalation of the war between two men of
pride.

The impure state of politics is the center of Achebe's novel.
Even the heroic Max, who dies for his party's cause, is willing to take a bribe from the rival party and then use the money
to fight the very party that has given him the money. Max's
rationale is that any means are good, if the end is good. Odili
argues that the acceptance of the bribe constitutes a moral
betrayal, yet Odili's wonderfully stated pedagogics seem akin
to the advice that the nice old absent-minded professor gives
to a class of students whom he has already lulled to sleep.
One of the charms of this novel, however, is that the author
does make us believe that Odili has some sense, and that,
like all men of principle, he is driven into action by his own
compromises. It is the seductive female who rouses the aca-

demic Odili, as much as the force of his political convictions. Max and Odili are thus both compromisers, but they have not sunk to that level of lying, murder, and thievery which distinguishes the other politicians in their country—in particular, the party of Chief Nanga.

Eventually in this novel, as in all of Achebe's novels, the resolution is to withdraw the hero from the world of politics and action, either by death or imprisonment. In *Things Fall Apart* and *Arrow of God* the strong tribal leader is defeated, and his end is tragic and inevitable; in *No Longer at Ease* the young modern hero is an admixture of corruption and principles, and his role must lead him to an external prison where he can shake free the prison of his ambivalence. In *A Man of the People* the hero has found a *modus operandi*. He has his girl, his job, and his political cause. But, it is important to notice, while Odili remains politically committed, he is not politically active. The novel ends with the abolition of all political parties in a military state. Thus Achebe, even in this novel in which his hero is able to achieve some triumph through compromise (all his other heroes have been tragic heroes or misfits), portrays the modern Nigerian in a state of abeyance. The implications of the divorce from stately tribal traditionalism in the union of modern Nigeria are still present.

Dr. Thomas M. Aluko, an engineer and town planner working in Lagos, constructed his first novel, *One Man, One Wife* (Lagos, 1959),[3] around the agitation of Afro-Christian conflict. Aluko's approach is satirical, as distinguished from Ekwensi's muted anger and Achebe's compassionate lament. The title refers to the concept of monogamy, but is misleading, for Aluko presents many other conflicts as well, among them the struggle between town and village, Christianity and African tribal religions, native customs and Christian missionary pro-

---

[3] Repr. as *One Man, One Matchet* (London, 1964).

hibitions, and the encroachment of urban customs on the pastoral way of life. Just as important as Joshua's desire to take a second wife, a decision which forces him to leave the Christian Church, is Royasin who forsakes Christianity to become an incipient nationalist force and helper of the "oppressed" through his public letter-writing service. Unfortunately Royasin's career is halted by lunacy due to smallpox, but the sequence of events over which he presides serve as the author's symbolic foray into the conflict between the second-generation Christian African and the already established, first-generation conservative Christian Church.

In the guise of the narrator, the author spotlights the particular conflicts he wishes to display:

> First came the new religion, with its confusing teachings and strange code of morals. Next, the annual epidemic of smallpox became more and more serious. Next, the long arm of Shango m'lord had reached out in justice and struck down a prominent citizen. Then the invasion of the village by the Shango worshippers at the funeral rites of Joshua, which completely upset the already tottering village economy. Then came the introduction by the "Smallpox gang" police of the sophisticated ways of urban life into an unspoilt rustic atmosphere. These are all by-products of the new thing they call civilization. Village life stood bent under these everlasting waves of adversity. And it looked as if it would stand bent forever.   (p. 148)

The book's lack of a central character mitigates its impact. The intertwining strands are too complex for Aluko's present ability, and the novel succeeds only in parts. It does, however, reveal a strong talent, and it exemplifies the pattern of Nigerian writing during the 1950's. It was, incidentally, the first novel written by a Nigerian to be published by a Nigerian publishing house.

Still another excellent novel by a Nigerian utilizing the elements in the conflict between tribal tradition and modern and urban African customs appeared in London in 1961.

Wand of Noble Wood was the first novel of Onuora Nzekwu, now a thirty-nine-year-old assistant editor of *Nigeria Magazine,* who came from an Ibo family in Northern Nigeria but who was educated in the Eastern part of the country. Its hero, Pete Obiesi, is a journalist who is willing to have an affair with a city girl but who wishes to return to his tribal home to select a virginal country bride. Pete's conflict is a profound one: on the one hand he accepts his professional status as a journalist engaging in the most modern practices of deception; on the other, he cannot accept the people who work in the city beside him. Yet, when on a return trip home he becomes betrothed to a lovely country girl, it seems possible that Peter will enjoy the best of both worlds. The gods, however, have their vengeance, for on the night before his wedding, disaster overtakes him. His fiancée believes herself to be under a family curse. She and Pete try to negate the curse by offering gifts to the priest of the *iyi ocha,* who then places the offering on the proper ground. However, just before her marriage the girl discovers that a jealous rival has stolen a white stone—the necessary object-offering—from the *iyi ocha* priest's bag. Without the stone the curse cannot be lifted, and the fiancée, rather than subject her husband-to-be to the curse, commits suicide.

The tragedy is complete; the curse has worked, for it has robbed Pete of the girl he desired. In desperation and anguish Pete returns to his Lagos mistress, who has now given birth to their child. He lives with her and tries to face life—a modern life—as best he can.

Wand of Noble Wood is another example of the Nigerian novel in English about the conflict of cultures. What distinguishes the book is Nzekwu's use of supernatural devices without irony. *The curse is meant to work: because the white stone was stolen.* The fact that Pete pays lip service to the modern world is not to deny the still tangible power and reality of tribal superstition. This supernatural element is difficult to comprehend by Western readers, and many have found *Wand of Noble Wood* a curious bag of tricks.

In Nzekwu's second novel the tricks are still there but are more plausible to the by now seasoned reader. *Blade Among the Boys* (London, 1962) is the story of Patrick-Okonkwo Ikenga, and the struggle between his family traditions and his desire for a wider future. That struggle is presented mainly in terms of Patrick's decision to become a Catholic priest: the choice opens up economic and diplomatic advantages to him; since, however, his choice of profession attacks the basic tenet of his people—that man's primary responsibility is to propagate his tribe—it also closes the family door on him. At first the struggle is one of a Christian education for Patrick, which Patrick's wily uncle sees as advantageous, even though he has no intention of allowing the philosophy of Christianity to pervade his nephew. Patrick is dismissed from the school, however, because of a quarrel with one of his teachers, after which he treats himself to an indulgent night with women and wine. Patrick returns to the Christian fold, when he miraculously avoids arrest for taking bribes at his railroad job. This decision costs him his family loyalty, and eventually causes the death of his mother, who wails for her son in front of the seminary and dies of a broken heart. As Nzekwu ends his novel, Christianity does not triumph, for Patrick, seduced by a beautiful girl who serves him a mysterious love potion (again Nzekwu indulges, seriously, in the supernatural aspects of tribal lore), impregnates her, and is forced to leave the seminary.

Like Pete in *Wand of Noble Wood*, Patrick is forced to live out his life in a modern Nigeria, in a city whose lack of tradition he does not admire. Yet like Pete he too is drawn to that very city, to its promise of a new order.

In his third novel, *Highlife for Lizards* (London, 1965), Nzekwu seems to have found a happy medium between the extremes of his previous books. The hero is a young man who brings the daughter of a priest of an ancient cult to his marriage bed, but who after five years of marriage finds that his wife has become both a modern and a traditional shrew. The novel is a comic affair in which Udezue, the hero, attempts to cut his first wife down to size by taking a second wife. Unfortunately the second wife turns out to be a child-like beauty who cannot understand the nature of good and evil, and who, in her self-destructive way, forces her husband to send her into exile. It is interesting that in this novel the power and mystery of the tribal past are presented as historic remnants to modern readers; that the tribal past, while retaining its fascination, is unable to provide a compromise with the rational forms of modern life. Only Agom, the first wife, who forsakes the tribal past to become a different sort of Nigerian woman, is portrayed by Nzeweku in flattering terms. It is she at the end of the novel who tries to scrap some of the tribal customs; and this action on her part is doubly significant, since she is now the sacred priestess of Ozoma:

> Agom had promised herself that, should the opportunity arise, she would ask for the scrapping of some of the practices or at least ask for a curtailment of the time set out for wives to mourn their husbands. Now was her opportunity and she knew from their bickerings that it was going to be an uphill task. However she called for attention and when she'd got it, spoke to the daughters of Ozoma trying to justify the reform.   (p. 188)

This time the novel ends with a happy hero—a husband with two wives again (for Agom has provided a new second wife for her husband, to free herself for other activities). And these two wives are women who move with the times. The hero even wonders, as the book closes, whether women are more adaptable than men, and whether, through this adaptability, they rule their reputed male rulers.

Two novels re-creating the milieu of West Africa fall outside the patterns described in the preceding pages and form the nucleus of the African political novel. One, *A Wreath for Udomo* (New York, 1956) is by a Cape Colored from South Africa, Peter Abrahams, but its fictional locale is a mythical West African kingdom resembling Ghana. Its hero, Udomo, is a fierce nationalist who tells a British peer in London, "It is our business to be irresponsible! A slave's business is to get rid of his chains, not to be reasonable! Only the free can afford to be diplomats!" (p. 32). Eventually Udomo returns to his country, and through the help of several African Communists manages to convince the British to grant independence to his land. Udomo's achievements live on, but he is assassinated by members of his own political party. The real enemy in Abrahams' novel is tribalism, and the book ends with a letter explaining the significance of Udomo's death:

> You can guess the reason for his murder. They wanted to go back to the days of tribal glory. You know there are people all over the world, whites as well as blacks, who are attracted to tribalism. Among other things, it has security, colour, and emotional outlets that the bleak, standardized, monotonous chromium and neon benefits of mass production civilization lack. You know also there are many, mainly among the whites, who say that the trouble in Africa today is due to the fact that Africans have moved away from tribalism too rapidly. They are foolish people who don't understand the true nature of tribalism. Udomo did. He worked against it, quietly, secretly at first, and then, as recent accounts of developments there show, more boldly, more openly. And so he had to be hacked to pieces in true tribal fashion. But they were too late. He'd carried things too far forward for them to be able to put the clock back.   (pp. 355-56)

The emphasis in Abrahams' novel is politics, and it is for this reason that it gives a very extreme, if also very graphic, picture. Like John Wyllie's *Riot*, it presents a varied set of characters, all in subtle shades of leanings left or right. The five Africans who lead the country to independence, the "Black Elite," are willing to work with Communists for the goal of nationalism. Mabi, a painter, says, "Life is an act of will for us. The strands are pulled taut. There is no room for weakness. I think we've largely accepted the Communist dictum of means and ends. To liberate Africa we must live by an act of will" (p. 50). And when one of the five complains about the enemy within, the "gradualists" willing to work with the British, another replies, "Africanization will get rid of them" (p. 227). Yet the means prove overwhelming for four of the five. Udomo is murdered; Mabi, the painter, writes to an English woman of his yearning for the days of innocence "before Udomo came and brought reality into our lives" (p. 356); Lanwood, the venerable theoretician of the revolution and an ex-Communist, dies a broken man in England, because no place exists for him in the New Africa; and Mhendi is defeated. Only Adebhoy remains supreme in West Africa—because he has joined forces with tribalism. He and the rich mammy-merchant Selena, who controls the politics of the country, are triumphant.

Like many African writers, Abrahams is aware of the ironies in the racial conflict. Udomo has two affairs in England with white women, who are actually close friends sharing the same apartment. One falls in love with him; the other, whom he makes pregnant, has an abortion. It is ironic that after Udomo has arrived in Africa he and his leaders take an oath not to marry white women—because they are too "fast," too corrupt.

Politics is everywhere on the surface of William Conton's novel, *The African* (New York, 1961), but at its core is a humanism. Conton, a Sierra Leonian now teaching in Ghana, has selected a mythical West African colony, Songhai, for his setting, but his hero in many ways resembles Kwame Nkrumah of Ghana. Kamara, helped by the contributions of his neighbors in a remote village, goes to England to complete his studies. There he meets an Afrikaans girl with whom he falls in love. The girl breaks her engagement to her violently racist South African fiancé. A few nights later a car runs down both Kamara and the girl; Greta dies but Kamara lives, vowing to avenge her death. He is sure that her ex-fiancé has murdered her and tried to murder him, but he has no evidence to support his supposition. After Kamara recovers from his injuries he completes his studies and returns to Songhai. The pattern which he follows is now one that has been seen clearly in African politics—from Christian mission school to an English university to a colonial post in his own land to leadership in a nationalist political party and finally to a position of honor in his newly independent country. Along the way the liberalism of his Western views is dropped for nationalist narrowness. All gradualism is suspect, and even a man's dress must no longer be European but "African." Kamara changes from his double-breasted suit to the Ghanian togalike national costume.

But with the British gone, the problems do not end. They simply have a new beginning. Abrahams showed the problem in terms of the conflict between tribal and centralized views of government. Conton is less political and more humanitarian. Kamara disguises himself as a diamond smuggler and crosses illegally into South Africa. He gets to the city where the suspected murderer of his first love lives, and takes a menial job at his club. But when the opportunity comes, when the odious Afrikaner is drunk, Kamara experiences an illumination. He takes the first step toward suppressing hatred. Instead of killing him as he had planned, Kamara carries the man home and puts him to bed.

Kamara's selfless act is unique in African fiction. Such acts of compassión can be found in Alan Paton, Nadine Gordimer, and Dan Jacobson, but their characters are not politicians. They are gentle people trapped in the prison of racism. Kamara is the prime minister of an independent land, the man with a clear vision, the nationalist who has everything to gain by hatred, who can even plead the biblical justification of an eye for an eye. Therefore his act of restraint may be taken as a hopeful sign of a new era of maturity in the political milieu, especially as it comes after Kamara has organized a South African Native Committee to produce unrest and eventual revolution in South Africa.

In Abrahams' *A Wreath for Udomo* the intensity of repressed hatred and resentment gives the book a furious pace. In Conton's novel, the pace is slow and easeful. Abrahams' style, a simulation of roughness and haste, shows a concern to speak loudly and quickly. It must be emphasized, however, that Abrahams, like Udomo, was not interested in fairness. In 1954 there was little time for consideration of hurt feelings. In 1960 the attitude, as exemplified by William Conton, seems to some extent to have been mollified, to show concern for sensibility.

Conton's willingness to see many sides of the complex social structure is expressed in his comment on the stratified societies of West Africa: "In its own way, the caste system in the towns of West Africa was in those days as rigid and as vicious as the Hindu variety, and as unquestioned. None of us schoolboys would dream of carrying our own luggage even a few hundred yards between home and school at the beginning of the term—a Fula laborer must be called for this purpose, and be given a shilling from which perhaps we could ill part" (p. 101). Conton is also one of the few African writers to portray an Englishman with the capacity to understand, and unselfishly to interest himself in Africa. Even Achebe and Ekwensi present the European as basically thoughtless in his dealings with the African. While they do not blame the European, they imply an intrinsic inability on his part (because of the limitations imposed by training and background) to grasp the subtleties of the African mind. Conton, in his relativistic view, sees the ignorance as a condition on both sides, and the result is again an affirmation that the gap between races can be bridged:

It is perhaps a pity that the British, with their traditional reserve, were the most successful of African imperial powers. For reserve shown toward a once-subject people is at once interpreted as prejudice. Two pairs of eyes meet across a ship's lounge . . . a copy of *The Times* is promptly interposed across the line of vision by the Briton, and the African sucks his teeth and curses him in his heart. In fact, of course, the Briton would have made exactly the same gesture if his eyes had met any other strange ones. And so gesture creates attitudes, and attitudes in turn give color to gestures, and the waters are soon poisoned almost beyond cleansing.

                                                                    (p. 46)

Lastly, Conton, like John Wyllie in *Riot*, shows an admiration and respect for Americans. His narrator Kamara says: "It seemed as if everyone were relieved to be able to get back into the more urgent business of making a living in a world incomparably faster, and more ruthlessly competitive, than that I had left. Only in the American mission compound did I find that the atmosphere of sanity and calm still prevailed—and the irony of this was faintly bitter" (p. 118). Conton's Americans and Wyllie's American missionary in *Riot*, as well as the female American missionaries of Louise Stinetorf and Elizabeth Warner, are thus shown to have their place in the sun of Africa just as much as the bumbling, naive Americans of Graham Greene and Joyce Cary.

Among recent publications demanding notice is a curious novel, *The Voice* (London, 1965), by the Nigerian poet Gabriel Okara. *The Voice* is an attempt at a poetic distillation of a by now traditional tale: the educated African (Okolo) who returns to his home village (Amatu) in Nigeria and finds his messages of progress are threatening the established order. Okolo is granted asylum by a young girl, Tuere, who has been branded an outcast and witch. Okolo's search for Truth and his attempts to bring that Truth to his people result in tragedy to the bringer: Truth is always rejected and the Truth-bearer destroyed. The force of *The Voice* is in its poetry. Gabriel

Okara speaks in mythic sounds, and his words have an individuality of expression.

Another Nigerian voice and undoubtedly one to be listened to is Nkem Nwanko, a young Onitsha-born writer (b. 1936). In his first published novel, *Danda*, Nwanko has produced an amusing and somewhat sad picaresque tale of a rogue, Danda, who cannot settle down to his responsibilities.

2

West African novelists writing in French achieved distinction earlier than their continental colleagues writing in English. At the time of independence of the former French colonies, several commentators spoke of the "enlightenment" of the French Civil Service in preparing the way for a peaceful and mature separation. Needless to say, many observers will differ on the degree of "enlightenment," and on the many motives that inspired the French imperialist attitude. Yet few critics will deny that the French system fostered a literary culture: the many novels and poems which French-language West African writers published is testimony to this fact.

Many of the novels were written and published before the Négritude movement swept the consciousness of French Africa and the French intellectual countryside; and some which were published in the 1940's and 1950's seem quite independent of the Négritude spirit. The novels of René Maran and Ferdinand Oyono are more similar in attitude to the Nigerian novels that followed them than to the Négritude-inspired poetry written by their countrymen. Even the novels of Mongo Beti, an intellectual educated into French-African culture, do not promote the nationalistic fervor characteristic of Négritude. The few novels of political protest are more concerned with humanitarian ethics than with a specifically political consciousness of racism. The brutal maltreatment of Africans in these novels is seen as an evil that afflicts all mankind and not as a uniquely African phenomenon.

Perhaps then as a genre West African novels in English and French render a portrait of humanity rather than a protest against antihumanism. The West African novel in French can best be characterized in terms of the themes of the corrupt city in opposition to the still-undefiled countryside; the idealized childhood in contrast to the ugly realities of adulthood; and the cruel politics of the white imperialists in their treatment of a weakened and subdued African people.

René Maran, who won the Goncourt Prize in 1921 for his novel *Batouala*,[4] was the first French-language "African" novelist to expose in his fiction the evils of colonialism to a large reading public.[5] Maran, a Negro born in Martinique, worked in the French Civil Service for many years before writing his novel. His titular hero, Batouala, is a Mokoundji chief of many villages who is bewildered by his public duties when they are challenged by the white man. Later, French- and English-language African novelists were to give their African heroes more dignity, but their protests were to be similar to the one implicit in Maran's novel: it is the cruel whites who have created the stereotype of the animalistic African and who then, under the convenient guise of "civilizing the natives," continue to exploit him.

Maran's novel did not fall on deaf ears, but there were few people who heeded it. It created a sensation in France, but the sensation produced little practical effect. Ironically the one tangible result it did have was to force Maran to resign from the Civil Service, because his book had created such a hostile and indignant response among the French bureaucrats.

---

[4] Maran's novel, tr. from the French by Adele Z. Seltzer, was published in the United States in 1922.

[5] Some literary historians consider the post-World-War-I novel, *Force-Bonté*, by Bakari Diallo, a Senegalese shepherd, to be the first African novel written in French.

Two novels continue this note of protest in a different spirit. The Camerounian writer Ferdinand Oyono, in *Une Vie de Boy* (Paris, 1956), showed the horrors and evils of colonialism in his portrait of a "boy" servant, Joseph, who dies as the result of torture by a sadistic police officer. Joseph is the innocent victim of his trusting nature; he has accepted the catechism of the priest who tutored him, and he makes attempts to reconcile the evil practices of Christians with their statements of virtue. He has no chance of success, however. The sadists are in control. Oyono's novel is more akin to protest literature than any other novel by an African writing in French, yet even in this novel the tone is pacific. In comparison with *A Wreath for Udomo*, the "political" novel of Peter Abrahams, the Cape Colored writer, Oyono's book is quiet and controlled, never sputtering into rage. Oyono's book is much closer to the Nigerian novel in attitude and tone.

The indignation of the Senegalese writer, Sembene Ousmane, in his portrait of a Senegalese native caught between his desire to help his people progress and the traditional teachings of his Moslem father, is also muted. Faye Oumar, in Ousmane's *O pays, mon beau peuple* (Paris, 1957), brings home a white bride from Europe, where he had gone to study. His father turns his back on his son, castigating him for his progressive ideas. Faye, in his selfless drive to improve the conditions of his fellow peasants, is betrayed by one of his own countrymen. When his ideas begin to threaten the dominion of the colonial business community, he is murdered. The split between the good black and the good white can be mended, however, or so the author seems to be saying. Faye's understanding remains as a legacy to inspire the peasants, and his son—born after his death—is to remain in Africa to carry on his father's work.

This theme of *rapprochement* is more characteristic of the French West African novel than of West African literature in English. Chinua Achebe, perhaps the greatest of the Nigerian novelists, accepts the history of European empire, but he has repeatedly emphasized the need for a return to the ideals of the African past rather than for a blending of European and African traditions; only in his fourth novel, *A Man of the People,* does Achebe admit by implication that Africans can be as corrupt as Europeans or Americans. For the African writer, educated and trained by the French, the role is a more difficult one and the ambivalences seem greater than for the native writer neglected by the British bureaucrats. Both Camara Laye and Cheikh Hamidou Kane from Senegal reflect this ambivalence, especially in their novels which have settings similar to those found in Achebe's fiction. Laye's *L'enfant noir* (Paris, 1953) [6] is a poetic reconstruction of an idealized childhood; it is a childhood seen by an African, with all its wonders and mysteries lit by hues of silver and gold. The man who remembers those magical times is now in exile, both physically and spiritually. He recalls the days before the white man came, those days of enchantment when all people seemed united in their traditions and at peace with their world. In *Le regard du Roi* (Paris, 1954), [7] Laye has a black man show the light to Europeans, but the separation between them—like the gulf between past and present—seems a separation impossible to reconcile. The cogency, the subjective evocation of the past, is achieved here through the placement of the narrative in a dream-vision rather than in a concrete locality.

A similar paralysis fills Kane's *L'aventure ambiguë* (Paris, 1961), [8] which by its very title indicates the author's painful doubts and ambivalences. Kane's hero, Samba Diallo, is an aristocratic Muslim from West Sudan who feels an exile in his own land. He has been away at school, and when he returns home after his father's death he finds he has no local habita-

---

[6] *The Dark Child,* tr. by James Kirkup et al. (New York, 1954; London, 1955).

[7] *The Radiance of the King,* tr. by James Kirkup (London, 1956).

[8] *Ambiguous Adventure,* tr. by Katherine Woods (New York, 1963).

tion. He fits in neither with the strangers nor with the natives still living in their traditional ways unbroken by new ideas. Diallo, in the hope born of despair, accepts his own death at the hand of a fanatic. Kane's book, though originally published in Paris in 1961, thus seems to harken back to a much earlier time, to Louis Aladai, the intellectual prince of Joyce Cary's *The African Witch,* and even to the time of Mary Gaunt at the beginning of the twentieth century when she was bemoaning the disorientation of the British-educated African native in his home territory.

The theme of lost innocence, of a time before the onslaught of the white conqueror and colonial expediter when the African tradition existed in a state of untrammeled harmony and beauty, can be found in many African novels. It is a theme that is intimately connected with the "city" novel. The city in novels of this genre becomes the repository of vice and corruption, and they are often written as protests against European exploitation and African decadence. Some novels are more plaintive and less shrill; the city or village becomes an adult world of compromise and limitation, expressive of the tragic loss of wonder and enchantment.

Probably the earliest example of this type of novel is *Karim* (Paris, 1935), by Ousmane Socé Diop of Senegal. It is a typical story of the provincial hick who comes to a big city. Karim, a good-looking, bright young man, but of very limited financial means, spends whatever money he has in the pursuit of a lovely young lady. Eventually, without much harm, Karim returns home to his native village, a chastened prodigal son, marries a lovely virgin in a traditional village wedding ceremony, and all is harmony again. *Karim* is witty and hopeful, and perhaps its implicit advice was the only sensible advice to offer, some three decades ago: stay out of the city. Today it reads somewhat like a charming fairy tale, because the bright young men can no longer avoid the opportunities of the city. Someone like Cyprian Ekwensi or Onuora Nzekwu might hate the city for its destructive powers, but both writers see the futility of turning their backs on a Frankenstein that is advancing even into the village compounds.

Mongo Beti,[9] from Cameroun, has written several novels in which the lament for innocence is sung to the tune of the countryside. Indeed all his work may be said to revolve around this complex of the city and village, childhood and dryness of age. His earliest novel, *Ville cruelle* (Paris, 1954),[10] is a direct attack on the degradation inherent in the city: it is a hell as potent as the hell of Cyprian Ekwensi's *People of the City* and, curiously enough, the endings of both novels are the same—flight rather than triumph or defeat. The hero and heroine of Ekwensi's as well as Beti's fiction leave the city for a new promised land on the West Coast of Africa, a place to be washed clean by the sea. Three years later, Beti refashioned this theme in a more subtle, ironic, and amusing vein in *Mission terminée* (Paris, 1957).[11] In this novel a young man thoroughly soaked in urban culture visits the countryside, where he experiences a tremendous sense of loss; his whole identity seems challenged by doubt, and he feels an overwhelming desire for roots.

Beti's as yet untranslated work, *Le pauvre Christ de Bomba* (Paris, 1956), presents the theme of innocence and compromise, harmony and duplicity, in a less clearly divided symbology of geographic locations. Here the locale is restricted to the country and village, and the main characters are a French priest, Father Drumont, and the child narrator, Denis. In this novel it is the child who helps the old man to see his beliefs change into illusions before his very eyes; yet, in some tender and ironic way, the novel is also a tribute to the gen-

---

[9] Pseudonym of Alexandre Biyidi.

[10] This novel was published under the pseudonym, Eza Boto, the name of Beti's uncle.

[11] *Mission Accomplished*, tr. by Peter Green (New York, 1958); British edn., *Mission to Kala* (London, 1958).

tleness of the old man and the old world he represents. Beti's
obsessive theme—the discovery of evil in a world held to be
pure—has undergone some bitterness with the passing of time.
In *Le roi miraculé* (Paris, 1958),[12] the child continues to lead
the way to awareness, and the old men follow; only the note
of hope usually in Beti's work is now eclipsed.

In general, it may be said that West African writers in English and French are pacific in their attitude and style. The
obsession with violence so characteristic of South African
writers, white and black, is for the most part absent from
their work, and in its place is a more hopeful outlook toward
the conflicts in the African milieu. West African writers also
at this moment are re-creating the spirit of present Africa in
terms of the two major symbols dominating the continent: the
forests and the cities. African literature thus captures the
vitality of a people struggling with their potential but caught
in the whirlwind of opposing forces. Even in a peaceful Africa
struggle is never quiescent.

This then is the history of the novel in English and French
in the twentieth century about West Africa. It is a history that
can claim some notable literary achievements. Chinua Achebe,
Joyce Cary, Wole Soyinka, Mongo Beti, Joseph Conrad, André
Gide, and Camara Laye have all intimately captured the spirit
of the region. The traditions of several individual genres have
been continued. Several figures are conspicuous in their portraits: the missionary, the journalist, the politician, the tribal
chief, the police officer, the priest, the prostitute, the noble
savage, and the homosexual. Two novels by Graham Greene
and Elspeth Huxley portray the defeatism of the Europeans,
but most other "colonial" novels fail to give their heroes a
heroism. Only in the work of Joyce Cary and Elizabeth Warner
has there been optimism in the depiction of two different

---

12 *King Lazarus,* tr. by Peter Green (London, 1961).

groups of people living side by side. Not even the works of the Nigerian literary renaissance can make an equal claim for optimism.

3

Although he is only in his early thirties, Wole Soyinka has already established a firm reputation in Great Britain, the United States, and Nigeria as his country's leading dramatist. He has also published his first novel, *The Interpreters* (London, 1965), and some poetry. In addition, he has been an actor and a theater producer—he formed his own company, the 1960 Masks, which in turn mounted his symbolistic work, *A Dance of the Forests*, in October, 1960, as part of the Nigerian independence celebrations. Soyinka has been a college teacher and drama critic as well. That he has accomplished so many things in so many fields in so short a time is in itself symptomatic of his great talent, but what is more exceptional is that the quality of his chief work—his plays—is comparable to the best work of contemporary playwrights anywhere in the world.

In the past it has been difficult to speak of African writing except as a parochial matter: the writer who was not an African and wrote on Africa presented an outsider's view, no matter how perceptive and profound that view might be. The African writer—before Soyinka and, to a lesser degree, Chinua Achebe—either tried to imitate Western works or else wrote in a style and/or language that was often incomprehensible to Western and Eastern European audiences. Since each nation and each subcontinent has its indigenous style, no Westerner has the right to criticize an African work for being "African" to the point of exclusivity. Yet it is only with the recent acceptance by literate Westerners and Africans of the mutual interdependence of their arts—and especially with the burgeoning of native literary African work in English and

French in the past fifteen years—that African literature has come to be studied as a comparative literature. Perversely enough it is not the influence of European and American literature on African writers that gives their work appeal for Western audiences: J. P. Clark's worst work, for example, is the result of pretentious schoolboy imitativeness of T. S. Eliot and Gerard Manley Hopkins. What has given African literature its greater cogency in the world today is the adaptability of English and French to convey the sense of the supple rhythms of a supple people shaping their human clay out of swampland, forests, and cities, of the bursting forth of an overwhelming energy.

Of all the contemporary African writers, Soyinka is the one who makes the least pretense of social instruction. Even Chinua Achebe, whose works have a classic simplicity, is obsessively concerned with blaming the white man for the corruption of the African Garden of Eden. Other African novelists and playwrights—Tutuola aside, since he is primarily a folklorist and fantasist—are even more involved in this instructional approach to literature. Since African customs have largely stressed the benefits of a communal and tribal society, this special approach to literature is not surprising and may even be a distinctive contribution to a certain kind of African expression. It is not likely, however, that any literature can remain based on the level of instruction without losing most of its other values. Literature primarily intended to convey a message is undoubtedly still literature, but it often results in sledge-hammers of expression. The early work of Cyprian Ekwensi and Peter Abrahams suffers from their imposing on it an all too deliberate exposé. Alex La Guma's *A Walk in the Night* (Ibadan, Nigeria, 1962) is another example of how literature is sometimes exploited—to its detriment—in order to reveal the evils of a society.

At one time or another, many writers criticize society. The great writers criticize it within the framework of a human comedy or tragedy. The lesser writers, on the other hand, start with a message, upon which they then proceed to super-impose their characters; thus the human element, the essence of all creative art, becomes subordinate to ready-made slogans. It is this propagandist approach—a feature characteristic of certain founding literature from the time of the American Puritan divines to that of the Communist revolutionaries of Lenin's time—that has until recently seemed the obsessive pre-occupation of many African writers. Fortunately the conscious-ness of nationalism and the need for public display of public unity have now receded into the background of African litera-ture and have been replaced by quieter and more subtle cries of pain and joy.

Soyinka is the best example of this continuing maturation of African literature in English (for the preceding remarks are not intended to characterize African literature in its many native languages). He treats most of the themes with which other and earlier African writers have been concerned, but unlike them, interweaves these themes within a humanistic fabric. Soyinka's plays are concerned with the mystery and fascination of a primitive countryside. His characters are either drawn back to the vital countryside or else never leave it, finding in its mystery and voraciousness their necessary ful-fillment. Often enough that fulfillment is doom, but in Soyinka's plays this magnetism of primitive life is so strongly projected that there is no accompanying sense of depression. The reader is too overwhelmed by the terrors of the infinite—whether forest or swampland—and pity for his own sake to concern himself with rational qualms or depression. He is shocked into the sense of disbelief in what is happening, but is power-less to resist following the playwright into that black-forested void that, in Soyinka's plays, always seems to be beckoning from just beyond the real stage. Even in his comedy, *The Trials of Brother Jero,* the reader is led into a black hell which a demagogue priest opens and closes at will. Soyinka paves his plays with pitfalls into which his characters stumble one by one, as if willingly embracing their emasculation or self-destruction.

Soyinka is one of the few contemporary African writers writing in English who does not introduce any white man into his cast of characters (with the exception of his recent novel). This feature, certainly a distinctive characteristic, points up Soyinka's disinterest in contemporary situations, on which the historicopolitical role of the white man in Africa has a direct bearing. Although almost all his work—with the exception of his early allegorical piece, *A Dance of the Forests,* and *The Lion and the Jewel*—is set in the present time, his essential interest lies in the primary emotions of hope, struggle, and defeat. In a sense, his people could as well be Asians or Americans or Europeans: their hungers and needs do not in themselves demand a specific local environment. This is not of course to deny Soyinka's ability to characterize peculiarly African folk beliefs and conflicts.[13]

The Strong Breed, one of Soyinka's later one-act plays, clearly reveals his purposeful ambiguity in the matter of time element. Here Soyinka tells of an educated man, a teacher in a small village who opposes the barbarous custom of human sacrifice. He takes the place of an idiot boy who has been selected to be the "carrier" or sacrificial victim at this year's festival of appeasement to the gods. In the wake of his surreptitious act, the hero relives his past while attempting to escape his pursuers. Ironically, the chief stalwart of the sacrificial custom is the father of the girl who is in love with the hero. Her attempts to get rid of the idiot boy, before he can cause trouble by arousing compassion and sympathy, prove fruitless. The hero, led off to his sacrifice, escapes but, stripped of his clothes, he begins to feel more and more like the caged,

---

[13] Soyinka's plays are available in two editions. For details, see bibliography at the end of this volume.

stinking animal he has been forced to become. One of the most appealing moments in the play occurs when the hero recollects his past love—a fourteen-year-old girl whom he had abandoned when first he ran away from his village to "discover" his identity. Thus, the hero, in taking on the role of the boy carrier, once again finds himself deserting a loved one, in this case the daughter of the tribal chief. In reliving his past, the hero attempts in another way to "go home" again and to make amends for his "desertion"—in this case by finding his father and, as a loving gesture, embracing him. His father, however, tells him to "go back" to the place he has already chosen. It is too late, the father seems to be saying, as he escapes the son by running through the forest back into his own past, and now the hero, the son, cannot choose his identity or place; it has chosen him.

The play ends with the primitive chief and his lieutenant aware that their days of sacrificial ceremony are about to end, but still clinging desperately to their own past. Also on stage are the women who loved the hero, and the idiot boy for whom the hero has made his personal sacrifice. The effect of this resolution is to suggest the humiliation by suffering of the chief's proud daughter caught between a lover and her father, and losing both. What she is left with is, on the surface, very little: an idiot boy and humiliation. It is little, but Soyinka seems to be saying it is enough to start on. Africa, its villages destroyed in the processes of progress, does not have to lose the best elements of its tribal life. That element is the sense of personal loyalty, of friendship, of human commitment to a higher ideal than personal gain and impersonal success. At the same time Soyinka seems also to be acknowledging the evil—attractive though it is in its forbidding and veiled mysteries—of the tribal life and the village: the superstitions that offer transient thrills and a proliferation of other superstitions.

The Strong Breed is an ironic title—ironic since all the reputed "strong" people are defeated: the chief by a sense that he is becoming an anachronism; the hero through his act of self-sacrifice, in order to make a point; the daughter by losing her lover and suffering loss of pride. Only the weak survive: the idiot boy and the young girl who have no real awareness of the forces of conflict.

This destruction of the "strong" and the survival of the weak, and perhaps more corrupt (for the girl who has not the courage to hide the hero from his pursuers is corrupt in accepting expediency and local custom as her spiritual guides), invades the atmosphere of Soyinka's other one-act masterpiece, *The Swamp Dwellers*. Here an old man and woman await the return of their son to a village in the swampland. The son has gone to the city to make his fortune and has lived there eight months; part of his pilgrimage to the city has been to find his brother, who disappeared into the caverns of the city some time ago and who has never written to his family. Over the family household is spread the fetid blanket of flower and decay, and human impassivity. Floods occur, lands are robbed and stolen, but the family, a blind beggar, and the local priest calmly cultivate the permanent swampland of their lives. Only the "Serpent of the swamps, the Snake that lurks beneath the slough" flashes his beauty and potency in this drab brown land. When Igwezu, the son, returns home, he is a defeated man; he has been defeated by the city ways, by having his wife and his landed property aggrandized by his city-dwelling and citified brother. Igwezu, like Eman, the volunteer "carrier" of *The Strong Breed*, is Soyinka's new hero, a brave man who holds on to the ideals of the past, both tribal and Christian, both chivalric and self-indulgent, and who is destroyed without flames of glory. When Igwezu leaves his home he does not know where he is going. He knows he will be no more suited to the crass city than he is to the passive farmland. He asks a blind beggar, a man who has stopped at the house, to remain and "take care of the farm." The beggar, in answer to Igwezu's question about faith in the harvest of one's sowing, has answered Igwezu, "In my wanderings, I think that I have grown a healer's hand." The beggar's suffering is complete Igwezu's, however, is yet to come. Igwezu cannot stay on the farm where, he says, "Only the children and the old stay. . . Only the innocents and the dotards," nor can he accept the help of the beggar in finding the road to the river's edge, since he and the beggar would be "blind men groping in the dark." Igwezu is unsure; yet, even if he has lost his old beliefs, he is still searching for self-fulfillment.

Soyinka, like other Nigerian writers, characterizes the conflict of his country in the broad terms of a revolution in culture and faith. Particularly he symbolizes this dilemma of cultural and religious choice in terms of the city and the country, the educated ways and primitive vitality. In *The Lion and the Jewel* his schoolteacher has education but lacks virility his chieftain has virility and shrewdness even if he lacks education; and the reader is aware that although the chieftain wins once more this time, his defeat by withering old age cannot be avoided much longer. In *The Swamp Dwellers,* the beggar the true representative of the old humility and the old faiths like the idiot boy in *The Strong Breed,* is the last one on the stage, but the onlooker and the reader are aware that although such people, in Soyinka's words, may "be here to give account," they do not provide any formula for the future no lead to a conciliation of opposing forces.

This tragic state of irresolution pervades all of Soyinka' work and gives to it a lyric and plaintive beauty. In his early work, *A Dance of the Forests,* the guests of honor—a dead man and a dead woman—in the magic forest of the under other-world see the past of Nigeria rise before them, but the past and its so-called moments of glory in the court of Mata Kharibu become as tawdry as their modern counterparts in the town. The wood carver Demoke is revealed in his previous guise as a fawning court poet; the courtesan Rola is the descendant of the evil temptress, Madame Tortoise. Adenebi the council orator, becomes the suspect court historian. Nor do the forest dwellers offer a more hopeful guide. Eshuoro is the wayward flesh of Oro, the spirit of terror and bestiality; Ogun, the patron god of carvers, is also a god of war, and the spirits of darkness provide chaos rather than direction. Soyinka's "dance" ends not with a stately resolution but in a whirl of bodies.

Soyinka's other long play, *The Lion and the Jewel*, posits the same conflict and irresolution. Sidi, the village belle, is courted by Lakunle, the schoolteacher, and Baroka, the "Bale" or chieftain of Ilunjinle. Sadiku, the headwife of the chieftain, spreads the tale of the chieftain's reputed impotency to Sidi, who, armed with this information, accepts a visit to the chieftain's tent. Sidi's head has already been turned by her having been photographed and then imaged throughout Nigeria in a magazine, while the "Bale" has been relegated to a corner of the picture. Thus the Jewel—Sidi and her beauty—is being sought by three forces: by the city, with its modern ways and its easy road to corruption (i.e., via the photographer); by the tentacles of education, which carries with it the danger of overintellectualization (via the schoolteacher); and by the old tribal chief, who offers primitive mystery and masculinity (hence the "Lion").

Sidi accepts the man she has fought and rejected—the tribal chieftain, whose suggested "impotency" appears to have been a trick to lure her, unsuspecting, to him. Both in his earlier play, *A Dance of the Forests*, and in this play, Soyinka pays homage to the strength of the tribal wisdom while at the same time exposing its cunning; the kind of ambivalence in which Soyinka engages frees him from either glorifying the past or berating its shortcomings. Indeed, Soyinka's half-mocking approach may well be one answer to the dilemma of the modern African writer who finds he cannot write about Africa without allying himself to primitivism or propagandizing modernism. This sense of humor, this ironic approach to his materials is most openly exemplified in *The Trials of Brother Jero*, in which a rogue "divine" by the name of Jeroboam styles himself "a prophet by birth and by inclination," linking his divine role to early portents: "I think my parents found that I was born with rather thick and long hair. It was said to come right down to my eyes and down to my neck. For them, this was a certain sign that I was born a natural prophet."

To meet any challenge Brother Jero plays a double-edged game. He refuses to allow a convert to beat his wife, until he secretly discovers that the woman is hounding him (Jero) for payment of a debt. When his (Jero's) duplicity is detected, Jero arranges to have his accuser committed to a lunatic asylum; this disposal of an annoyance (the husband in his rage at having been duped by Jero attempted to beat him) is accomplished by Jero through his influence on another of his converts, a Member of Parliament. The comedy ends with Brother Jero supreme, a rogue whose native cunning has outwitted all who have crossed his path. Jero is a masterful con man, as good a knave as any picaresque hero from the eighteenth-century novel, and as splendidly individual in his way as Joyce Cary's Gulley Jimson. What is significant again in this play is that both traditions of Soyinka's town and country come in for a drubbing—the foolish village natives and the foolish, overintellectualized modern Nigerians. The Member of Parliament is no less immune to guile than his supposedly less fortunate uneducated backwoods brother. The rogue wins hands down; his primitive craftiness and vitality remain the only constant in a world of shift and change.

Soyinka's latest play, *The Road*, closely parallels his earliest published full-length work, *A Dance of the Forests*, and makes even more vivid the dichotomy between the forces that play out their dreams and struggles in the quasi-timeless present of Nigeria. Perhaps his use of the same material in changing shades of expression is Soyinka's greatest gift; certainly no sense of familiarity dulls the reader, and acquaint-anceship with his subject matter takes on a growing intimacy with each encounter.

In *The Road* several rogues appear. The setting itself is a motor-park in which various "layabouts" (i.e., idlers; in Amer-ican slang, "bums") visit each other. The chief rogue is the Professor, who has grown fat and rich on "The Word." He uses "The Word" the way Brother Jero used his charm to seduce and fleece his flock. The Professor dresses in Western-style clothing, and undoubtedly Soyinka's "Word" is meant to convey the sophisticated, divisive teaching of Western propa-ganda; perhaps it also bears an overtone suggesting the self-interest and hypocrisy of missionary teaching in Africa. One of the Professor's adversaries, a young driver-trainee who has little spunk, gathers up the courage to declare to his friend that he doesn't believe in the Professor or his "magic." When the Professor hears of this outrage, this affront to his reputa-tion, he swears at the young driver and orders him out of the park. The "Word" this time will be vengeful, not protective.

Just as in *A Dance of the Forest*, where the conflict is be-tween the forces of Nigeria's past and present, the forces in *The Road* range themselves in tribal and urban fashion. Par-ticulars Joe is an expedient local policeman with little regard for the spirit of the law but much for its city and worldly dicta. He tries to arrest a "masquerade"—a spirit of "Death" that comes into the tent in the park in which the characters sit. In describing the culprit who gets away, Particulars Joe sig-nificantly says of him, "Are you sure you know who I mean? Sort of tall but a little on the short side. Tribal marks, but beginning to wear off . . . in fact, unless you looked closely you might think he had no tribal marks at all." (Part Two)

The greatest significance for all the characters is the death that lies in wait for all of them, whichever road they take, tribal or modern. And just as in *A Dance of the Forests* the play ended with a dance—half-frenzy and half-pavane—so this play ends in the whirl and frenzied acceptance of the irreconcilable conflicts of life. The Professor, before "Death" reaches him, yearns for a timeless situation, a time analogous to timelessness, an open space for his mind behind the closed door of a prison. He does not find it, because the mask, the masquerade of Death, is more powerful than any one of the opposing forces of life. The Professor's personal servant, ironically a mute, merely waits on his master without contributing to his welfare or safety. The mute does not stop the Professor's enemy, "Say Tokyo Kid," from stabbing the Professor with all the violence of frustration.

"Say Tokyo Kid" is a modern thug, a motorcycle sadist with the special characteristics of the kind of young person who finds in senseless violence his own curious brand of concord. "Say Tokyo Kid" cannot stand being rivaled by the Professor's quasi-educated talk, and he acts in the only way open to his character: with violence. Thus the Professor is beaten, as all of Soyinka's educated or self-styled educated characters are beaten, by the remnants of barbarism. In the case of "Say Tokyo Kid" this barbarity can be traced to tribal primitivism.

Soyinka's "liveliness"—or at least his sense of the grand grotesque, of dark, malignant forces—is matched by another young Nigerian poet and playwright, John Pepper Clark. Clark is both more worldly and more traditional than Soyinka: his poems follow a modern British pattern, and his often-produced play, *Song of a Goat*, is more familiar to Western eyes than is any of Soyinka's work. Clark, at least initially, treats of themes that are part of the Western heritage. *Song of a Goat* is the story of an impotent husband, his frustrated wife, and the husband's younger, virile brother. In this *ménage à trois* the inevitable occurs, and tragedy results: the wife, the husband, their child, and the husband's brother all die, purging themselves by heartbreak or suicide. Judith Illsley Gleason, in *This Africa* (Evanston, Illinois, 1965), posits the theory that an indefinable humor, a kind of elusive grand comedy, pervades the play, and that this "spirit" illuminates a work which might otherwise be considered imitative. However elusive its quality—whether it is the spirit of comedy, of the grotesque, or whether it is something that is engendered by the sheer breakneck speed of a young writer who stops for tragedy, out of deference, as it were, to his characters but who, one senses, is anxious to move on to more momentum, to the tragicomedy of life—it is this adroit evanescence that gives *Song of a Goat* its distinctiveness. For, surely, J. P. Clark is that most puzzling of all writers: a highly individual African who tries to show that he can equal the best writing in English of any Commonwealth citizen; who succeeds in displaying an intrinsically indigenous talent in spite of his aptitude for Western "learning." His play treats an eternal theme: woman's need for sexual fulfillment and man's desire for exclusive possession of his love-object. The African motifs, too, are present: the goat in the clutches of the leopard's claw; the serpent entwining itself around an unsuspecting village; the calabashes and the blazing fires. Intermingling with the African symbols are strains from Western climes: the marine sorrows of J. M. Synge's *Riders to the Sea,* the Greek choral rhythms, and the sin-and-guilt Puritan strain of Eugene O'Neill's *Desire Under the Elms.* These "Western" elements, whether conscious or not, rob Clark's work of an easy identity.

Since African custom has until recently shown a propensity to societal priority and multiple marriages for men, it may seem that the loss of a wife would not suggest the same kind of tragedy to an African as it would to a Western audience, attuned as the latter is to the theme of the one-man-one-wife relationship. Soyinka, in *The Lion and the Jewel,* has his hero slink away when he loses his "fiancée." The cuckolded hero feels shamed and bitter, but his anger is essentially comic, not tragic.

Two of Clark's other plays reveal this playwright's unique talent for lyricism. In these, *The Masquerade* and *The Raft* [14] —one almost plotless, the other with a familiar pastoral setting—Clark captures a plaintive and lyrical note without any shrillness or comic disharmony. Although they are more integrated as poetic verse dramas, it is doubtful if either *The Masquerade* or *The Raft* would play as well as *Song of a Goat*, since from a purely theatrical viewpoint they are essentially static. *The Masquerade* has its share of horror. It opens happily enough on an attractive, physically beautiful young couple, idyllically in love, who soon marry with the blessing of the girl's family. What destroys their marriage is a rumor, apparently based on fact, that the young man's mother died at his birth and that his true father was actually his uncle—his father's brother. On hearing this rumor, the new bride's father demands the dissolution of the marriage, a proposition to which the young lovers refuse to accede: for them, their love for each other, not societal strictures, takes priority. The bride's father, in a fit of fury and despair, murders his daughter and son-in-law. Thus, like *Song of a Goat*, the play ends with the death of the leading characters. It is perhaps its brevity that gives the play its unity of tone, such that even the choral elements seem indivisible from the dramatic movement.

Clark's absorption with the demands of the individual in conflict with those of the family demonstrates itself in *The Masquerade*. The conflict is an eternal one, that of individuals who break their societal code however outmoded its impositions may seem. When the father learns of the shame that is now his to bear, the shame of the boy's family's history, he accuses his son-in-law of "masquerading." The boy replies that for his part he has been honest. He himself has only learned of his father's adultery through the "rumor." Yet the boy's innocence of this past deed does not dissuade the father from demanding a just punishment. All drama may, in essence, spring from the collision between society, or social norms, and

---

[14] Both published, with *Song of a Goat,* in *Three Plays* (London: Oxford Univ. Pr., 1965).

the individual. In Clark's work the dilemma takes on added significance because of its historic associations. Though he reaches back to the village and a distant past, his theme is contemporaneous: that of the individual caught in a community that punishes him for a crime of which he is not guilty but for which, nevertheless, he bears a responsibility. The dilemma is carried into a discussion of values in *The Raft,* in which several men are lost on a river, searching for a home port. At the end of the play, only two are left on the raft, and they cannot stop, because of the fog and the current, at the banks of the city which lie on either side of them. The men drift on, hopelessly; theirs is the human predicament of being adrift in an indifferent, or hostile, world.

As a poet, no less than as dramatist, Clark can be brilliantly lyric or merely adequately imitative. Various shades exist between these two extremes, and often Clark succeeds in spite of, or because of, his derivations—as in his gem of an imagistic poem, "Ibadan." The Websterian-Jacobean lines of "Passion is a fuel/driving me a rudderless ship" (from his poem, "Passion is a fuel . . ."), or the conscious play of "Ama, are you gall bitterpent?" in "Variation on Hopkins on Theme of Child Wonder," or the compressed *Waste Land* echoes of

> Is it not late now in the day
> Late late altogether late,
> Turning our doubled backs upon fate,
> To pluck out of honey
> Fresh milk fangs?

from his long poem "Ivbie," [15] are each in their own way good imitations; but imitations they are, nevertheless, for none of these poems transcends its intellectualized conception. The whole of "Ivbie," a long poem of despair at the rape of African culture by white men, loses in intensity because of its author's

[15] An eight-page poem in the Mbari publication, *Poems* (Ibadan, 1962).

self-conscious, Eliot-like posture. Granted that in themselves
the title and its image—signifying Nigerian women holding
their hands above their heads and sobbing with pain—capture
from the reader an immediate and sympathetic response. Yet,
like *Song of a Goat*, the narrative itself is warped by all too deliberate artifice, by the poet's facile use of European allusions.

The problems of communication vis-à-vis reader/audience,
which plague the novelist, beset the poet and dramatist as
well. An African is free to choose his language—English or
French, Serer or Sotho, Yoruba or Zulu, to name only a few
African tongues, or an even more regional vernacular. Even
if he chooses such a widely spoken tongue as Yoruba, however,
he will only reach a limited number of his fellow citizens in
Nigeria, and the world outside his country will be deaf to his
words. If, on the other hand, he opts for English or French,
he has to write in an adopted idiom and will therefore be
subject to the dangers inherent in any substitution of one's
frame of reference. Poets like Adeboye Babalola, the late Jean-
Joseph Rabéarivelo, and Flavien Ranaivo have attempted to
overcome this dilemma by adapting the vernacular poetry of
their folk traditions and villages to English or French. Babalola, a professor at the Institute of African Studies of the University of Ife, Nigeria, has rendered in English poetry many
Yoruba folk tales, while Rabéarivelo of Madagascar and the
Malagasy poet Flavien Ranaivo have adapted the traditional
Malagasy poetic form, *hain-teny*, to that of French prose-
poems. Other poets, David Rubadiri of Malawi, for example,
have used the traditional European rather than African models
in their English-language poems. Rubadiri, in transposing the
still, intransient wonder of T. S. Eliot's "The Journey of the
Magi" to his "Stanley Meets Mutesa," [16] creates a strong sense

---

[16] This, and other poems referred to in subsequent pages, are to be
found in several anthologies now available to the American public.
For details, see bibliography at the end of this volume.

of the metaphysical: it is a thrill as hair-raising as the bracelet
of hair on the lady in John Donne's poem.

Other poets have attempted to meet the tastes of two different audiences. James Jolobe, now a Presbyterian church
minister in South Africa and a Xhosa tribesman by birth, has
written poems in the Xhosa tongue and translated them into
English. His narrative poem, "Thutula," originally written in
Xhosa and translated by him into English, recounts the adventures of a beautiful maiden who falls in love with a prince,
marries a rival chieftain, and is then exploited in a plot to
destroy her husband's power. Jolobe's translation, which is
often reprinted in anthologies, carries the mood of a folk epic,
and it is possible that Jolobe's practice—translation by the
original poet into the languages of English and French from
the African vernacular—will become a new wave in African
literature, though the difficulties of such an approach are immediately evident.

Until very recently Négritude inhabited a large room within
the structure of modern French poetry. Léopold Senghor and
Aimé Césaire's influence is evident in any reading of the poems
by Africans in French. This flavor of Négritude may be compared to the propaganda novels of Africans through the 1940's
and 1950's, with their confrontation of white brutality and
black economic deprivation and cultural oppression. African
poets writing in English have also dealt with Africa as a symbolic entity related to a social cause—among them, Abioseh
Nicol and Sam Epelle. Other African poems in English have
as their theme the soil of Africa, seen as a beautiful plaything
of Nature, or the simple, joyous routines of life. Lenrie Peters
of Gambia shows an ironic simplicity of mood and an indestructible sense of humor in his poetry. A Ghanian poet and
playwright, Albert Kayper Mensah, born in Sekondi, Ghana,
in 1923, is more simplistic in his approach than the deceptively
coy Lenrie Peters; but Mensah, like Peters, sees the crisis of
personal awareness as the starting point of social and cultural

growth. His poems usually move to the rhythms of walking or riding, a counterpart to the progressive awareness on the part of the narrator. One of his poems concerns the reaction of the poet to the vision of a new Lazarus walking through the streets of a new city. In another and much longer poem, "The Ghosts," Mensah becomes almost allegorical in positing the ghosts of the past and a young Ghanian man of the present-future in a taxicab ride through a modern city. The poem ends with a plea of hope by the ghosts to the young man that they may look to him "to save the day." Mensah's poem draws its strength not from abstract symbols but from personal observations of real difficulties, a quality beautifully expressed in these lines:

> And lovers have to part at sundown
> If they want to meet tomorrow.

Even a poet like Christopher Okigbo from Eastern Nigeria, who startled African writers and critics at a university conference in Kampala, Uganda, in 1962, by insisting on a definitive measurement of "African" literature, is more concerned with the essentials of personal emotion than commitment to a social or national cause. His poems are universal in appeal, drawing on nature and natural acts, and can only be labeled "African" because their creator happened to be born and still lives in Nigeria.

No overwhelming characteristic has pervaded African poetry in the past decade, certainly nothing comparable to the Négritude of an earlier one. Enriching are the many approaches by which African poets writing in English and French reach their goals. Often the obstacles seem insurmountable, but the impulse for beauty and the dedication to craft are not to be quenched. Gabriel Okara, another talented Nigerian poet, wrote an ode for his thirty-first year, in which he lamented the babble of tongues and the flames within his head that seemed to be engulfing him. He concluded his ode with a wish for silence and a stone retreat. The stone and the silence are symbolic of a spiritual altitude, a height from which to accept the world; they suggest Okara's final acceptance of, and not evasion from, the personal and social world. The pain Okara bears is the pain of all African poets and thinkers and could be said to symbolize their struggle to create an eternal and contemporary literature not only for their world, but for the world at large.

FOUR

East and Central Africa:
Comedy and Psychoanalysis

1

The East Coast of Africa, stretching from Abyssinia to Tanzania, has been intimately entwined in the skeins of Swahili and Arabic culture. Perhaps this explains the paucity of literary culture in English (and, to a lesser extent, German, Portuguese, and French) on Africa's East Coast, an area more completely under the domination of British culture than any other area in Africa. This paucity is reflected in the fact that (1) this territory has been and still is a popular haunt of the romance, adventure, and political escapist novels; (2) East Africa has been the home of a particularly virulent escapist comic literature; and (3) ironically, many novels about the "native mind" in East Africa have been the work of authors born outside the tradition they are describing.

Most of the popular novels have been written by women, especially during the 1930's. Among these writers are Gladys St. John-Loe, Inglis Fletcher, F. E. Baily, Florence Riddell, Margery F. Perham, E. M. Mordaunt, and Jan Godden. The most significant of these writers is Florence Riddell, whose early novels (*Castles in Kenya, Suspicion, Wives Win*), all written and published during the 1930's, showed promise of a serious talent. Miss Riddell was able to convey the disillusionment and loneliness of the Kenya mountain settlers and farmers who struggled to create the customs of "home" in their new surroundings. In her novels the emphasis was on romantic love and on the inevitable challenge of Africa to young émigrés. These novels portray Africa as vast and grim, not because of social and racial problems but because of the isolation of white settlements. Black Africans rarely enter the pages, and, when they do, they usually appear as servants.

Other popular fiction of note from the early part of the century to contemporary times include Edgar Wallace's *Sanders of the River* (1909) and *Mr. Commissioner Sanders* (1930); H. F. P. Battersby's *Edge of Doom* (1920); Harris Dickson's *Old Reliable in Africa* (1920); Jeanie P. Thorndike's *Not to the Strong* (1941); M. M. Kaye's *House of Shade* (1960); and Gwyn Griffin's *Something of an Achievement* (1960) and *A Scorpion on a Stone: Six Stories of Loyalty and Betrayal in Modern Africa* (1965). These popular adventure fantasists follow a similar pattern. The Noble Savage either aids the white man, or is tragically defeated by him. The theme of the quest for identity is also utilized. Graham Greene, in an interview with the present writer in London in April, 1962, revealed that as a boy he had been one of many who read Rider Haggard and his imitators. While these novels are not thesis-ridden, they portray Africa as a challenge which makes the hero a better man for having searched into the darkest pit or most mysterious cave. At the center of such explorations is the self, and while Joseph Conrad was to explore this concept with supreme insight in *Heart of Darkness,* it was Haggard who presented it in popular form and whose heroes gained a world of pleasurable knowledge for their pains. Not until the 1940's, with Jeanie P. Thorndike's *Not to the Strong,* did the fictional European in Africa come to be defeated by his environment; by that time the consciousness of a new, dawning Africa was producing a different type of popular novel, the political "New Africa" novel. The best of these writers is Gwyn Griffin, whose stories and novels about Africa have shown an increasing seriousness of purpose and maturity of craft.

Recently Miggs Pomeroy, in *The Janus Lovers* (New York, 1966), continued the tradition of the well-made popular novel, in which Africa is imbued with the spirit of romance and remoteness. Significantly, her novel deals with the isolation of people who live side by side but who, nevertheless, do not gain any empathy for one another. In earlier novels of this type, isolation was a physical affair and the mountains and forests were regarded as personal foes as well as subjects for adulation; in the present decade the sense of isolation has little to do with the physical boundaries of one's habitat.

Miggs Pomeroy, a naturalized American citizen who was born in England and who has lived in East Africa, placed the action of her novel in a mythical village somewhere in East Africa. It is a small country that she describes, and the hero she selects is a familiar Western one, the doomed and neurotic intellectual. Aden, a bright young man, a Moslem nationalist, is courted by both the Russians and Americans. In his early thirties, Aden comes to realize the futility of personal comfort, that life demands allegiance to a more worthy ideal. Aden joins an underground rebel group while still accepting aid from both the Russians and Americans. What immensely complicates matters is a love affair which develops between Aden and an American girl; this affair, Aden's first experience of love, becomes the cause of his death. Miggs Pomeroy is far better than most popular women writers who have simply used the African locale as a runway for their romantic imagination. Admittedly her people are typical without being real, are little more than the superior creations of an intelligent mind which has, with compassion but without depth of passion, set them in motion. Yet if *The Janus Lovers* is largely a superficial book, it is also a well-written one that, however gingerly, touches on many of the explosive problems of the milieu it describes.

Ernest Hemingway, whose followers exploited Africa and its reputed savagery, is not really a writer in the Conradian tradition of Africa. Yet he has certain elements that tie him to Conrad, and to H. Rider Haggard also. And, unlike the love of his followers, his love for Africa is genuine. *Green Hills of Africa* is an autobiographical fiction in which "none of the characters or incidents . . . is imaginary." [1] The book is a search for "the shape of a country." Hemingway's love for Africa is a love of the unspoiled, of the natural beauty of green hills and cool lands, of heat and the "beautiful killing" by the hunter, of the untutored impulse to nobility. In his shorter fiction, like the stories, "The Snows of Kilimanjaro," "The Short Happy Life of Francis Macomber," and "Hills Like White Elephants," where the natural beauty of Africa is a backdrop to the neurotic destruction of life by the two major characters, Hemingway reveals his love for Africa as a love of the primitive. Africa is the last remaining place for the man who wants to escape the corrupted industrial world. Africa is still young, though her people may have populated the land for thousands of years; she is young in her joy and idealism.

If Africa for Conrad is the key to self-revelation, for Hemingway it is the key to contentment. Africa is a mask—perhaps in itself a greater reality but still a reality one puts on—which provides the illusion of the unspoiled, paradisiacal Garden. In *Green Hills of Africa* the real Hemingway can forget the cities and the neurotic urban citizens he wants so desperately to flee. He can create a jungle of that ideal in which kudu, camp fires, books, and a ready supply of achohol are the in-

---

[1] Hemingway, in his Foreword to the first edn. (1935).

gredients. In "The Short Happy Life of Francis Macomber" the white hunter who loves Africa remains the symbol of masculinity and purity; the wife who shoots her husband is a bitch from the American city. In "The Snows of Kilimanjaro" it is the mountaintop in Africa which beckons to the dying American writer. That writer has "sold out" to success, money, fame, and rich American wives, but, dying in Africa, he is able at last to face himself. Hemingway's Africa is a combination of the real and the imaginary—it is an heroic Africa, unlike Conrad's stripping of the veils of illusion. If Conrad had to go to Africa to face the degradation within himself, Hemingway's African quest was a means of releasing the pure in himself. Hemingway could not live without Africa because he needed its illusion, and that illusion gave him a sense of purpose which enabled him to work. Conrad had to go to Africa to put to rest the illusions and rationalizations of his social and private world; the reality beneath the illusion sustained him in the shaping of a lie for those who could not face the truth of Africa. In both Hemingway and Conrad, Africa was the crux of land in which they found their identity.

A novel which exploits the Conrad-Haggard-Hemingway theme of identity without a deep understanding of the African milieu is *Rain Doctor* by Peter Wingate. The first assignment of the Scottish doctor hero, Tom, takes him to the British-ruled mythical colony of Chidyiko, a region of six thousand square miles populated by 130,000 Africans and less than twenty-five whites. Among the recognizable types he meets are the helpful District Commissioner, the snobbish native who claims his superiority over "the raw African," the liberal Catholic priest, and the pretty nurse also new to Africa. Tom soon succeeds in his duties: he sets up a mission station in the bush; he cures a man whose foot has been torn away; he saves a girl gored by a buck; and he delivers a baby, using brandy in place of an anesthetic at the confinement. Tom's

major battle is the conquest of tsetse fly sickness in Chief
Lukosi's compound, a battle he wins practically and symbolically when Chief Lukosi's people switch their belief in witch
doctors to an acceptance of the power of modern medicine.
What has helped Tom's cause is the fortuitous advent of rain
wherever Tom appears. A superstition soon grows that Tom
has godlike powers, and he is named the "Rain Doctor." Father
Adrian, the priest who does not commit himself to any solution of the rain puzzle, nevertheless insists that Tom come to
his church so that the Africans will believe Tom's rain-making
powers come directly from Christ. It is such peripheral observations that give Wingate's novel authenticity, but the novel
fails to imbue any African character with human depth, particularly in its treatment of the conflict between black and
white people in Africa. Even the sympathetic African characters remain symbols in Doctor Wingate's crusade to bring
"enlightenment." Wingate's novel is one of the better examples
of the popular English novel about East Africa which never
touch art because they never grasp at real life.

The political novel is an evolution of the adventure novel.
From exploits in the jungle, where the white man had to sub-
due rebellious natives or wild animals, or in the forests, where
he found a hidden kingdom, the novel has progressed to adventures where courage and personal heroism are less needed
than wisdom and patience. But in most of the political novels
written about East Africa it is wisdom that both sides lack,
while courage abounds.

The political novel is also an extension of the colonial or
empire novel, the novel dealing with the political and sociological problems of outposts of the British Empire. What distinguishes the political novel from the colonial novel is the
advent of nationalism. Most colonial novels treat Africa,
Asia, and South America in terms of the Noble Savage, the
"wronged" black man, and the dissolution and decadence of

colonial life. They have not, because of the limitations of history, dealt with contemporary native dominance in African affairs.

The early political (or late colonial) novels are optimistic about solutions to the many problems of empire. This optimism was undoubtedly due to the contemporary impregnability of British power, a situation changed in later years by economic and political reversals, particularly those following World War II. Yet recent as well as early political novels suffer from a similar imbalance or lack of realistic objectivity. Their propaganda is not integrated into their fiction; the rupture between the author's attitude and the artistic creation of events is never healed. In trying to be tracts, these novels concentrate heavily on a plotted message, and most of the characters become stereotypes.

One of the most distinguished colonial novels which show this kind of attitudinizing is The Man Who Did the Right Thing (London, 1921), by Sir H. H. Johnston. Johnston was a journalist, scientist, and administrator of wide experience. In 1883 he visited Henry Stanley in the Congo; in 1884 he led a scientific expedition of the Royal Geographical Society and British Association to Mount Kilimanjaro; in 1888 he tried unsuccessfully to acquire the territory for an all-British route from Cape Town to Cairo. Johnston wrote many studies of African problems and British imperial policies. In The History of a Slave (London, 1889), a fictionalized biography, he showed compassion for the African uprooted from his home by the greed of white and black hunters. In The Man Who Did the Right Thing Johnston's sympathy is with the administrators and missionaries who work together in Africa, while he is critical of the politicians', peeresses', and diplomats' string-pulling in England. But he was not blind to the political activities of missionaries; his German missionaries, like the German missionaries in Sarah Gertrude Millin's novels twenty years later, see patriotism for the fatherland as quite relevant to

their religious zeal. The hero, Captain Roger Brenham, arrives
in Africa during the Victorian reign and remains there, trying
to restore the situation as it was after the holocaust of World
War I.

Johnston's attitude toward the African is set forth in the
Foreword to his long study, *The Negro in the New World*
(London, 1910):

> In Chapter I, I have set forth the theory that the Negro should be
> regarded as a sub-species of the perfect human type—*Homo
> sapiens;* that his sub-specific differences from the Caucasian or
> White Man, the Yellow or Mongolian, are largely, but not en-
> tirely, in the direction of his being slightly more akin to the
> lowlier human stock which preceded in time and development
> the existing *Homo sapiens.*

> At the present time the generality of Negroes (leaving out of
> account exceptional individuals) are inferior in mental develop-
> ment and capacity to the peoples of Europe and their descend-
> ants in America, to the Eskimo, the Red Indian, the Japanese,
> the Chinese, the natives of India and of Tartary.   (p. vi)

This attitude of condescension pervades all of Johnston's
work. However, unlike Sarah Gertrude Millin, who held the
same view, Johnston was unable to give his African Negro
characters any individual reality.

Several recent political novels have attempted to present
the white man's point of view, partly as justification and partly
in response to African prejudice against white civilization.
Elspeth Huxley in *A Thing to Love* (London, 1954) portrays
the white-settler attitude in a country (Kenya) where the
natives no longer want their white bosses, and where the
white bosses feel they belong as much to the land as the men
from whom they have taken it. Elspeth Huxley again uses the
Kikuyu tribe as her African spokesmen. From them spring the
nationalist Gitau, who organizes the Mau-Mau movement in
his farming community, and Matthew, the Christian son of a

tribal chief who tries to effect a compromise between his own
and the settler people. This novel, like her earlier *The Walled
City*, presents a group of varied English citizens trying to find
some means of remaining in a country they have grown to
love. But the antagonisms and resentments spring up at any
given moment.

In the opening chapter Gitau is riding in an airplane. Riding in the same plane is Sam, a callow young man "running
away" to a new experience because England has become "old
and cold and weary" to him. Sam is another visitor come to
Africa in search of the exotic. He is a hunter whose game is
experience. Innocently enough in his own eyes he asks Gitau
if the African likes flying. Gitau answers that he thinks of it
simply as a convenience. Sam then asks Gitau if he finds it
"miraculous." Gitau replies that religion has nothing to do
with it, and adds, "Don't you think an African could fly this
aeroplane if Europeans were willing to train him?" (p. 17).

Although Gitau becomes the villain of the piece, the opening chapter reveals the author's attempt to understand the
causes of black nationalism. Sam, who takes no responsibility
for African affairs, is in the novelist's eyes as responsible for
the tragedy as any extremist. Only when the moderates—Sam
and the Christian native Matthew, who suffers grotesque torture at the hands of Gitau for refusing to eat the Mau-Mau
oath—accept their role, does an Africa for black and white
become possible.

Like so many novelists writing of the contemporary African
scene, Elspeth Huxley does not conceal her reaction to dilet-
tante commentators. While other novelists berate journalists
who misrepresent facts, or anthropologists who mistake primitivism for vitality, or sociologists who collect data without
understanding, her dislike for the amateur African observer is
more generalized. She offers, in the concluding pages in the
person of Sam, her plea for a less black-and-white view. It is
not simply white tyranny against black independence, but the

vestiges of a violent past which threaten to overrun the advances of civilization:

> He saw himself as he had been when he first came to Africa: a man groping and confused, above all running away. He had come here to escape. . . .
>
> So he had decided to put it all behind: to turn from a world grown old and cold and weary, to leave the sick hearts and the half-men and adopt a world that was old and new at the same time: not yet drained hollow, devitalised, wasted by the disease called civilization.
>
> But just lately he had come to see things differently. Confronted for the first time by life without civilization he realised that, while from the outside, it might look simple, decent and pure, as perhaps it had been in the days of man's infancy, now, when that infancy was past, and those left behind were not primitive but retarded, in truth, it was complicated, piteously poor and stunted, without hope for the future. (p. 252)

Gerald Hanley has written three novels dealing with the political and social problems of East Africa. Each of these novels has for its overtone the deterioration of Englishmen in the African milieu. In *Consul at Sunset* (London, 1951) a group of English officials break down in a desolate African outpost near Somaliland. In *The Year of the Lion* (London, 1954) a young Englishman succumbs to the influence of the Kenya drunken-settler lot. In *Drinkers of Darkness* (London, 1955) a group of colonials preparing for a Christmas party expose their petty rivalries and rationalizations. The Christmas party turns into a shambles as murder, rape, and a riot greet the holiday. Hanley's novels have that sense of commitment to the spirit of a place which is an essential part of creative writing, but his novels are tracts rather than illuminations. His characters are stereotypes in the eternal war between whites and blacks, between Communist exploiters of nationalism and Western moderates, and between gradualists and conservative imperialists. Even his dialogue reflects the heavy symbolism.

One of the best political novels whose locale is East Africa was written by an American. In *The Day of the Monkey* (New York, 1955), the familiar pattern of plot, violence, nationalism, and riot, and of stereotype characters, the black rebel and the white liberal whose moderate view is rejected, is again apparent. But David Karp does more than resort to clichés. In their awareness of the racial milieu his two heroes, the rebel Luba, leader of a nationalist movement, and Lysander Pellman, the British Governor of the Protectorate, reflect levels of consciousness that create complex human beings. Luba and Pellman are good friends, but their friendship does not interfere with their conflicting political views. Luba, like Peter Abrahams' Udomo, believes a nationalist must be "irresponsible." Yet Luba, jailed and then freed by his friend the Governor, calls off preparations for a native uprising. He comes to realize that blood once spilt cannot be bottled up. The forces of sanity, and of friendship between black and white, seem to have won, but Luba's enemies within his own party (again the situations of this and of Abrahams' novel, *A Wreath for Udomo*, are similar) kill him. A riot breaks out, and the Governor is forced to resign.

In *Honey for Tomorrow* (New York, 1961), another political novel which succeeds in probing beneath archetypal characters, Robert Lait examines the forces that constituted Zachio Shabani, a brilliant young mission-schooled East African rebel. As the novel opens, Zachio is being led to prison. He has been sentenced to five years' imprisonment for contempt of court and embezzlement of funds from the Fiscal Department where he had worked. When Zachio is asked if he has anything to say, he replies, "What protection does an African get? You wish to find me guilty. I don't believe what you say. I spit at this court" (p. 183).

Yet Lait's novel shows that as overlords the British were fair. This quality forms the irony of the colonial romance, for Africans like Zachio are no longer content with fair play.

They want independence. The title, which comes from an East African legend about a bird called the "honey guide," epitomizes Zachio's attitude. In the legend the bird guides a person to a beehive, but this person must leave a little for the honey guide to eat. If he doesn't leave it its rightful portion, the honey guide will lead him to a hippopotamus the next time. The British, in Zachio's eyes, cannot escape the paths they have created.

A subplot of the novel shows a literary allegiance to E. M. Forster's *A Passage to India.* The frustrated, bored wife of the Surveyor-General tries to seduce Zachio into her bedroom. Zachio flees from her, yet a charge of rape is lodged against him. Like Forster's Doctor Aziz, Zachio is faced with insurmountable evidence of guilt, but at the crucial moment the woman in the witness box admits that nothing had happened.

Lait's point of view is extreme. Zachio is shown to be a hot-headed and narrow-minded nationalist, yet his attitude is wholly justified by the author. The displaced colonials, no matter how devoted and benevolent their service to Africa has been, must be driven out. Because of the scandal attaching to his wife, the Surveyor-General is transferred to a new post, yet this official has been considered one of the liberal voices in East Africa. The old-fashioned liberal no longer has a place in the new Africa.

This point is underscored in Lait's portrayal of another mission-schooled educated African. Andrew, who has been given Zachio's job as tax-collector, discovers Zachio's duplicity. He is presented with the dilemma of betraying Zachio to the police or flouting his own morality. In despair he turns for advice to Zachio, who mockingly advises him to report him.

Andrew is an African spoilt and misled by Christian and Western teachings. He is the confused idealist so brainwashed by his white captors that he is reduced to mental paralysis. Zachio, who knows the realities of politics, remains freer in his prison cell than Andrew who, in his cluttered mind, can neither denounce Zachio nor accept his practical view of politics.

The revolution in politics and the social fabric of the Kenya village lie under the surface in James Ngugi's first two novels, *Weep Not, Child* (London, 1964) and *The River Between* (London, 1965). Ngugi, born in Limuru, Kenya, in 1938, and widely published as a journalist, is probably the best-known Kenya writer (except of course Jomo Kenyatta) in English today. His two novels were published only a year apart; yet, while the narrative skill in *The River Between* is that of a master, *Weep Not, Child,* on the other hand, is an interesting but unpolished story. In both novels Ngugi has as his central character a young man—intelligent, sensitive, and somewhat apart from his tribal group—who hopes to heal the breach between the warring factions of his social milieu. In several chapters of *Weep Not, Child* Ngugi describes the intimacy between his young hero and his girl friend who is tragically isolated from him because her father has become a tool of the British colonialist. The hero, a brilliant student, gets to know the son of the British governor, and the old theme of children overcoming (or not feeling in the first place) the prejudices of their elders is conveyed in Ngugi's story. The irony of the white boy wanting to remain in Africa, in order to know the people of Kenya, is told in the simple tones of a childhood encounter between the child-hero and the white boy at school; it is the white boy who feels envious of the black boy, of the latter's *opportunity* to remain in Kenya.

Ultimately the political situation erupts into the novel. The hero's family is torn apart by divided loyalties—desire for peace, and desire for national independence. When the father is tortured because one of his sons is exposed as a member of the Mau-Mau, the climax of familial loyalty is reached. The hero, at the end of the novel, does not run away from home even though flight means safety; he stays with his family to create a hymn of loyalty to his African ideals.

If the conflict between black and white provided the *modus operandi* of *Weep Not, Child,* the conflict between black and white reveals a deeper tonality in *The River Between.* Ngugi's themes are intimately connected with the division of people's loyalties, with the eternal conflicting claims of allegiance. In *The River Between* he tells the story of a young man, Waiyaki, who tries to bring the two opposing groups of his village together. The river between—in this case, the divide between the belief in tribal laws and Christian laws—is never bridged; even Waiyaki, at the conclusion of the novel, is to be sacrificed to the prejudices of his people.

Ngugi's novels treat the same themes as those of Chinua Achebe and Onuora Nzekwu; his settings—a village in conflict with old and new customs and approaches to life—are also similar to the ones found in the novels by the two Nigerian writers. Where Ngugi differs is in his tactile imagery, and in the coolness of his prose. Ngugi's landscape is filled with growth and vegetation; the demanding sun and sultry flatlands have not yet desiccated hope, even for a union of understanding with the white settler.

2

Although Evelyn Waugh was not the first satirist of Africa, he has had a greater influence on British satiric writing about this continent than any other Englishman. The reason may be that he was alone in investing it with the ridiculous. All the other writers who poked fun at Africa's foibles, such as Joyce Cary, David Garnett, Bernard Shaw, and Sylvester Stein, were to become seriously concerned with its problems. Waugh is content to laugh only, though the laugh becomes savage and bitter at times. For this reason he has almost no relevance vis-à-vis Africa today, and yet his influence can be seen in a large number of comic novels which appear fre-

quently on the British booklists. Waugh's satire, while virulent
and destructive, is not without truth: he attacks the insincerity
of both the whites and blacks. He criticizes black nationalism,
which, in the 1930's, he considered absurd, and also white
humanitarianism. There has been a tendency to dismiss Waugh
as a bombastic reactionary because of such misguided statements as "In East Africa as yet there are no negroes in positions where they could possibly contemplate equality with
the whites; Anglo-Saxon sanity remains undisturbed in that
direction. . . . It is just worth considering the possibility that
there may be something valuable behind the indefensible and
inexplicable assumption of superiority by the Anglo-Saxon
race." [2] Waugh's relevance, however, is to be found elsewhere:
Africa for him was but another area of human folly to be in-
dicted; his sharp scorn was poured on pretentious intellectuals
and ineffectual humanitarians.

Both of Waugh's novels about Africa followed a visit to
Abyssinia. Waugh also wrote a travel memoir after each visit.
In *They Were Still Dancing* Waugh celebrated the overthrow
of Haile Selassie's regime by Mussolini because he (Waugh)
hoped the new fascist power would bring a decent European
influence into the country. The following comment helps explain his attitude:

> We drove out to the ruins of the Arab house where Stanley and
> Livingstone had spent three weeks together in Tabora, a region
> inhabited by the Kikuyu tribe. On the way we passed the resi-
> dence of a local chief whose history illustrates the difference be-
> tween English and African ideas of justice. A few months before
> my arrival he had been arrested for very considerable defalca-
> tions of public accounts. There was not the smallest doubt of his
> guilt in anyone's mind. He was sent down to the coast for trial
> and there acquitted upon some purely technical legal quibble

---

[2] *They Were Still Dancing* (New York, 1932), pp. 253-54. Quotations
are from this edn. The original London edn., published in 1931, is
entitled *Remote People*.

To the European this seemed an excellent example of British impartiality; anyone, black or white, guilty or not guilty, got a trial according to law on the evidence submitted. To the native there was only one explanation; he had bribed or intimidated his judges. Under German administration justice was often ruthless but it was delivered arbitrarily by the officer on the spot and the sentence executed immediately in a way that the natives understood; English justice, more tender and sophisticated, with its rights of appeal and delays of action is more often than not confusing and unsatisfactory to the African mind.   (pp. 283-84)

Antagonism toward the social democratic, "liberal" line is prevalent throughout Waugh's two African novels and is one of the underlying reasons for Waugh's savagery of style. Waugh rejected "enlightenment" as well as gradualism toward African independence because he saw no hope in contemporary progressive schemes. His attack took the form of satire of the insincerity and inconsistencies of British civil servants, African leaders, American "liberal" journalists, and titled English ladies—"do-gooders" who wished among other homespun activities to spread the word for antivivisection.

Waugh's African novels are located in mythical East African colonies: *Black Mischief* (London, 1932) on Azania, an island off the African coast; *Scoop* (London, 1937) in Ishmaelia, a territory of the mainland. Azania is ruled by a young and foolish Oxford-trained emperor who gets all his knowledge from European books and destroys himself and his country by his "advanced" theories. In *Black Mischief* Waugh also savagely attacks the French and British ambassadors to Azania. The French representative is a paranoiac who believes the British ambassador is plotting to bring Azania to its knees; the British ambassador is an even more foolish man, a bored nitwit who has neither concern nor knowledge about the happenings outside his rose garden. Dame Mildred Porch and her traveling companion Miss Tin also come in for a share of the satire. They are journeying round the world in a crusade to promote antivivisection, but, as Waugh reveals them, they are selfish creatures of comfort indulging in a diversion. The end of the novel finds the foolish emperor dead, and a new emperor installed in his place. Nothing has been learned or gained. European ideas have made no impact on the African consciousness, and the only one who has profited at all is a Syrian merchant who has played with both camps to suit his own ends.

Waugh continued his satire of African politics and European "benevolence" in *Scoop,* but here he concentrated on exposing the vices of journalism. In *They Were Still Dancing* he wrote, "My complaint is that in its scramble for precedence the cheap press is falling short of the very standards of public service it has set itself. Almost any London newspaper today would prefer an incomplete, inaccurate and insignificant report of an event provided it came in time for an earlier edition than its rivals" (pp. 60-61). In his second African novel he attempted to expose the indecencies of this kind of journalistic behavior. In the process Waugh knocks almost all of British and European society, which he views as existing on the same level as the journalistic maw. The revolution in Ishmaelia which brings in a host of newspapermen is but a cover for the machinations of mineral hunters. Russians and Germans are intriguing against each other, but both are defeated by an Englishman who jumps from skies like Superman and sets everything aright. The irony in the novel is that none of the sides approaches from the right, or correct, angle. Ishmaelia has gained nothing from its association with European culture, as represented by the various European residents there, and the Europeans have exploited the African milieu without thought or sensibility. The result in both novels is that experience has taught nothing. This disgust with the decadent Europeanization of Africa is what gives Waugh's comedies a bitter taste and which helps to rationalize his neofascist declarations.

In a letter to the present writer (dated April 23, 1962),

Waugh wrote, "Recent changes in Africa have changed the raw material of the comic writer and impoverished it. Farce has become melodrama of a rather commonplace kind. Very few (if any) negroes have any sense which corresponds to the European sense of humour. They are merely jolly." But if Waugh lost interest in the African locale, his literary companions and descendants carry on his tradition of mockery in somewhat diluted form. Among these confreres are Winifred Holtby, Ian Brook, and Anthony Burgess.

In *Mandoa! Mandoa!* (London, 1933), Winifred Holtby satirized the tourist agencies which, even in the 1930's, were trying to turn Africa into a diversion; the International Humanitarian Association, which investigated charges of Mandoa's engagement in the slave trade with Arabia; and Members of Parliament, who jumped onto the "liberal" band wagon and hopelessly confused the issue. Like Waugh, her blast is scattered on two sides, but since the blacks count for little in her scheme of things, she fires away continually at the whites who bring nothing but decadence and amorality wherever they go. As Waugh mocked the humanitarians who pretended an interest in dogs, Miss Holtby derides the International Humanitarian Association which cares more about its public image than its public duties. Again, like Waugh, she is particularly hostile to sentimental observers of the African scene. In the concluding scene of her novel, she presents a fatuous humanitarian who says she wants to help "the driven slaves, those poor little girl prostitutes" in Mandoa. She is answered by Fanshawe, another tourist who has returned from Mandoa, "Has our own civilization no victims? Frustrated human appetites, perversions, miseries? What you are trying to do, forgive me, is to substitute one form of evil for another" (p. 282).

Fanshawe is an anthropologist who had decried the modernization of Africa because such progress promised the destruction of the quaint social habits of a "primitive" people.

Winifred Holtby would undoubtedly have found funny the
recommendation of E. E. Evans-Pritchard in *Social Anthropology* (London, 1951) that a department of anthropology be a
permanent feature of colonial administrations. She has greater
scorn, however, for Cardover, an effete convert to the imagined orgiasticism of African rites:

> "If you could know how we envy you! We, who are the victims
> of an effete intellectualism. You, who still dare to retain the—
> shall we say—purity of primitive sensation. You, who lose your
> individual consciousness in your corporate dances. My dear
> Talal, if you knew what anguish we suffered through the loss
> of our power of spontaneous and corporate ecstasy . . . your
> natural, sinless, cool, lustful completion of bodily bliss. Unself-
> conscious, unafraid. Your wholeness with the community! Your
> deep tranquil blood-unity!"   (pp. 284-86)

In the end nothing changes in Mandoa. The African Prince
Talal, who was the first of his tribe to come in contact with
Western civilization, builds a "Hollywood Hall" and agrees to
enter into partnership with Prince's Tours, Ltd., an English
outfit advertising the safari to Mandoa as "the last of its kind"
into primitive Africa. Talal's brush with Western civilization
brings only the white dregs to his land. At the conclusion of
his first tour, Talal reflects on his failure:

> The hotel and the ballroom, the stadium and cinema, were not
> what Europeans and Americans wanted. His arrangements had
> been too good, his people too docile. All that he had planned,
> all that he had paid for, was unnecessary. He had drained the
> resources of his country. He had aroused dissatisfaction among
> the younger men. And at the end of it all, the visitors were dis-
> appointed. For the men, it appeared, desired violence, and the
> women expected rape. They had wearied of their well-conducted
> cities.   (p. 291)

Winifred Holtby's novel is a rejection of hypocritical Western policy in Africa. Through her hero Bill Durrant, the black

sheep son of a rich and titled English family, who bears a
resemblance to Basil Seal of Waugh's *Black Mischief,* she sums
up the lack of values which British policy has engendered in
East Africa. Bill does not believe that anything European—
the hospital, the dispensary, the mission school, the store—will
survive the departure of the Europeans from Africa. In almost
the last line of Miss Holtby's novel comes Bill's self-accusing
question, "What had Europe and America to offer these alien
people?"

Two more recent comic novels carry on the tradition of the
Waugh comic novel. In *Jimmy Riddle* Ian Brook (the pseudonym of a British diplomatic officer) makes fun of progressive
and liberal spokesmen who fail to grasp the complexity of
politics in Africa. His hero Jimmy Riddle is a Kiplingesque
fighter who gains the love of African chiefs because he treats
them and everyone else with a strict, fatherly sense of disci-
pline. Brook has Riddle join forces with a tribal chief and
declare war on the corrupt, modern African leaders and the
naïve British colonial administrators. Brook also makes fun of
the social anthropologist who comes to Africa to improve the
lot of the African. This anthropologist, a foolish lady in Brook's
novel, tours around the country, gathering hordes of material
for her study of inhumane prison treatment. Like Joyce Cary's
Marie Hasluck, in the novel *An American Visitor,* this British
visitor soon learns that her academic ideas will never pass the
test of reality. The lady anthropologist mends her ways, even
to the point of falling in love for the first time in her life;
naturally, it is with a black "primitive" leader, the antithesis
of all her teachings and the kind of man she had come to
Africa to educate away from his beliefs.

Devil of a State (London, 1952), by Anthony Burgess, which
is dedicated to Graham Greene, is also reminiscent of Waugh.
The British are effete, bureaucratic sops; the Africans, on the
other hand, are good-natured bumblers and smiling liars. Ultimately Burgess envisages a plague on both houses, and a

clean sweep as the only solution. He places his demihero, a self-centered passport officer, in the mythical colony of Dunia where he must battle with the corrupt caliph, with British businessmen after uranium concessions, and even with an American representative from the United Nations, who is of course too nice for words. Burgess, who has only visited Mediterranean Africa, gives his locale the dimension of a concept rather than that of a living place. Africa has become—like the Africa of the psychological writers and of the political exploiters—a repository for ideas, but it is a repository full of comic irony.

These comic novels reflect one side of the British attitude to the African. In them the African is never a man but a comic butt. He has to be dealt with, not as a human being, but as an obstruction. The good African in these novels is one who wants to return to the past without the corruption of European exploiters. It is the inevitability of progress, a progress which these English writers see as the loss of English and African culture and sensibility, that causes such a bitter defeatism in their comic bites.

As late as 1965 the comic novel about East Africa was still in vogue. Harold Beaver's *The Confessions of Jotham Simiyu* (London, 1965), however, reveals a shift of emphasis, the key to which lies in its author's sympathetic attitude to the African rogue. Simiyu in Beaver's novel is more than a foil to provide laughter: he is the incurable rogue, the rascal who provides such a reminder of the charm and zest of life that his "crimes" become glorious follies. If Waugh reduces Africa to a mad world in which all values have been lost and inanity is the ruler, Beaver gives to his African rascal the stature of a picaresque hero filled with the gaiety of life's paradoxes. Waugh's comedy is dark-edged; Beaver's is filled with the sunshine of human foibles.

Many novels have been written in English about the mind

and psychology of the native East African. These novels present for the most part a compassionate picture of the problems which have beset the African as a result of the Christian and Western invasion of his land. Many of these novels are romanticized pictures of noble black warriors, picturesque heroes seven feet tall, and barbarous natives fighting a last-ditch stand against the mightier gunpower of the British. Haggard and Bertram Mitford were writers of this kind of novel, which was so popular in the early part of the twentieth century. Perhaps the need for such fiction arose from a sense of guilt at having all but exterminated the native East African. Certainly the British during the nineteenth century had stripped him of effective power, but now there were moves to idealize him in his natural state.

By 1930 a new type of "native mind" or socioanthropological novel was evolving. In British West Africa, Robert Rattray was writing *The Leopard Priestess* (London, 1934), the reputedly true story of two lovers who paid the price of defying juju customs. In East Africa, Jack H. Driberg was describing the Didenga tribe which inhabited the mountainous regions of the Sudan. Driberg, employing a folk tale style, wrote a series of psychological sketches entitled *People of the Small Arrow* (London, 1930). This book marks a turning point in the anthropological novel about the African native. No longer is he merely romantic (though for a long time he will continue to be strange), but an individual struggling for personal fulfillment within an ordered way of life threatened by foreign culture.

A far more ambitious attempt at the anthropological novel was made by Elspeth Huxley in *Red Strangers* (London, 1939). This writer has since written several more novels, each revealing a different aspect of form and a much greater political awareness of the role of the displaced white settler. In this first novel the author re-created the life of a Kikuyu community before the "red strangers" arrived. The novel spans three generations of one family, and ultimately it is Christian and Western rule that triumphs over them. The triumph of these twin forces does not benefit the Kikuyu natives, however. One family suffers great poverty but continues to believe that benefit will come of contact with the white man. The novel ends with the third generation of the family converting to Christianity; the hero marries a Christian girl, and takes his first ride in an airplane. The daughter born to this generation is called "Aeroplane," and the father thinks: "His wife . . . would never be able to pronounce such a difficult word; but educated people would know, and would understand." Thus the final note suggests that the hero, and other Kikuyu natives like him, are gaining a share of Western progress in exchange for the loss of their past. It is a theme of *rapprochement*.

Two more recent novels show a less neatly ordered approach. Richard Llewellyn's *A Man in a Mirror* (New York, 1961) examines the role of the Masai in an industrialized world. The hero, educated in England, engages in local and national politics and must face again, as is the case in so many other novels, the conflict of world, tribal, and personal loyalties. In *The Brothers M* (London, 1961) Tom Stacey, a correspondent for the London *Sunday Times*, also attempted to give a picture of the native mind, but Stacey's canvas is much broader than that of an anthropological novel. Stacey placed two men, a black and a white, in the remote, lonely Ruwenzori Mountains of southwest Uganda. The black is a "been-to," an Oxford-trained intellectual who has achieved total integration in England with his friends, his professors, and his English female companions. The white is a Canadian Rhodes scholar who journeys to Africa to live with the primitive tribe from which his educated African friend is descended. The white man's visit is in the nature of a sojourn in a strange land; the black man's is a return home to his past.

Stacey's book is as much a psychological and symbolic tale

as a re-creation of native life. The search for the lost relative in "The Mountains of the Moon" becomes a search for the self. The novel is in the tradition of Conrad and Haggard, an initiation through the dark pits of the forests and jungles to awareness.

Like Elspeth Huxley, Stacey suggests that the educated African is going too fast, that a period of maturation is necessary before all that he has learned can prove fruitful. His depiction, however, lacks any ulterior rationale: he does not argue or suggest that the answer is the benevolence of the white-settler government. Stacey's desire to emphasize the general theme of alienation probably explains what is surely a shortcoming in his novel, the assignment of a double tribal allegiance, half-Muganda and half-Mukonjo, to the African hero. One of these tribes has its foundation in a fixed aristocratic tradition, the other in a static primitivism. Stacey's choice no doubt reflects his desire to give all Eastern Africa a symbolic unity, but the symbolism weakens the plausibility of his character's behavior.

Ebony and Ivory (London, 1923) and *Black Laughter* (London, 1925), by Llewellyn Powys, are imaginative essays that have their base in Powys' five-year experience in East Af.'ca as a sheep farmer. Powys was never a popular author, but he was well respected by influential writers and critics. Units of shorter writings combining to form a novelistic federation, these books turn Africa into a mysterious, primeval place, beneficial to the soul. Their style and the views they express are much like those of later imaginative observers such as Isak Dinesen, Lawrence Green, and Laurens van der Post. They strip away the illusions, but they do not strip away the mysteries. In Powys' Africa, wild creatures and man live side by side in mutual harmony. Violence cracks the placid surface, but it is never out of tune with the essential harmony. Even the inexorable African rhythm of "Kill! Kill! Kill!" produces "the sublimest cadence" when "backbones are being snapped and throats cut." [3]

3

Few of the novels in English which have their setting in Central Africa deal with real or actual problems. Those that have done so have usually been written by people who have never lived in Africa. Central Africa, and especially the Congo, is a symbolic state for the English and American writer rather than a milieu or a neighborhood. Significantly enough, most Americans, when they write on Africa, turn to the Congo for their setting. For it is the center of Africa, the "heart of darkness," which inspires these novelists. They are searching for an idea, a mystique, a revelation; they are looking for the flame in the blackness that will signify an end and a beginning to their restless psychological treks. They do not have to be experts on the African scene or even basically concerned with real problems of Africa.

Such novels have been influenced by Conrad's *Heart of Darkness*, which explored the need of one man to taste the forbidden fruits of primitivism, and of another man's need to discover the secret of degeneration. Conrad set the action of his novel in Central Africa because he knew the territory, having traveled up the Congo River in 1890 and having kept a diary of his journey.[4] He knew the model for Kurtz, a Monsieur Georges-Antoine Klein, the agent in charge of a company station at Stanley Falls who was buried at sea near Bolobo by the ship's company.[5] Yet Conrad's choice of setting was not simply fortuitous. Africa was a shape and an image

---

[3] Powys, *Black Laughter* (London, 1925; rev. edn. 1953), p. 57.
[4] See Chapter One, note 7.
[5] G. Jean-Aubry, *The Sea Dreamer* (London, 1957), p. 170.

to him long before he began his writing career. When he was a nine-year-old boy in Poland, he pointed to the center of a map of Africa and said, "When I grow up I shall go *there*." [6]

With the exception of Graham Greene, who researched his African novels by extended visits to Sierra Leone and the Congo, and Francis Brett Young, who lived in Johannesburg and East Africa for five years, most writers attracted to Central Africa have not even visited the continent. Other exceptions are of course the French writers on the Congo. From Gide's *Travels* in the Congo to the latest French novels, Frenchmen have been voyaging to Central Africa, fascinated by its beauty and paradox of meaning. The three most recent novels detailing the racism of black and white were written by men who lived and worked or traveled in Africa: Georges Conchon, author of *L'état sauvage*; Philippe Diolé, author of *L'Okapi* (Paris, 1963); and Jean Lartéguy, who wrote *Les chimères noires* (Paris, 1963).[7] English and German writers, however, have concentrated on the Congo from a psychological standpoint. They see the exotic dark continent in terms of a journey inward, an acquaintanceship with the mysterious path of the self. Two recent novels, in particular, owe this psychological orientation to Conrad. In *The Sun Doctor* Robert Shaw takes a Schweitzer-like doctor who has sacrificed fame for selfless work and devotion to his native patients in a remote region of Angola. Dr. Halliday is pursued not so much by "abomination" as by his narcissism. Only after he experiences a love affair in England does he feel capable of serving his natives in humility. Shaw's variation on Conrad—it is England which provides the epiphany and Africa the neurosis—does not obscure this writer's debt to the psychological genre that Conrad's influence extended.

Henderson, the Rain King, another novel by a man who

---

[6] *Conrad's Diary*, p. 6.
[7] *The Hounds of Hell*, tr. by Xan Fielding (New York and London, 1966).

never visited Africa, shows a similar psychosymbolic pattern. Saul Bellow's novel is a comic allegory whose hero is fifty-two years old, weighs over two hundred pounds, wears a size-22 collar, and raises pigs on a gentleman's farm near Danbury, Connecticut. He is on the road to Africa because for him it promises a secret, though Henderson does not know what it is he hopes to discover. Before he completes his African odyssey, Henderson suggests that he is seeking spiritual rejuvenation through the animal forces of the African mystique. The work of Bellow, like that of Shaw, suggests that the psychological novel of the great man who goes to Africa to rediscover his small, unique self is intimately connected in English and American culture with the historical fact of Albert Schweitzer's journey to Lambarene. When Henderson says, "Here we are in the farthest African mountains" (p. 87), it is apparent he is already thinking of Schweitzer.

Elspeth Huxley, who has journeyed extensively through Eastern and Western Africa, chose the interior of French West Africa for her novel of a Schweitzer-like character, *The Red Rock Wilderness*. The great Clausen, a Nobel Prize-winning biologist, has retired to a post in Luala, where he has set up a native hospital compound. Clausen is dangerously under the influence of Dr. B. Roland, an educated French West African biochemist who uses the primitive rites of his tribe to trap the gullible doctor. Clausen, like Kurtz, succumbs to the final "abomination." In Conrad's novella Kurtz crawls on all fours to a meeting in the jungle. In Elspeth Huxley's novel Clausen is traumatized into stabbing and killing his devoted nurse, whom he has bound and stuffed like a pig. The doctor is shot and killed, shortly after his orgiastic consummation, by Andrew Colquhoun, a young journalist who cannot bear witnessing the degradation. Clausen's quick death after surrender to primitive evil is parallel to Kurtz's demise when he is taken aboard ship to England: both men no longer have a place in Western civilization. Colquhoun is the Marlow of Elspeth Huxley's tale. He narrates the story some time after the actual adventure, when he has had time to ponder its meaning; he goes to the heart of darkness to find Clausen, because, like Marlow, he feels compelled to confront this famous man. He passes through several stages of psychological understanding, and, at the final moment of revelation is able to cross the darkness without being caught up in it. Like Marlow, he escapes to a bigger world through having witnessed a man's downfall.

Graham Greene set the action of his novel *A Burnt-Out Case* in the Belgian Congo. He said in a personal interview [8] that his choice of setting was dictated by his knowledge of Africa. There were two possible regions for the remoteness Greene desired—Central Africa and British Guiana—but since he knew little about British Guiana, Greene decided on the Congo—"And besides, I knew a doctor in a leper station in the Congo, which of course made things easier." Yet Greene's explanation, one which on the face of it may seem to negate any symbolic insinuation vis-à-vis the Congo, is a gloss on his many comments on Africa as a psychological necessity. In his early travel book, *Journey Without Maps,* he wrote of Africa as the Mecca of a weary soul; while in his two African journals, published under the title *In Search of a Character* (London, 1961), he states, "How strange it is that for more than a hundred years Africa has been recommended as a cure for the sick heart" (p. 17). The title of his first novel about Africa, *The Heart of the Matter,* refers as much to the African milieu as to the romantic affair that forms the crisis of the hero's life. The symbolism of Africa in *A Burnt-Out Case* is as intense: Africa is "one of the dark places of the earth" which gives off light. Even Querry's name suggests the symbolism of the man in search of identity in Africa.

Two earlier writers who reveal their debt to the novel of regeneration in Central Africa are Francis Brett Young and

---

[8] In London, April 1962.

C. S. Forester. Young, a prolific romantic writer, set the locales
of many of his novels in South Africa, in what he called the
"African obsession" following a five-year stay in that continent.
In *The Crescent Moon* (London, 1919) he placed an English
missionary and his sister in German Central Africa on the eve
of World War I. The missionary is defeated by the African
acceptance of life. All the puritanical teachings of his creed
are rejected casually by the people he has come to help. The
lack of understanding in the missionary and the futility of his
religious endeavors are contrasted with the secret power of a
German coffee farmer, Herr Godovius. Godovius has allowed
himself to partake freely of primitive rites and orgies; his sensuality fascinates the missionary and his sister, despite their
puritanism. When James, the missionary, ill and weary, crawls
to a jungle fire where he sees Godovius dressed in a white
robe presiding over an orgiastic ceremony, the novel gains a
Kurtz-like atmosphere. James's cry, "I've been in hell. There
can't be anything worse than hell" (p. 181), equates with the
third stage of Marlow's journey. The last lines of the novel
sum up Godovius and Africa in Conradian terms: "Godovius
consumed in the flames which he had kindled. . . . I knew
that this was the land above all others which men of European
race have never conquered. It was a strange moment, full of a
peculiar, half-bitter ecstasy. I gazed at the stars and murmured
to myself: 'This is Africa. . . . This is Africa!'"

C. S. Forester's novel of regeneration, *The African Queen*,
is a comic escapade describing the transformation of a rodent-
like ne'er-do-well into a man. It is never threatened by the
earnestness of a message, but it reveals the exploitation of
Africa as a psychic journey. Allnut and Rosa travel down the
long river in Central Africa: when they start out they are a
prudish spinster and a lazy self-centered wastrel; when they
end their journey they are on their way to aggressive middle-
classdom. Forester pokes fun at military men and earnest
missionaries, and has reservations about the success of the

marriage between Allnut and Rosa; he also recognizes the inspirational effect of Africa on the European.

Forester's second African novel, *The Sky and the Forest* (New York and London, 1948), is an attempt at exploring the native mind. It concentrates on the indignities and tragedies engendered by Arab plunder and the slave trade. It encompasses the black man's forced venture into the exterior. Like Conrad's anti-imperialist protest, it recalls the days of glory of the black man and pleads for recognition of the black man's achievements. In all, it is a romantic lament for the disappearance of the Noble Savage.

Most other novels written in English whose locale is Central Africa have been written by Americans. Stewart Edward White and Charles Beadle both treated German imperial activities in the Congo before the outbreak of World War I. Emily Hahn, in *With Naked Foot* (New York, 1934), dealt with the affairs of a native girl who goes from one lover to another, each time losing more of life's sad sweetness in exchange for the awareness of pain. Peter Viertel's *White Hunter, Black Heart* (New York, 1953) is a fictional account of what is commonly believed to have been the activities surrounding the cinematic production of *The African Queen* by a Hollywood company earlier in the 1950's. A comic novel, utilizing the Congo as another kind of Mississippi River Valley basin, is Ben Lucien Berman's *Rooster Crows for a Day* (New York, 1945). Berman's idyll saw Little Doc, a red-haired Mississippi river pilot, and his friend Poppy, battling fever and disease as they traveled up the Congo River. Success awaits them, and they return to the United States to become bonafide members of the Cotton Valley Booster Club.

Charles Mercer and Louise Stinetorf both turned to Central Africa for their novels about missionary workers. In *Rachel Cade* (New York, 1956) Mercer told the story of a missionary nurse who arrives in a village ruled by tribal superstition. In

Pilgrim Strangers (New York, 1961) he portrayed the revolution in the native attitude toward missionaries. His Schweitzer-like American missionary doctor is stoned by former African students, and the mission station is wrecked. The fourteen-year-old American girl who narrates the story is an innocent who had loved Africa for its elephants, crown princes, and folk dancing. She is shocked into recognition of the new Africa.

In *White Witch Doctor* (New York, 1950) and *Beyond the Hungry Country* (New York, 1954) Louise Stinetorf treated the theme of the American missionary and his triumphs in Africa. Especially in her second novel, she dealt with what has become an increasingly important theme in nonfiction writing (but not yet in fiction): the ambivalence of Americans and American Negroes in Africa. Both Mercer and Louise Stinetorf have lived and worked in Central Africa. Miss Stinetorf was a missionary, while Mercer traveled throughout West and Central Africa as a reporter. Their novels thus describe a reality as well as create an image.

This chapter perhaps suggests some demarcation lines useful in reaching an overall assessment of literary trends: that American, French, and English writers, by some kind of conscious or unconscious design, carved up literary spheres of activity in the African scene. The Americans chose the Congo as a battlefield of morality; the French spawned in West Africa a tolerant bureaucracy that promoted a Frenchified African imagery and the consciousness of a French-African culture; the English in East Africa concentrated on an ivory tower of fantasy and comedy till the realities of politics brought it crashing down.

FIVE

The Color of
South African Literature

Over all of modern South African literature hangs the ugly shade of color. No other national or regional literature is as infested with the racial problem. "South Africa . . . is primarily a land of racial problems," writes Sarah Gertrude Millin in *The People of South Africa*,[1] and in its literature this concern has become almost paranoiac. Practically every book, whether by white or black, or by foreign or native writers, treats the color problem in one or more of its aspects. Even popular romances and thrillers have not escaped the racial virus. And it was always so.

South African literature differs from other literature in English about Africa in that so much of it is written by native authors. South Africa can claim what no other region in Africa can claim: a white native population, a white native literature, and an indigenous white native intellectual movement. Leaving aside the valuable Afrikaans cultural scene, white South African literary history is remarkable for its artistic accomplishments no less than for its sheer profligacy. Although in recent years it has tended toward exploitation of

---

[1] London, 1951, p. 13.

surface violence rather than study in depth, a number of serious writers have portrayed South Africans as caught *in* a political situation rather than *by* it. And even in such politically oriented writers as Doris Lessing and Sarah Gertrude Millin, the novelistic art survives the sociological enthusiasm.

Before the policies of *apartheid* drew world attention to its government, South Africa had several vogues. In the continuing rivalry between the British and the Boers, which erupted into the war of 1899, the region was represented variously as glorious, dangerous, dark, and vast. In the nineteenth century such distinguished visitors as Anthony Trollope and Rudyard Kipling toured the territory. Trollope's comment in 1887 that "South Africa is a country of black men—and not of white men. It has been so; it is so; and it will be so," [2] foretold the major conflict in South African literature that would grip the twentieth century.

South Africa, mirrored in English literature since 1900, gives off several reflections. This literature may be grouped in three classes: (1) novels of isolation; (2) novels of violence; and (3) novels of forgiveness. The writers of these novels are natives and foreigners. Yet differences in nationality and color play no definitive part in the determination of these writers' attitudes. The lesson that is to be learned from the image of Africa evolved from these novels is not found by separating the writers into national or color groups. The significance lies not in their different beginnings but in their similar development and aims.

1

Olive Schreiner was born in a mission station in Wittebergen, South Africa, in 1855. Her father was a mission-

---

[2] Quoted in Millin, *The People of South Africa*, p. 2.

ary who was later dismissed from service for engaging in trade. Her mother, who had met her father at a London Missionary Society meeting and who had come to Africa with high hopes of selfless service to the natives, later dismissed her early religious beliefs as foolish.[3] It is likely that most of the inspiration for the kind-hearted, impractical man found in her novels, especially the old German teacher in *The Story of an African Farm* (London, 1883), came from her father. He, like the German Otto, was self-effacing and impractical; generous to a fault, he had no idea of practical business techniques. The rational and intellectual side of Olive Schreiner, the clear-sighted, ambitious urge that drove her to write her novels under the appalling conditions of fatigue, overwork, and illness, was inherited from her mother. Olive at sixteen was reading Herbert Spencer, John Stuart Mill, Emily Brontë, Charles Dickens, George Eliot, and Thomas Hardy. Although she never had a formal education, her intellectual curiosity gave her a deep grounding in philosophy before she was twenty-one.

Olive Schreiner wrote much but published little. Of her three full-length novels extant, two were published after her death. One, *From Man to Man, or Perhaps Only . . .* , was never finished; she had worked on it for forty years but left it in a state of chaos. Ultimately her husband, S. C. Cronwright-Schreiner, presented it in edited form with notes.[4] Her first novel, *Undine* (London, 1929), was the last of her works to be published. Written before *The Story of an African Farm*, it was a juvenile effort that revealed again the lifelong questions she asked in her fiction.

---

[3] See Vera Buchanan-Gould, *Not Without Honour* (Cape Town, 1948); Marion V. Friedmann, *Olive Schreiner: A Study in Latent Meanings* (Johannesburg, 1954); D. L. Hobman, *Olive Schreiner: Her Friends and Times* (London, 1955); and A. C. Partridge, "Olive Schreiner: The Literary Aspect," in *South African P.E.N. Yearbook 1955* (Johannesburg).

[4] London: T. Fisher Unwin, 1926.

Every native-born South African writer of importance has admitted that Olive Schreiner was an early ideal. William Plomer has said of her in his autobiography, *Double Lives,* "Such is the power of the written word that she [Olive Schreiner] was in fact a closer companion to me than those beings with whom my life was passed." [5] Doris Lessing has said in conversations with the present writer that the only South African novel she can return to is *The Story of an African Farm.* This work, written by a girl who at the time had never traveled beyond the geographical limits of the South African veldt, is the cornerstone of South African literature. When Olive Schreiner brought her manuscript to George Moore, a reader for the London publishers Chapman & Hall, in 1882, neither she nor her friends could have anticipated the world-wide attention it was subsequently to create.[6] Its success was slow in coming. Reviewers called it an "agnostic novel"; they were not to know that Lyndall, one of the two heroines, was to become a representative figure in modern British fiction, the free woman defeated by a world imprisoned in its social prejudices.

Olive Schreiner's influence is still pervasive. Doris Lessing, who as a writer seems at first glance so far removed from her literary mentor, follows the same tradition of portraying the intellectual woman in South Africa. Characteristically, Doris Lessing's heroines are set adrift in the desert not of the physical country but of its intellectual current. Another novelist

---

[5] London, 1943, p. 155.

[6] Although South African fiction has been published more regularly in England, it has had its spectacular successes in the United States. Among the best-sellers in the United States were *The Story of an African Farm,* Sarah Gertrude Millin's *God's Step-Children* (London, 1924 [Am. edn.: *God's Stepchildren* (New York, 1925)]), Stuart Cloete's *Turning Wheels* (London, 1937), and Alan Paton's *Cry, the Beloved Country* (London, 1948) [original English publication dates given].

whose work seems cursorily to be a far cry from *The Story of an African Farm*, with its lonely veldt and saintly people, is William Plomer; his *Turbott Wolfe* (London, 1926) is a violent tale of miscegenation and police-state bureaucrats. What unites Plomer with Olive Schreiner is his understanding of the oppressive beauty of the South African landscape.

It may be said that *The Story of an African Farm* is the seminal novel of modern South African literature. Joseph Conrad created a mystique out of Central Africa; Rider Haggard constructed a magnificent fantasy in the wilds of East Africa; but Olive Schreiner painted the real colors of her land. In her own words in the Preface to the second edition of *The Story of an African Farm*, she could not create "those brilliant phases and shapes which the imagination sees in far-off lands," but she dipped her brush into the "grey pigments" around her and painted what lay before her.

In her writing, Olive Schreiner is the foremost example of the literature of isolation which has grown into a South African literary pattern. In large measure this image of South Africa as a "wide, lonely plain," a "dry, sandy earth," with low-lying hills and stunted karroo bushes—terms which are found on the first page of *The Story of an African Farm*—derives from her novels. It is the image found in more current anti-city novels, whether it is the black farmboy come to Johannesburg in *Cry, the Beloved Country* or the white seeker after truth in Daphne Muir's *A Virtuous Woman* (London, 1929). It is the country of "level waste" and "rounding grey" that is the ultimate salvation of these people. They journey to the city, where they find destruction and waste. They return to accept the unquestioning peace of the countryside which they had earlier rejected. Their resolution is not defeatism but quietism.

In this hymn to machineless space, Olive Schreiner is also to be identified with another major South African literary

image—the soundness of the Boer stock. Contemporary newspaper accounts have led to gross caricatures of Boer racialists;
but in literature until the last decade the Boer farmer was
presented as hardworking, tenacious, and imbued with those
traits of individualism associated with rural struggle. It is the
exploitation of this image, largely through historical novels,
that has led to the figure so prevalent today in literature, the
South African farmer as a wicked bully fond of his whip.

This literature of geographic isolation, of physical apartness,
has its racial analogue. The clash between black and white is
sensed but not felt in the gray desert. The lack of violence is
not due merely to chronology. In the historical novels written
by Stuart Cloete and Daphne Rooke, and in Rider Haggard's
quest novels, wars and murders occur frequently. Against the
lonely mountains and "kopjes" of the Karroo, however, hate
bows its head. White and black wait alike, in patient suffering,
in the African countryside; only in the cities does the vital
issue explode. This literature of aloneness is the least race-
ridden of any South African literature.

Olive Schreiner gave the subtitle "A Queer Little Child" to
her first novel, *Undine*. This book reveals what several critics
have called the neurosis or inner conflict that plagued its
author. Undine cannot reconcile the cruelty of God with His
benevolence. She cannot love a God Who ordains that mil-
lions of people go to destruction. The result of Undine's conflict is pain and depression, and rejection by her society. At
many points in the novel, the narrow and rigid South African
society misjudges her. Even her silence is interpreted as the
spite of a cold creature. Undine marries a rich, lecherous
widower so that she may give away his money to his son,
the man she really loves, but the son marries a rich woman
simultaneously and has no need of Undine's sacrifice. When
the old man dies, Undine sails to South Africa where she gives
away whatever pittance she has left. At the end of the novel

she is seen crawling, her face in the dust, a wretched, dying woman.

This note of pity and pain is found in Olive Schreiner's two other novels. Waldo, in *The Story of an African Farm,* in the same fashion as Undine, ponders on the souls going to damnation with each tick of the clock to which he is listening. Characters in both novels open the Bible for a "sign" and then toss the Good Book away in disappointment. *The Story of an African Farm,* like *Undine,* is a record of the frustrations of people who strive for wider horizons than those of the veldt. Waldo, Lyndall, Em, Gregory, and Otto—in the former novel— are defeated when they venture beyond their garden, and those who survive their experiences return chastened and grateful to live on their isolated farms.

Olive Schreiner was dealing with people of infinite psychological complexities, but the intention here is to focus upon their specific relationship to the South African milieu. Their neuroses are an integral part of that milieu—and in some cases spring from it—but all of them come to terms with their inner conflicts by returning home, to a country house, to a little world they had left for a bigger one. Psychoanalysts may see in this solution a desire to return to the cradle, the womb, and one literary critic has suggested that Olive Schreiner's work is a reflection of its author's inability to accept her ambivalence toward her mother.[7] The psychoanalytic interpretation is not at variance with the interpretation presented here: that Olive Schreiner's Karroo valley is a beginning and an end—but not the struggling middle—of life; that while it is described in naturalistic terms, it is a mythopoeic resting place. It is this image that has been especially influential on other writers, loosening in them surges of personal and subconscious memory.

In many of her letters to her friends, Olive Schreiner ad-

---

[7] Friedmann, *Olive Schreiner, passim.*

mitted that she drew her characters from actual experience. Of Rebekah and Bertie in *From Man to Man,* she stated: "Rebekah is me, I don't know which is which any more. But Bertie is me, and Drummond is me, and all is me. . . . Sometimes I really don't know whether I am I or one of the others." [8] Her husband said of Waldo and Lyndall in *The Story of an African Farm* that they were "two sides of Olive, though she had more than two sides." [9] Since these characters represent the dominant themes of her fictional work, it is instructive to see what happens to them when they journey into that wider world they yearn for in their ignorance. Waldo, like his venerable father Otto, the resident preacher, is saintly and naïve. He allows others to exploit him without nursing any rancor toward them. Indeed, he is almost ready to sacrifice himself for them. When the sadistic opportunist Bonaparte Blenkins finds Waldo working on a sheep-shearing machine he has perfected over several years' labor of love, Blenkins crushes the machine in the sand before the boy's eyes. Yet Waldo's spirit is not embittered to the point of hatred, and when Blenkins is at last discovered to be a scoundrel—when the proprietor Tante Sannie heaps a barrel of pickles on him and orders him off the farm—Waldo gives Blenkins his hat and his last two shillings.

Thus ends the first part of *The Story of an African Farm.* The veldt is a cruel and lonely place, yet it does not inspire cruelty. Within the grimness of the farm world lies a yearning in Waldo for knowledge, for education, for initiation into the mysteries of the adult world. A stranger appears on the farm

---

[8] Olive Schreiner to Havelock Ellis, January 24, 1888, *The Letters of Olive Schreiner,* ed. S. C. Cronwright-Schreiner (London, 1924), p. 129.

[9] Preface to *The Story of an African Farm* (1924 edn.), p. 6. All subsequent quotations pertaining to this book have been taken from this edition.

and speaks to Waldo; he tells him of the great world outside the veldt, and urges Waldo to see it. Waldo lives with that dream till it gives him the strength to travel beyond the desert into the cities. Yet what he finds in the cities leads him back to the farm. He is boxed on the ear, forced to work in a factory, and initiated into the confines of an industrial society which allows no room for nonmaterial thought. The city destroys Waldo's ambition, and the dream which the stranger had planted in Waldo is put to sleep when Waldo returns to Tante Sannie's farm. He is content to be a shepherd; he wishes no part of the mean grand world.

Lyndall is the bright and penniless cousin who lives with Em, a passive, kind, pretty girl. Em's father, an Englishman, has died and left his farm to his second wife, Tante Sannie, a fat Boer woman whose animal vitality is matched by her vulgarity. Lyndall, like Waldo, is moved by the spiritual majesty of the veldt and by an intense dream to voyage into the imagined wealth of intellectual spheres. When she returns home from college, she tells Waldo he is the only man she considers to be her intellectual equal. Such a confession shows the plateau on which their creator wished to place them. Waldo and Lyndall are elevated to a higher plane than the other characters in the novel. In her journey outward, however, Lyndall carries more than selfless love in her baggage. As a female she is a symbol and an issue as well as a human being. Lyndall must prove that woman is not a dependent creature, that she is as free as any man. This determination to be free and uncommitted to another human being is the reason she refuses marriage to her lover, even after she is made pregnant by him. She tells Waldo she will never forget the beauty of their "three hours," but she cannot bear the thought of having to depend on him. She forces him to leave her, and travels alone to an inn where she lies down to die. Her odyssey has ended in defeat, and on her deathbed she yearns to see the mountains of her childhood, yearns to return to that world of innocence she rejected. It is a world of simple piety: "I see the vision of a poor weak soul striving after good. It was not cut short; and, in the end, it learnt, through tears and much pain, that holiness is an infinite compassion for others; that greatness is to take the common things of life and walk truly among them; that . . . happiness is a great love and much serving" (p. 320).

It has been said by some critics that Tante Sannie, the owner of the farm on which Waldo and Lyndall live, is a vulgar, boorish, and even distasteful woman. She gleefully enjoys the prospect of having Waldo beaten; she has no conception of the intellectual niceties which plague Lyndall, and in her fat, gross face lies the soft hypocrisy of daily self-indulgence and Sunday sermons. Undoubtedly the picture Olive Schreiner meant to present of Tante Sannie was not idealistic, but the portrayal may be construed as being grudgingly fair. Tante Sannie in her ignorance has learned how to cope with the world. Family and home provide enough to satisfy her needs. She is the counterpart of the black African, the equal of the American Negro Dilsie in William Faulkner's *The Sound and the Fury.* Tante Sannie endures. She leaves her farm for another farm and remains content. This is the side of the Boer which Olive Schreiner admired, and her admiration again reveals her ambivalence toward the gross stability of Boer life. She is attracted to it, yet she cannot accept her love of it.

Olive Schreiner was not engaging in an anti-city war. Her novels were reflections of the state of a world which had no place for the ennobling spiritual and intellectual ideas of Waldo and Lyndall. She was not urging a return to the farm, but imaginatively Olive Schreiner did crawl back there to gain a rest from her frustrating battles with the sophisticated world.

That Olive Schreiner's attitude to the arid farmlands of the South African veldt was similar to the ambivalence of Waldo and Lyndall is evidenced by her letters and journals. In 1889, when she returned to Matjesfontein for reasons of health after a ten-year sojourn in Europe, she wrote, "No place but the Karroo will ever be home to me." [10] Ten years earlier, on the eve of her departure, she wrote to her former employer, Mrs. Cawood, "This dear old quiet parlour has been my study so long I feel as if it isn't right I should leave it. With all my physical suffering, I think the time that has passed here has been the quietest and best in my life." [11]

When it is remembered that it was in "Ganna Hoek," the farm of the Cawood family, that Olive Schreiner wrote her three full-length novels (and all before the age of twenty-one), there is little reason to doubt her fond memory of the place. While still in her teens, she worked there as a governess for the children of the Cawood family. Her restless journeys in Europe and South Africa following her initial world fame did not end in the same death struggle as Lyndall, but they were as painful. She was wracked by asthma and nervous disorders, and she was unable ever again to complete a full-length novel, a task she was constantly putting before herself and just as constantly thrusting away.

If it is argued that *The Story of an African Farm* is a very early work and that it does not represent the mature Olive Schreiner, a reading of *From Man to Man* will reinforce the thesis that Olive Schreiner thought of the South African countryside as a refuge and haven. Though the latter work is unfinished, it reveals her attitudes concerning art, politics, feminism, and race relations, passages on which subjects she devotes more than a third of the book. She is less explicit about her attitude to the South African veldt, but it is not difficult to see the conflict between ambition and selflessness, worldly knowledge and satisfied simplicity, in operation again.

From Man to Man is "the story of a prostitute and of a mar-

---

[10] Quoted in Buchanan-Gould, *Not Without Honour*, p. 118.
[11] *Ibid.*, p. 61.

ried woman who loves another man, and whose husband is
sensual and unfaithful." [12] The novel opens with a "Prelude"
called "The Child's Day," in which the childhood of one of
the heroines is described. Rebekah, like Undine and Waldo,
tells an imaginary baby not to be afraid of the ticking clock:
"*Don't* think it means any of those dreadful things—it doesn't!"
(p. 17). Rebekah is more like Lyndall, however: she reads
philosophy and serious literature, studies nature with a keen
and intellectual eye, and discusses sexual issues freely. She
suffers great conflict even after she has decided to marry and
enter a sophisticated world:

> What was she leaving it for, that quiet, peaceful life? That life
> in which the right was pleasantest, and easiest to do, and lay
> right ahead; in which there was no being torn asunder, living
> between "I would" and "I must"; a life in which there was just
> as much to be done for others as might yield a grateful sense of
> satisfaction, yet leaving space for the individual life undisturbed;
> a placid, peaceful life, into which the noisy, babbling, worried,
> worrying world crept only once a week through the post-bag
> when the boy brought the letters and newspapers from the town;
> a life in which news from the outer world came to one with a
> freshness it could never bear for those living in the hurry and
> turmoil of the great streams of life; a studious life, in which one
> might grow exceedingly wise over plants, and seek whatever
> joy there was in insects and stones; a thoughtful life, in which
> one might read and creep into when the wheels of the daily life
> are grinding soft and low; a life in which suffering was small
> and pleasure, if grey-tinted, calm and constant. What was she
> leaving it for? She looked back again into the room, and then out
> into the dark. The scale looked heavy.   (p. 85)

This conflict in Rebekah is part of the recurrent battle in

---

[12] Olive Schreiner to Havelock Ellis, October 29, 1884, *Letters,* p. 43.

Olive Schreiner's fiction between aggression and withdrawal, between the attraction of the city and the country retreat. Although Rebekah's whole development is toward an immersion in a bigger world than her farm birthplace, she comes to regret her marriage. The other heroine, Rebekah's sister Bertie, is much like Em of *The Story of an African Farm*. She is beautiful, gentle, and naïve. She suffers the wrongs with which stupid but good women are afflicted. Seduced when quite young by her tutor, she babbles the truth to her fiancé some years later and is rebuffed by him. The story of Bertie's unfortunate sexual experience hounds her even when she goes to live with an aunt in a distant village. To avoid further scandal, Bertie accepts the invitation of a rich old Jewish man to join him in London. In London, however, she is turned out of his house because of a false rumor that she is having an affair with the old man's handsome young cousin. The novel traces Bertie's pursuit from a brothel in Soho to another in Cape Town, and, in its unfinished state, ends with Rebekah and her platonic lover Drummond searching Cape Town for the dying Bertie. S. C. Cronwright-Schreiner, in his introductory note to the novel, said the story was to end with Rebekah finding her dying sister too late to save her. Thereupon Rebekah was to find the strength to leave her dissolute husband and live at Matjesfontein with her children. His note continues:

There is a little koppie in the flat at Matjesfontein, some distance west of the lonely station, towards the bare and rocky mountains Olive so loved. This koppie she often referred to in her letters as "my koppie." From the station, away across the vast and barren flat to the koppie, was a favourite walk of hers. There we see the last of Rebekah. As the sun sets, flooding the Karroo flats with radiance and glowing the brilliant mountains as it disappears behind them, Rebekah stands on the summit of the lonely koppie in the soft effulgence of the evening light, in . . . unutterable beauty of wild nature.   (p. 482)

It is not mere plot manipulation that sends Rebekah back to Matjesfontein (where Olive Schreiner herself had gone for her peace of mind after a bout with world fame). This constant return to the Karroo bush, kopjes, and sunsets, that ended in subsiding inner turmoil, is a characteristic note to be found in all this writer's fiction. As Vera Buchanan-Gould has affirmed, "Only in the rocks and stones, the lonely miles of Karroo bush and in the everlasting blue depths of the sky, did she hear a voice which had any significance for her. Otherwise, she was alone." [13]

Olive Schreiner has been called a psychological realist and a crusading feminist, but she was also a romantic harking back to the Adamic universe before the capsule of knowledge came to infest it. It is this romantic image of the gray-tinted veldt, innocent of everything save space, that was to become, in one guise or another, the prevailing image of South African literature for the first twenty years of the twentieth century.

Three important writers—Pauline Smith, Daphne Muir, and Doris Lessing—have carried on the Olive Schreiner tradition, as well as have such lesser figures as Bertram Mitford, W. C. Scully, Ernest Glanville, Francis Bancroft, and F. E. Mills Young. Pauline Smith wrote of the Boer farmers and their bare wood houses, in which were found a Bible, a wood table, and cups of strong black coffee, in her first book, *The Little Karoo* [sic] (London, 1925), a collection of short stories. In "The Pain" she told of a Boer farmer who journeys into a town in order to bring his sick wife to a hospital. The pain and anguish of the wife increase, however, as she lies isolated in the efficient inhumanity which furnishes the hospital room. The husband finally steals into the hospital one night and puts her in the "feather bed" he has put together in his oxcart, then starts back on the journey to the Aangenaam valley. When

---

[13] *Not Without Honour*, p. 63.

they reach "the top of the Groot Kop, the highest of the low, flat-topped hills that surrounded Platkops dorp," they stop for a moment in "the clear pale moonlight." They do not look behind them at the quiet village, but gaze across the river "at the grey stone building standing there alone. A moment only they halted, then turned and went on." The wife, "in her little nest in the feather bed . . . lay content" (pp. 40-41).

This image of the land as reaper-and-fulfiller is continued in "The Schoolmaster," and here, as in the work of Olive Schreiner, the implicit attack is on the rootless intellectual who has broken from the veldt but who has been mortally wounded by the rupture. The schoolmaster is a wanderer, whose cheeks "were thin and white" (p. 43). A stranger who had "neither relative nor friend in the colony," he is destroyed by the veldt. Because in anger he killed a mule, he bears in penance the burden of a beast. He buys a cart and straps himself in a harness to it, and drags the cart like a mule across the country. He finds peace finally in death.

Pauline Smith's first novel, *The Beadle* (London, 1926), is also set in the Little Karoo, in "Aangenaam valley, poorest of the Platkops valley." Aalst Vlokman, the beadle, has crushed all emotion in himself and has tried to do the same with the three women with whom he has daily contact. When a young man he had been in love with one of them, but in a night of passion had seduced and made pregnant her younger sister. The girl born of that night, Andrina, is the heroine of the novel.

Andrina, at seventeen, is a lovely, innocent maiden who falls in love with an Englishman on a visit to the country. The beadle tries to wreck their romance, even to the point of offering his own property as bait to a young farmer for proposing to Andrina. But the veldt, though exacting, is not inhuman, and Andrina's love triumphs over everything—the opposition of the beadle, the callousness of the Englishman she loves, and the death of her beloved aunt. Although Andrina's lover leaves her, she bears his child proudly. The beadle, who had been absolving himself all these years in cold, clerical renunciation, comes to Andrina to try to help her in her new life.

The Beadle, like *The Story of an African Farm*, creates its conflicts out of the romantic urges of youth and its wanderlust in opposition to the calm acceptance that comes with age. Andrina, however, is not defeated by her conflicts; in her innocence she embraces the world and adds a new touch of human warmth to the impersonal countryside. At the core of both novels is the growth of a sensitive individual in an indifferent, majestic environment.

A Virtuous Woman, by Daphne Muir, shows the influence of Olive Schreiner more clearly. This novel is the record of the life of a young girl just before her wedding day till her death as a grandmother and very old woman. Sanni, like Lyndall, has urges to leave the veldt and to taste the delights of a civilization softened by fashion and worldly culture. Like Lyndall, she dreads marriage because it promises to destroy her freedom of spirit. On her wedding day "Her white veil fell round her like a tent, closing all that was living within its folds. She alone was alive, the last thing left on earth" (p. 21). Yet Sanni does not regret her marriage; it becomes the focal point of her life, and at one point she rejects the opportunity to leave the heavy round of familial duties and the invitation to flee to a garden with her husband's brother, who all the time has adored her secretly. Sanni is so morally outraged at the brother's proposal that her response to his outpouring of love is withdrawal from and denial of him.

This proposal and its aftermath mark the climax of the novel, for Sanni has now become the prototype of the good Boer woman, the virtuous woman who sacrifices her own interests to those of her husband and family. Like Olive Schreiner, Daphne Muir sees the value of the stolidity of Boer life. Sanni regretfully forsakes her sensitivity to art, but she gains an entire world of belonging. And Klaas, the brother who dedicates himself to appreciating art, to seeking knowledge, ends as a weak and spiritually bereft man. Klaas, like Waldo in *The Story of an African Farm*, left his farm to enter the world of the city in search of wider meanings to the things he has begun to notice, and like Waldo he returned a chastened and disappointed man. On his return home,

> . . . looking out into the garden, he wondered why it had been so necessary to go so far to find peace, when peace seemed to be enclosed here, between these two houses, in the very village he had left to seek it. He had gone away, with a thousand undefined illusions, vague dreams of a new life, the only life beyond the mountains. And beyond the mountains, everywhere, he had found the same life from which he had run away. Always unreality, always a passionate interest in material things, things that pass and change, and die, and disappear. Nowhere an interest in things that last. (p. 65)

Klaas's daughter Judith, whom Sanni takes into her family, is also infected by this same disease that spreads from contact with new ideas: "She was too young to understand that this unrest was only the burden of Civilization, not peculiar to the people of her town or country but a punishment laid upon all countries, because the progenitors of the human race partook of the Fruit of the Tree of Knowledge" (p. 242).

Several years separate the work of Daphne Muir and Doris Lessing, but the influence of Olive Schreiner on both writers bridges this gap in time. Doris Lessing is a contemporary novelist and playwright who often treats the subject of politics in urban and rural settings. In this she differs from Olive Schreiner, who limited her expressions on politics to her nonfiction work. The influence of Olive Schreiner on Doris Lessing is most apparent in the latter's similar treatment of the intelligent female frustrated by a conventional order. Doris Lessing's work has also shown a progressive shift of interest away from the African milieu, but always at the heart of her work is a Lyndall-like woman. This character, whether she is Martha Quest of the "Children of Violence" series [14] or Anna Freeman Wulf of *The Golden Notebook* (London, 1962), has her roots in Africa: her personal dilemma is the emptiness that faces her in Africa, and the irrelevance that greets her as soon as she leaves her home place. Martha leaves the parochial town life of her childhood in quest of a more significant experience; Anna Wulf leaves South Africa for England where she hopes to discover a deeper intellectual current. Both women fail in their quests. Martha is merely confused, though she has been through a marriage, a passionate love affair with a Communist agent, and years of reading. Anna writes her notebooks because she cannot write her novel; she is using the notebooks to scatter her writer's block.

The parallel between Doris Lessing and Olive Schreiner may be seen even in their life stories: Olive Schreiner's first published work, *The Story of an African Farm,* brought her world fame and a ten-year restless sojourn through Europe; Doris Lessing's first published novel, *The Grass Is Singing* (London, 1950), earned her praise and commercial success and made her a literary celebrity. The income from that novel enabled her to live and write in England during the next ten years, when all the rest of her books had very small sales until, with the publication of *The Golden Notebook,* her writing met once more with material success.

Doris Lessing was in fact born in Persia and spent almost all her early life in Southern Rhodesia; nevertheless, her work falls into the tradition of white native South African writing, and the action of many of her novels is set in South Africa. The problems she treats are those found in South African literature, and the milieu she describes is almost indistinguish-

---

[14] Of the five planned volumes, the following have been published: *Martha Quest* (London, 1952); *A Proper Marriage* (London, 1954); *A Ripple from the Storm* (London, 1958); *Landlocked* (London, 1966).

able from the social fabric radiating from Johannesburg to the Karroo. The first part of *Martha Quest* is dedicated to Olive Schreiner, whose statement, "I am so tired of it, and also tired of the future before it comes," is quoted on the opening page. In her autobiographical reminiscence, *Going Home* (London, 1957), the record of a return trip to Salisbury, Southern Rhodesia, she tells of an old man, afflicted with blackwater fever, who refused to go to hospital. He preferred dying on the plains, like Pauline Smith's married couple in "The Pain." Doris Lessing comments, "It seems to me that this story of the man who preferred to die alone rather than return to the cities of his own people expresses what is best in the older type of white men who have come to Africa. He did not come to take what he could get from the country. This man loved Africa for its own sake, and for what is best in it: its emptiness, its promise. It is still uncreated" (pp. 14-15). Here again is an expression of the attitude that permeates Olive Schreiner's fiction.

Five character-types emerge from Doris Lessing's work: the white woman and the black servant; the Jewish businessman and the Jewish intellectual; the faithful Communist Party member; the sexually virile black man; and the confused, restless, "free" woman.

The Grass Is Singing is the story of a marriage which cannot succeed. Mary Turner, the only daughter of an ineffectual father and shrewish mother, hates the Rhodesian farm on which she grows up. As soon as she can she leaves for the city, where she gets a job in an office as a typist, buys smart clothes, and eats in immaculate, fashionable restaurants. She refuses to see her parents, who make life convenient for Mary by dying. But Mary, in her desire to flee the aridness of the veldt, the emptiness of the dusty farmhouses, never reaches beneath the superficialities of urban life. She continues, at thirty, to live in a girls' boarding house; she wears teen-age-styled clothes; and she remains virginal and frightened of sex. When she overhears her friends ridiculing her immature emotional state, she determines to prove them wrong. Her first experience with an older man is abortive. He proposes, and she accepts, but, when he tries to embrace her, she is repelled and runs away. When, months later, a poor farmer asks her to marry him, she accepts, though she has always hated farm life. Her husband and she do not really love each other, but each is determined to try to come out of his narcissistic world and give and gain pleasure from a shared experience. The experiment proves a disaster, for Tom is incompetent even as a farmer, and Mary sees herself in a horrifying vision on the road to becoming the aggressive nagger she so despised in her mother.

Mary's downfall comes finally as the result of her sexual frustration. Since neither she nor her husband is able to hate but only pity the other, each sinks into a spiritual anarchy. Mary at first gets pleasure from whipping a black servant, then succumbs to his physical presence which awakens all her repressed sexual desires. She sees him washing behind the house and gazes at him, fascinated. She does not understand her reaction, for

> . . . she had never come into contact with natives before, as an employer of her own account. Her mother's servants she had been forbidden to talk to; in the club she had been kind to the waiters; but the "native problem" meant for her other women's complaints of their servants at tea parties. She was afraid of them, of course. Every woman in South Africa is brought up to be. In her childhood she had been forbidden to walk out alone, and when she had asked why, she had been told in the furtive, lowered, but matter-of-fact voice she associated with her mother, that they were nasty and might do horrible things to her. (p. 61)

Within a few days, however, Mary succumbs to the gentle, powerful touch of her black servant.

The portrait of Moses, the servant, is sympathetic, though lacking in subtlety. Moses is a familiar example of the white

man's image of the black—a sexually potent male who rapes
white women. Moses is more important in revealing the white
South African writer's attitude toward what has become a real
and literary problem—the relations between whites and their
African servants. When Mary brings down the whip on Moses,
she has these thoughts:

> And she was beyond reflecting that her anger, her hysteria, was
> over nothing, nothing that she could explain. What had hap-
> pened was that the formal pattern of black-and-white, mistress-
> and-servant, had been broken by the personal relation; and when
> a white man in Africa by accident looks into the eyes of a native
> and sees the human being (which it is his chief preoccupation
> to avoid), his sense of guilt, which he denies, fumes up in re-
> sentment and he brings down the whip.   (p. 166)

With the exception of the historical novels, the "native problem" in South African novels is the servant problem. In the
work of Doris Lessing, Nadine Gordimer, Sheila Macdonald
(a popular novelist of the 1930's whose works include *Sally
in Rhodesia* [New York, 1932], *The Outsider* [New York,
1933], and *Mr. Crusoe's Young Woman* [New York, 1935]),
and in Daphne Rooke's *Mittee* (London, 1951), the emphasis
on African servants becomes a central feature. The problem
first mirrored in fiction is now considered so important that
the South African government, through its Non-European
Affairs Department, issues booklets of suggestions, one with
the title "Your Bantu Servant and You." In the latter, this advice is offered: "Much of the tension which exists between
the different racial groups in the country can be eased by your
playing your part in giving serious attention to the human-
relationship factor in the handling of your Bantu domestic
servant." Women are asked to be "exceptionally careful" in
their treatment of male servants.[15]

---

[15] See Leonard Ingalls, "Bantu Servants Aided by Booklet," in *New
York Times* (February 5, 1962), p. 7.

In Doris Lessing's novels the journalistic surface treatment of the "servant problem" is stripped away to reveal the complex depth of fear in the white masters towards their black servants. In her novel *A Ripple from the Storm* the author describes her heroine Martha finding her landlady at 2 A.M. with her ear "bent to the keyhole of the door that led to the verandah. . . . 'Did you hear a noise?' Martha had recognized a form of neurosis only too familiar to her. The widow Carson's life was a long drama played against fantasies about her servants" (pp. 27-28). The male black servants in *The Grass Is Singing* and in the novella *A Home for the Highland Cattle* [16] are superfluous; the women could do the work. Employment of the black servants actually produces frustration and endless hours of boredom for the women, while the Africans' powers are put to scant use in the kitchen. Doris Lessing's fiction suggests that the use of healthy men in the kitchen is but another aspect of the white man's fear of the dangerously potent black man.

In the series "Children of Violence" Martha is the heroine, and the first volume—*Martha Quest*—is devoted to her adolescence and young maturity. A restless, intelligent, inquisitive girl, Martha reads Havelock Ellis, Engels, and Marx. She considers herself a firm opponent of anti-Semitism, nationalism, Christianity, and the color bar in South Africa, and an unswerving believer in socialism. Like Olive Schreiner's Lyndall, Martha considers herself adrift from her society. She has no place in it, and does not yet want one. Her feeling of apartness is carried to the point where she deliberately exaggerates the weakness in her eyes so that she need not take the examination for college. Martha is in rebellion against her aggressive mother, her ineffectual father (the parents are similar to those found in *The Grass Is Singing*), and the whole world of the South African town she inhabits.

---

[16] This novella was published in *Five Short Novels* (London, 1953).

Several conflicts are introduced into the novel. An Afrikaner family and Martha's English family are constantly engaged in a social rivalry; and a Jewish family, with which Martha becomes involved, is composed of a father who is a successful businessman and his two sons who are members of the Communist Party. Martha's first boy friend is an effeminate young man who wants to be a dress designer but has bitterly resigned himself to entering his father's business. He has a great many of the traits assigned by Olive Schreiner to Gregory Rose, the English overseer who dressed in woman's clothes in order to nurse Lyndall on her deathbed.

Martha's introduction to socialism comes through her contact with her Jewish friends, the Cohen brothers. Her mother and many of her friends urge Martha to give up these Jewish friends, but, due to her rebellious spirit, this incitement serves merely to increase her devotion to them. Her first affair is with an East European Jew ashamed of his background; the experience reveals Martha's tendency to masochism. Martha is also accused of being a Kaffir lover because she defends a native in a conversation with her friends. The color issue, however, is only touched upon; much more significant in the novel is the social conflict between English, Afrikaner, and Jew. At the end of the novel Martha marries a thirty-year-old drunkard who is afraid of responsibility.

The novel is quite a step away from *The Grass Is Singing*. Here the emphasis is on politics and political and social issues; the racial-sexual question, for the moment, is almost nonexistent. The novel reveals what was to become a major development in Doris Lessing's career—a turning away from South African thematic material to global issues and psychological probings of confused intellectuals. Martha's marriage, the point toward which the novel is structured, is coupled with allusions to impending social and world crises—"Martha Quest married on a warm Thursday afternoon in the month of March, 1939, in the capital city of a British colony in the centre of the great African continent. Afterwards she could remember very little of the occasion" (p. 318).

A *Proper Marriage*, the second volume of the "Children of Violence" series, continues the concern with the Jewish issue. The color issue is introduced, again in a slight role, when Martha's mother warns her now married daughter about African workers, "You can't trust them" (p. 328). The most important portrait is the depiction of Communist activity in the city where Martha comes to live in Zambesia. When Martha leaves her husband, her mother blames the rupture on Martha's left-wing friends and political views.

A *Ripple from the Storm*, the third volume in the series, concerns itself with Martha's enchantment and subsequent disillusion with Communism. She finally gets her husband to consent to a divorce, then marries a Communist proselytizer. She and her new husband quarrel over a joke she invents about Stalin. Martha is astounded that this joke sours Anton, to the extent that afterward it creates a film of polite hostility between them. It marks the beginning of her disbelief in the Communist movement and methodology.

After this novel Doris Lessing's work has largely centered on English settings, and there was an interval of several years before the fourth volume of the "Children of Violence" series —*Landlocked*—appeared. Instead, the author turned to *The Golden Notebook* (London, 1962), to a new "free" woman, Anna Freeman Wulf, a writer who was a member of the Communist Party in South Africa and who came to England to deepen her knowledge. Like Martha, Anna's name is symbolic —she is as "free" as any man, and she goes through her sexual and intellectual affairs determined to prove her equality with the male sex.

Anna keeps four notebooks, in one of which she records her views on world politics and Communist activity in South Africa, while in another she sets down her literary impressions. A third notebook contains her views on sex. Each of the notebooks contains information about the same affairs, the overall purpose in dissecting her activities for special comment in categorical impressions being, as the author has described it, "an attempt to break a form; to break certain forms of consciousness and go beyond them." Though Olive Schreiner would have disagreed with much that Doris Lessing has to say in this novel, on the other hand she would perhaps have been flattered to learn that it follows in the pattern of development of *From Man to Man*. The significance of *The Golden Notebook* lies not in its narrative, nor in its characters, but in the author's commentary on sexuality, neurosis, and art.

2

If the work of Olive Schreiner, Pauline Smith, Daphne Muir, and Doris Lessing represents the spirit of apartness in South African literature, then the work of Alan Paton, Peter Abrahams, Dan Jacobson, and Nadine Gordimer may be said to represent the spirit of forgiveness. Significantly, while the writings of Olive Schreiner and her literary descendants centered on farms and small towns with the concomitant of psychic loneliness, the emphasis in the novels by the second group of writers mentioned above is on the city with its obstacles to social harmony. The conflict in the novels of Olive Schreiner and Doris Lessing is mainly within the characters; in the work of the second group of writers it takes place outside the characters, in the working out of a peaceful entente between them. The most famous expression of this literature of forgiveness is Alan Paton's *Cry, the Beloved Country*.

On the same level as these "novels of forgiveness and adjustment"—that is, preeminently situated in the racial and social tensions of South Africa—are what may be called "novels of violence." Novels of adjustment generally deal with conflicts and daily frustrations of a nonviolent nature. Novels of violence, on the other hand, deal with the explosion of these frustrations. Some of these novels of violence end on the same note of compassion, the same plea for understanding, as the novels of adjustment, but they tend to be more black-and-white in their portraits and closer to propaganda literature, whether of the Left or Right, or pro-Boer or pro-Black. The essential difference between the two types is this: novels of adjustment and forgiveness see the ultimate sanity and spirit of humanity triumphing over racial misunderstanding, violence, and bitterness. Yet they do not see or present an easy solution. Actually their view is less hopeful of an immediate solution than novels of violence, which end the problem by the facile riot and sentimental lament. Among the writers of novels of violence are: John Buchan, Sarah Gertrude Millin, Stuart Cloete, Nicholas Monsarrat, William Plomer, Laurens van der Post, and Harry Bloom, all natives of South Africa with the exception of Buchan.

Novels of violence tend to fall into three categories: (1) those written as adventure thrillers in which the black native is in revolt personally or tribally but not for any reasoned political cause. He is the primitive or idealized savage; (2) those written as historical novels, a genre that differs from the adventure thriller in that it is based on historical fact and presents, in many cases, a more serious literary study of native violence; (3) and those written as political novels, the most contemporary development of the historical novel. In this last kind of novel, hacksaws, metal pipes, smuggled guns, and bare fists replace the *assegai* (the traditional long-pointed spears) of the warrior tribe; the desert carnage is transformed into an urban riot.

Utilizing these points of reference, the fictional work of Sarah Gertrude Millin, Stuart Cloete, and Nicholas Monsarrat may best be delineated or suggested in terms of their themes and especially their fear of real or potential miscegenation. Although the styles of these writers differ—Stuart Cloete, for

example, romanticizes the male ego while Sarah Gertrude
Millin is an intellectual destroyer of romantic illusion—their
work forms a clear pattern in which the predominant fear of
miscegenation and uninhibited contact between black and
white becomes an obsessional theme. This theme in large
measure reduces their work to tracts urging a gradualism in
personal, social, and political relationships between black and
white in Africa. Together they form what I have termed the
"novelists of violence." The conflicts which in other novels are
based on the quiet, invidious frustrations of human life are
absent here. In their place are the open anger and the am-
munition of racial prejudice. John Buchan's *Prester John* (London, 1910) may be considered as belonging to this group,
since it employs the motif of the novel of violence—a riot and
bloodshed; but *Prester John* is more significant for the contrast it provides between nineteenth- and twentieth-century
fiction in English about Africa. Buchan idealized his African
warrior while at the same time describing his defeat. S. G.
Millin, Stuart Cloete, and Nicholas Monsarrat all fear and be-
little the African, because in his defeat he has become a permanent, invidious member of the white-conqueror world.

The influence of Rider Haggard lives on in *Prester John*,
which many readers remember fondly as a straightforward
adventure story they read in their youth. Buchan makes of
his African rebel a twentieth-century version of Prester John,
the black Christian King of Abyssinia whose empire encom-
passed the eastern half of Africa from Ethiopia to Lake Victoria in the fifteenth century. The legend of Prester John was
carried by the Zulus as they advanced southward in the six-
teenth and seventeenth centuries to Natal and Cape Town
provinces in South Africa. The favorite Zulu word for Prester
John was *Umkulunkulu,* signifying that he was the father of
all Bantu tribes and that he watched over his flock even after
his death. Strictly speaking, Prester John has never left his
empire, for to "the African mind men, when they die, become

midzimu, or spirits in the air, and continue to live in the places
where they lived in the flesh. They actually continue to live,
only in a different way, and are in constant and intimate contact with the living. The dead and the living form a chain that
must not be broken. There is no division of the worlds between them." [17]

Part of Buchan's idealization of his native hero stems from
the author's use of the fetish cult of the Zulus. All African
tribes have a fetish. Wars fought between them were not for
territory but for the spiritual (which in the African mind is
equivalent to the actual) leadership symbolized by possession of the fetish. The Zulus' fetish was *Ndhlondho,* or the
Great Snake, which was lost in the battle which resulted in
the death of Chaka, the "Black Napoleon" of South Africa,
who, during the nineteenth century, was reputed to have
killed nearly two million people. Buchan's black hero, the
Reverend Laputa, is the new Prester John spiritually and actually because he has found the fetish; in one scene he puts
the beautiful, heavy-weighted necklace—his chain of office—
round his neck and stands godlike before his followers.

Laputa is in the British tradition of the Noble Savage. He is
"a noble figure" (p. 151), and "if he had been white he might
have been a second Napoleon. . . . He has the heart of a
poet and a king, and it is God's curse that he has been born
among the children of Ham" (p. 138). Like Kensa Muda of
Mary Gaunt's *The Uncounted Cost,* Laputa is a Christian
minister who reverts to primitivism on returning to Africa.
Stalwart and physically brave, even on the point of dying he
is able to strangle the white traitor who has shot him. Laputa's
death is mourned by Buchan as the passing of a noble enemy.
When he dies, the last of the kings of Africa has died, thinks
Davie Crawfurd, the young Scottish boy who played the major
part in Laputa's downfall.

---

[17] Wulf Sachs, *Black Hamlet* (Boston, 1947), p. 107.

In literature, as well as in Davie Crawfurd's mind, the passing of Laputa is the end of the noble black kings of South Africa. For the Noble Savage was largely a creation of the English nineteenth- and early twentieth-century writer, and Buchan, a Scotsman and creator of many romantic adventure novels, was in line with this tradition. In the later historical novels or adventure stories of white South Africans the black man is not only defeated; he is ignoble. The novels of Sarah Gertrude Millin and Stuart Cloete depict the black warrior as a treacherous and sadistic enemy. When the Boers defeat him, they suffer no compunction at his extermination. Since Buchan, the Noble Savage in the twentieth century is not to be found again in South African literature until a Cape Colored writer, Peter Abrahams, published *Wild Conquest* (New York, 1950), and here it is Cubuza, a man dedicated to peace, who is idealized while the warrior, Mzilikazi, is criticized for his savagery.

The influence of Olive Schreiner is apparent in the work of Sarah Gertrude Millin, a Jewish South African author who published her first novel *The Dark River* in London in 1920. S. G. Millin writes of the lives of people in small cities and on farms whose bleakness of attitude is matched by the austerity of the land. Frustration is the keynote of the lives of most of her characters, a frustration compounded of a hostilely indifferent land and a cruelly ironic universe. Her heroines are women with ambitions beyond the reach of fulfillment, and to her depiction of their defeat she brings a bitter, austere tone and style. It is in her style and outlook that she reveals the distance that separates her from Olive Schreiner.

Olive Schreiner was a romantic writer whose depiction of worldly defeat was enshrined in a saintly triumph. Undine crawling in the mud to her death, Lyndall dying on the plains, Bertie closing the fitfulness of her tubercular life in a Cape Town brothel—these women could all glory in the purity and innocence of their outlook in a corrupt and expedient society. S. G. Millin's heroes and heroines are different: they are shown as weak, but neither pure nor innocent. She does not idealize their defeat; Gideon Aab, Miriam Hugo, Mary Glenn, Johannes van der Kamp, Henry Ormandy, Edith and Barry Lindsell resent their frustrations and get no compensatory pleasure from their pain.

It is in the delineation of the differences between the lives, emotions, and potentialities of white and black men that is found that spirit which unites S. G. Millin's work with the novels of violence. S. G. Millin does not believe that understanding will triumph over the differences of race in South Africa. While most of her novels avoid the motif of the riot, the underlying tension of racial conflict is present. Her lifelong fascination has been for the black and Cape Colored man, but she has preferred to keep the black enigma unilluminated by any notions of equality. Instead, every one of her novels is at least in part an attempt to show the limitations of the black man.[18] In this she shares a similarity of outlook with Stuart Cloete and Nicholas Monsarrat who, like herself, have professed an affection for the black man tempered with paternal restraint. She is also allied with them in her belief that miscegenation is the prime cause of disturbance in the black-white, subject-master relationship. In one of her autobiographical works, *The Measure of My Days* (London, 1955), she has this to say:

---

[18] In this context she has summarized her views as follows: "If the past is the standard, then the Negro breeds of the world have not established their right to be considered as equals of the Asiatics or Europeans. . . . Their civilisation is the white man's clothes, the white man's religion, the white man's education, manners, systems, hopes. They have never made an original contribution towards thought, towards art, towards the mechanical conveniences of life. Those of them who, in America, are in some ways distinguished, have nearly always had white blood in them, so that one cannot tell whence their distinction came.

"It must therefore be denied that the black race are today the equal of the white." (*The People of South Africa*, p. 315)

I had written about colour since I was sixteen. *The Dark River—*
The River of Colour, the River of Life, the Dark River itself, the
Vaal River—was the name I had given my first novel. . . .
Where I lived on the Vaal River, among the remnants of tribes
that had fought one another and the Boers in Voortrekker days,
I saw drunkenness, disease, hunger and miscegenation; and to
talk to these stepchildren of the vote would have been like offering them the cake Marie Antoinette suggested for the poor who
had no bread.   (p. 265)

This attitude of paternal benevolence and justified supremacy
is the essential element found in all of S. G. Millin's novels.
Yet combined with it is a curious attraction to what she so
fears.

The Dark River, her first novel, has its action set in the Vaal
River diggings where the author lived as a child. Although the
main theme of the novel is the quiet desperation in the lives
of three women waiting for marriage in a dry land, the informing milieu is the damp fungus of native life. The white
women in this novel do not admit it, but they yearn to know
the secret which allows the black people to be free of white
neurosis and frustration.

The Dark River was noticed by Katherine Mansfield, who
praised it highly in a review she wrote of it for *The Athenæum*
in 1920. But it was not until three novels later that S. G. Millin achieved any popular following. The novel which established her fame and made her a world celebrity was *God's
Stepchildren*. Before this novel appeared, she had written and
published three others, *Middle Class* (London, 1921), *The
Jordans* (London, 1923), and *Adam's Rest* (London, 1922),
the action of all three being set in the Vaal River area.

In *Adam's Rest* she presents the color problem in several
aspects, but beneath each level of awareness is the horror of
miscegenation. Miriam, the heroine, says:

"There must be something wrong at bottom. Look at their an-
cestry. It means a bad type of white man and a bad type of black

woman to begin with. You know yourself, Janet, decent Kaffir women have nothing to do with white men. So that's one thing. Besides, it doesn't matter what it is. I can't work it out, but I have a feeling about colour as if it were a catching disease—perhaps it is—and I don't want to be near it." [19]

Yet at the same time Miriam envies the Kaffir his calm ability to accept himself. The last scene of the novel shows Miriam watching a Kaffir woman who has just burnt a pot of coffee. Suddenly through that image Miriam becomes aware of the endurance of the Kaffir women, of their peaceful possession of the spirit of the earth. Her insight does not dissipate her fear of the natives or of miscegenation or of the specter of sexuality, but at least it leavens her earlier outbursts of hate.

This novel, like the one which immediately followed it, shows the author abiding by and relying on the standard mistress-servant relationship so frequently found in American literature as well as in the specific context, with its perhaps more cogent innuendoes, of fiction about Africa. The Kaffirs are not civilized, so they must be treated like children. And, since they are childlike, the masters love them and mete out treatment that is better, their portraitists advocate, than the treatment afforded by apostles of equality for the black man. In *The People of South Africa* S. G. Millin is explicit on this subject: "Even when the Englishman is strong enough in spirit to maintain his national tradition of justice, the difference remains that which once existed between the Northern and Southern United States. The Northerners fought for the rights of the Negroes, but the Southerners had an effectional intimacy with their darkies not customary among their more highly principled countrymen" (p. 255). This justification of South African behavior by a comparison with the treatment

---

[19] From the London edn. of 1922, p. 40. All subsequent quotations pertaining to this book have been taken from this edn.

of Negro slaves in the United States is also found in the work of Stuart Cloete, Nicholas Monsarrat, and Daphne Rooke, and shows again a similarity of attitude in the work of those writers whose fiction falls within the category "novels of violence."

S. G. Millin, however, does not deal only with blacks. To a large extent, the color problem in her novels has to do with Cape Colored people, the descendants of the Hottentots of Cape Town province who were indigenous to the land when the Dutch arrived.[20] The main theme of *Adam's Rest* concerns Miriam's development from a young girl to a widow afraid of dying without having truly loved. The two people for whom Miriam has had the greatest affection—her reckless, handsome nephew, and an ineffectual painter who chose a Kaffir girl for a bride in preference to herself—are dead, and she is left alone in her house without any sense of having given or belonged to a vital cause. When the Kaffir wife gives Miriam a painting by the untalented painter, Miriam accepts it with a measure of satisfaction. It is in effect an acceptance of banality; this time Miriam does not run away from the commonplace.

The subplot and secondary theme deal with the Croft family, the offspring of a marriage between an Englishman and a Hottentot wife:

> Mr. Croft was not a man of profound emotions or exalted philosophy. He was a blond, stout Yorkshireman without any inherited prejudices against colour, and he had married his half-caste woman without love and also without any soul-searchings on questions of miscegenation. His ancestors troubled him little and his descendants less. He never saw himself as the progenitor of a long line of beings inferior from the standpoint of civilisation. He wanted someone to make his bed and mind his clothes.
>
> (p. 65)

---

[20] She holds that the Dutch or white South Africans arrived in South Africa as early as the Zulus, who invaded the area from the north.

Of Mrs. Croft's three children, two are fair and one very dark. The fair ones, according to Miriam, put on airs, but their fate is tragic. They do not succeed in rising above the social scale—Carrie, the fair daughter who wanted to pass for white, is forced to move back to her mother's shanty house, while Freddie is brutally beaten by his own brother.

While S. G. Millin's heroine is aware that Hottentots suffer like white people (their blood flows, too, when their skin is pricked), she does not find any social injustice in their sufferings. Their fate is pitiable—but, since they have "colored" blood, nevertheless justifiable. "Miriam was sorry for everyone. For the wretched Kaffirs, the hopeless bijwoners, even the aspiring Crofts. Was it, after all, their fault they had black blood in them? How awful it was to be born damned. That boast of theirs—they *kept* themselves white, how pathetic!" (p. 116).

This tragic fate, this justification of *apartheid,* is the subject of S. G. Millin's next and most famous novel, *God's Stepchildren,* which traces the result of the Reverend Andrew Flood's decision to marry a Hottentot woman in order to prove that in God's eyes all people are white. The basic argument of this novel is that not everyone is God's child. Only white people are, as its author illustrates by a conversation between Flood and the Hottentot woman, Calchas:

"We are all God's children," the Rev. Andrew Flood said.
"But is not God himself white?" asked Calchas.
And, as the Rev. Andrew Flood hesitated for a reply, she made a suggestion:
"Perhaps we brown people are His stepchildren," she said.[21]

Flood's decision sets in motion a family history which ends in the sacrifice by its last descendant of his wife and child and his comfortable family home in Johannesburg. To make

---

[21] New York edn., 1925, p. 44. All subsequent quotations pertaining to this book have been taken from this edn.

restitution for his great-great-grandfather's transgression, Barry Lindsell goes back into the desert to preach Christianity to black and Cape Colored natives. Barry is the son of a seventy-year-old white man and teenage part-Hottentot mother. After his mother deserted him and his father died Barry was brought up by his spinster half-sister, Edith. When Barry returned from England at the end of World War I with an English wife, his half-sister felt it her moral duty to reveal his Cape Colored origins.

Miscegenation in this novel is not a social problem but a moral crime. The author's attitude is identifiable with that of Barry and Edith, both of whom accept the fact that Barry is guilty of sin for having "colored" blood. When Barry is summoned to the deathbed of his mother, whom he cannot remember, he is embarrassed by the dark creature who lies before him. The author describes his reaction as a repetition of "the attitude of every successful coloured generation, approaching white, towards its predecessors. As Elmira had been ashamed of her father, Kleinhaus, as Kleinhaus of his mother, Deborah, so was this child ashamed of Elmira" (p. 258).

Barry's English wife cannot understand the moral issue that plagues Barry and Edith. She is matter-of-fact in her approach and tells her husband that all they need do is to suppress the unhappy fact of his heredity. In the war that ensues for Barry's spirit, it is Edith who triumphs. Her fervor is that of the fanatic, her shame that of the Puritan: "Down the future generations would run that black blood mingled with her father's. And Barry spoke as if the colour of his child's skin was all that need trouble Nora [Barry's wife]" (p. 278).

The terrible specter of miscegenation is again the dominant image in the mind of S. G. Millin's heroine.

Several years later S. G. Millin published a sequel to her most popular work, *The Herr Witchdoctor* (London, 1941).[22]

---

[22] The American edn. of this work is entitled *The Dark Gods* (New York, 1941).

This novel opens in Canaan near the border of Southwest Africa, where Barry Lindsell has gone to minister Christianity to Hottentots and Zulus. His act of restitution is complicated by the arrival of a half-brother, Carl Schmidt, born of the same mother. Carl, who is blond and blue-eyed, thinks of himself as an Aryan, and sleeps with African girls as if he were a god dispensing favors. Set at the time of the advent of World War II, part of the book is concerned with the conflict of loyalties in South Africa as regards its peoples' attitude toward the British empire. Carl allies himself with a Nazi movement trying to bring South Africa into the war on Germany's side; he forms an alliance with the native witch-doctor and tribal chief. Barry, ever pacific and humble, avoids politics, though he is loyal to the Commonwealth. His failure is evidenced in the departure of John, the only native intel-lectual leader, from the Christian religion. John, who at first saw himself as the Booker T. Washington of Africa, rejects this image for that of the martial Prester John and joins the Nazi movement because it promises a bigger and more work-able dream of African nationalism.

Although the Nazi scheme for revolt fails in Southwest Africa, the book is an indictment of missionaries like Barry. The author's attitude toward missionaries is that of the prac-tical lady who sees them as well-meaning dunderheads. In *God's Stepchildren* she reduced the Reverend Andrew Flood to a pitiable state, walking barefoot in a Hottentot hovel; in *The Herr Witchdoctor* Barry Lindsell is incompetent to cope with the practical politics of German aggression. And Barry's sin, for which Flood is preaching Christianity in the wilder-ness, is not vitiated; for, his half-brother continues to wander on the path of miscegenation.

If S. G. Millin sees the Reverend Andrew Flood as a fool, she has also some genuine pity for him. For the miscegenists like Carl, however, she has only scorn, but the scorn is ex-pressed in an hysterical form. The obsessive intensity with which she returns to this issue of miscegenation as a moral crime mars this novel and most of her later fiction. The obsession can be seen even more clearly in her historical novels, where she links missionaries with miscegenation, and paints attractive African women as forces of destruction. In *The Burning Man* (London, 1952) an intelligent female missionary concludes her discussion with the confused missionary hero of the novel, who is trying to effect a social equality in his planned community in the lonely veldt, with these words: "Here the difference in race is so strong that only the power of sex seems able to overcome it" (p. 118).

The Burning Man is an examination of the motives prompting the true-life Johannes van der Kemp to preach in the interior of South Africa, an examination which ends not in vindication of van der Kemp's teachings of equality but in condemnation of his disguised sexual drive for union with black flesh. Van der Kemp, who had been a rich young cavalier soldier in Holland in the late eighteenth century, surrendered his commission in the army and his inheritance for the love of a simple, poor girl. When the girl and child of his union with her were drowned, Johannes, turning to religion, joined the London Missionary Society. Sent to Africa, he walked into the interior to convert the heathen black to Christianity, but he succeeded with only one person, a Hottentot woman, whose reasons for conversion are made suspect by the author: "Johannes van der Kemp, an officer, a doctor, a philosopher, a scholar, a minister of God, was sitting in a hut in Kaffirland beside a half-naked savage woman, the mother of three children, whose husband had beaten her because he, Johannes, was Nyengana, one who stole in—one who stole into a country, into people's houses, into the home of a vagrant Hottentot" (p. 222). Forced to leave the kraal because of the jealous Hottentot husband, van der Kemp tries proselytizing in Cape Town where he refuses a position in a segregated church. At last he is given Bethelsdorp, an isolated spot in the north where his utopian plan, including freedom for all men and the right to intermarry, can be put into operation. At this station he marries a girl he has bought out of slavery, but the union does not provide bliss or equality. Although Sally bears him several children, she grows to hate him and even refuses to convert to Christianity. The end of the novel finds van der Kemp in as pitiable a state as the mad Reverend Andrew Flood. His experiment in equality has ended in havoc.

The fictional Andrew Flood was genuinely motivated in his crusade for equal rights regardless of color, but the historical figure of van der Kemp is stripped even of sincerity. His intelligence, his charm, his abilities, all these are warped by his strong sexual drive toward what were, for his time and society, socially scandalous partners. In the beginning of the novel, it is a Dutch girl beneath his social class who forces him into poverty and ridicule. From the middle of the novel, though he claims to be free of the demands of sex and to be a holy tool of God, the author suggests that the lure of the forbidden—the temptation of the black or Hottentot girl—is his true motivation.

The climax of the novel is the "defrocking" of the statements with which the minister burning to bring equality to Africa has clothed his crusade. This "defrocking" is executed by a Dutch outlaw leader who has lived with African tribal women and is the father of at least a hundred half-caste children. The book is thus a slashing attack on one of the few Christian "integrationists" in South African history. In her antagonism to the principle of racial equality, the author slanders the motives and conduct of van der Kemp, and in her fear of van der Kemp's sexual partiality she reduces him to a pitiable hulk walking in the wilderness. Beneath her rejection of van der Kemp's egalitarian philosophy lies her deep-rooted fear of miscegenation. Much more strongly than in her earlier novels, S. G. Millin here reveals that what disturbs her profoundly about interracial progress is the possibility it would seem to encourage sexual union between black and white.

In *King of the Bastards* (New York, 1949; London, 1950), another historical novel, S. G. Millin attempted to describe the life of Coenrad de Buys, the rebel Dutch leader who fought the English rule of Cape Town Province at the beginning of the nineteenth century and who married a Hottentot woman and later lived with a Xosa tribeswoman. The novel opens on the scene of a council composed of three hundred offspring of de Buys. Twenty of them can pass for white and the rest are "coal black." The council has convened, according to the first sentence, to "decide at last whether they may still hope to become white or must give up the struggle and go black." The story becomes a flashback into the life of Coenrad, and points to the possibilities for his descendants in a modern South Africa. The attitude of the author is one of sympathy for their plight but disgust with what brought it to pass, and the book as a whole—which includes a foreword by Field Marshal Smuts, the former Prime Minister of the Union of South Africa—is little more than a poor rendition, and repetition, of her horror of black sexuality. Her sentence describing the half-caste family, "Now their name was pronounced *Base*" (p. 4), is a statement of profound attitude, not merely a phonetic detail.

S. G. Millin's most recent novel, *The Wizard Bird* (London, 1962), is a shrill threnody. In this work the eldest son of an African chief takes part in a ritual quadruple murder, blackmails a white woman into marrying him, and atones for his sins by setting a lit match to his oil-soaked body. Miscegenation occurs, as always, as a horrible, loathsome fact; and the political and intellectual immaturity of Africans is again emphasized. Written as it was by a woman in her seventies, the novel is remarkable for its tautness of style, but the fury of the author's conservatism turns the book into lurid propaganda. It is dedicated to Sir Roy Welensky, once head of the former Central African Federation (comprising Nyasaland, and Northern and Southern Rhodesia), whom the author has privately declared to be "the greatest man Africa has produced in the twentieth century."

Among other novels of S. G. Millin which show this envy-hate and tense fear relating to a sexual urgency are *The Coming of the Lord* (New York and London, 1928), *Mary Glenn* (London, 1925), and *What Hath a Man?* (New York and London, 1938). *The Coming of the Lord* is a violent novel employing a riot motif. The hero, a restless World-War-I veteran, leads his white army against a millenarian sect of black natives. *Mary Glenn*, S. G. Millin's shortest novel, is another tale of frustration on the veldt, and the realistic compromise with their environment which women must accept. Mary Glenn flees from her small town of Lebanon but returns to it and accepts as satisfactory what she had formerly regarded as failure. *What Hath a Man?* is a character study of an introspective Englishman who becomes a member of the Chartered Company of Rhodesia and lives under the shadow of Rhodes for many years, but who ends his life as a bewildered man in England, sensing himself to be an anachronism in the modern world.

And it is for these novels, as well as for her other writings—she has written war diaries, a study of South African culture, autobiographies, and a biography of Cecil Rhodes—that S. G. Millin received the honorary degree of Doctor of Literature from Witwatersrand University in Johannesburg in 1952. The degree was conferred upon her with this appraisal: "Mrs. Millin has become *par excellence* the interpreter of South Africa to the English-speaking world. This is not only because of such an essay in objectivity as *The South Africans*—it is also, and chiefly, because of her novels of South African life." [23]

---

[23] Quoted in Edgar Bernstein, "Sarah Gertrude Millin: Trail-Blazer of South African Realism," in *South African P.E.N. Yearbook 1955*, p. 101.

Such is the official South African view of its most prolific writer.

By virtue of her narrative skill and restless literary explorations Sarah Gertrude Millin would be held a major writer in any national literature. Two of the other writers whom I have grouped with her, Stuart Cloete and Nicholas Monsarrat, remain some distance from her in stature, but all three writers share a similarity of attitude in their obsessional interest in miscegenation and in their praise of a superior white civilization in Africa. Monsarrat is a propagandist exploiting standard character types and what may now be called a standard African plot issuing from racial tensions and ending in a riot. Stuart Cloete is more ambivalent in his attitude. Like Sarah Gertrude Millin, he is capable of showing love for Africans in menial positions, and sometimes he displays an understanding of such people. His output has been prolific, and so far he has published some thirteen novels, five books of biography and travel, one volume of poetry, and one collection of short stories. Although he has been guilty of sensationalism and glib exploitation of racial issues, he cannot be ignored as a force in South African literature. Even his worst books are well-written, while the best of his novels show him worthy of serious study.

Cloete has written five novels based on South African history, four of which are remarkable for their narrative qualities. He has also written one serious novel of African life, *The Curve and the Tusk* (Boston, 1952), the action of which is set in Mozambique, and at least three popular potboilers. Cloete's novels, when they venture beyond South Africa, are not written for a very demanding audience. *Congo Song* (Boston, 1943), *Mamba* (Boston, 1956), and *Gazella* (Boston, 1958) utilize the mysteries of sex, jungle life, and native superstition on much the same jejune level that typifies the armchair fantasies in certain men's magazines. In his South African novels, with the exception of *The Fiercest Heart* (Boston, 1960), Cloete's tendency to vulgarize is balanced by his healthy regard for the ideals of his characters.

Cloete's first novel, *The Turning Wheels* (Boston, 1936), is the story of the Boers' great trek in 1837, and of the people who took part in that adventure—of Mevron Anna de Jong, the old woman who outlasted most of her younger companions; of Hendrik, who murdered his son because he coveted the same woman as his father; of Swart Piete, "The Hunter" who stole Sannie away from her husband; and of Sannie, the beautiful, dark-haired young girl, whose offspring, in Cloete's eyes, are the *Herrenvolk* of the world. The novel gives a perceptive view of the Boers' need to trek: they leave Canaan after having built it out of the jungles to start a new colony. There is no reason for their departure but an indestructible spiritual urge to travel again into the wilderness and build a new place unspoiled by the encroachment of civilization.

Watch for the Dawn (Boston, 1939), his second novel, continues the history of these Boers but goes back in time to 1815. Kaspar, the young hero, travels to the north because he hopes to find freedom in the wilds. Instead, he finds carnage. The novel describes the Slagtersnek Rebellion of 1815, when the Boers, in their opposition to British rule and especially to British policies of racial equality, were slaughtered by British military forces. Cloete presents the English as on the side of the black natives without any understanding of the Boers' rights and needs, but he does not end the novel in a denunciation. Instead, the old man Van Ek concludes the theme, "Nee, I hated them [the British] once, but I hate them no longer. They acted according to their lights and I according to mine. It is in my heart now that both were right: that in all matters there are two sides and little to choose between them" (p. 488).

The third novel in the series, *The Hill of Doves* (Boston, 1941), sets its action in the Transvaal during the Boer-British

War of 1880-1881, and continues the story of Sannie's family, and in particular Lena du Toit. A fourth novel, *Neck of the Tortoise,* which was to carry the series into the Boer War and its aftermath in the beginning of the twentieth century, has not yet appeared. The novel *Rags of Glory* (New York, 1963) centers upon the action and theme of the Boer War of 1899-1901. Although Cloete did not indicate that this novel was a continuation of his earlier series into fictionalized Boer history, *Rags of Glory* may be considered an integral part of his ambitious attempt to reconstruct Boer life in the nineteenth century.

Cloete has written two other historical novels. *The Mask* (Boston, 1957) also deals with the trek of the Boers into the interior of South Africa in an attempt to flee from British taxation and racial policies. According to Cloete's foreword, *The Mask* describes events as they happened in 1852-1854. Cloete compares the extermination of the natives to the extermination of the American Indians by settlers and pioneers and claims that the white man's conquest was inevitable because it represented "Progress." This view, whether in the serious historical novels or in his more popular fiction, leads Cloete to oppose the Boer to the Zulu as the representative of a more splendid race. Although he presents sympathetic portraits of Zulus and other black men, these portraits are only of natives who have capitulated to Boer hegemony and become its servants.

In *The Curve and the Tusk* the religious beliefs of one Kaffir tribe become the chief villain of the piece, resulting as they do in the destruction of a young, intelligent, Westernized native. The stupidity and primitivism of this tribe cause its victim to revert to an animal state of penance for having "progressed" into Western civilization. The Boer, on the other hand, is seen as exemplifying the strong, beautiful force of progress.

Much in the manner of Hemingway, Cloete glories in the

physical beauty and strength of his white heroes. Simon, the
painter in *The Mask,* looks at a Boer trekker and thinks:

> Every day Simon became more attached to Potgieter, who
> seemed to him the ideal voortrekker, one of those who went in
> front, a strong, bold, resourceful pioneer, a wonderful shot and
> horseman. He embodied all the virtues of the frontier. Looking
> at his enormous frame, at the muscles that bulged under his
> shirt, at the great thighs that gripped his bay horse, at the
> grizzled black virility of his beard, Simon felt that here was one
> who was more than a man, one who would not die but could
> only be killed in some terrible adventure.   (pp. 122-23)

Man as a splendid, heroic animal may also be seen in Cloete's fascination with hunting. In two of his novels, the elephant hunt is utilized to show the bravery, courage, and
spiritual strength of some men against the weakness and base-
ness of other more "civilized" types. In *The Curve and the
Tusk* an old British hunter and a young Portuguese hunter
take to the forest to bag the fabled elephant that returns periodically to the spot where it had once been pierced by a
bullet. In *Gazella* the conflict is expressed in terms of the
hero and heroine's love of elephants, and the fear of them on
the part of base and unworthy men. Chimboro the elephant
kills the villain, but Chimboro dies of old age. Its death is part
of Cloete's theme: the splendid individual heroism of the past
is being replaced by a more mundane technological civilization.

In his attitude to miscegenation, and in his praise of Boer
standards, Cloete shows his greatest similarity to Sarah Gertrude Millin. Miscegenation in Cloete's novels is an inevitable
part of the African scene, because man's physical nature cannot be denied. Thus in *Gazella* his half-caste heroine says:
"Miscegenation is proximity. I am a mulatto, a half-caste, the
product of what is called miscegenation. What went on be-

tween Mark Antony and Cleopatra was miscegenation. My
father's marriage to my mother was miscegenation, though
for him it was probably the choice between miscegenation
and death. Death from loneliness, drink or disease, or a combination of all three" (p. 55).

Cloete sees miscegenation in many places (though not
everywhere, as S. G. Millin does), but he implies its solution
is not a matter of restraint between the two races but of love
within each of them. The old man Van Ek in *Watch for the
Dawn* expresses the theme as follows: "There is no new thing,
no new feeling. Fear, cold, anger, love, remain the same. A
full belly still gives satisfaction; young men and maidens still
lust after each other. It was thus that they were made and is
in fact beyond argument, no matter what the predikants may
say. What folks seek is peace: and when they find it not, they
pass on, not as whoremongers, but as children seeking comfort" (p. 489). As in his idealization of physical beauty, Cloete
glories in the beauties of sex. In *Gazella* a "white Kaffir," an
Englishman who has adapted to the native ways of Mozambique, is serenely happy with his three native wives and their
children.

Cloete's more recent work shows a degeneration of his talent. His novel *The Fiercest Heart* brought him back to Boer
nineteenth-century history, but it was more a popular "Western" than a perceptive work. An old woman braves a deserted
valley to kill a lion, a young man is ordered a whipping by
an evil half-brother, the beautiful heroine saves her lover from
death and herself from rape—these are the elements of *The
Fiercest Heart*, which ends with the Boer community shedding
its association with the outside world and settling down into
splendid isolation. Yet Cloete is a writer and apologist to be
reckoned with. His Africa is for the most part a continent long
since passed, and his work is steeped in the romantic glorification of physical activity, violence, and war. He is the de-

scendant of Rider Haggard, with this important distinction: he denigrates the black warrior, whereas Haggard idealized him.

Cloete is also a novelist of violence, in that his work sees little hope for equality between races. Like Sarah Gertrude Millin, he believes the blacks to be incapable of taking on what they are shouting for. Or, as he put it in *The African Giant* (Boston, 1955):

> It seemed to me they [Africans] were capable of doing almost any job provided they had some white direction and assistance. But they were also, I felt, incapable of doing any job for long without it, particularly when it came to management, direction or finance. The remarkable thing was how much, not how little, they could do, what marvels they had achieved in so short a time. But they do not see it this way. They know so much more than they did that they think they know it all, and are not ready to wait and learn the rest.   (pp. 372-73)

The Tribe That Lost Its Head (London, 1956), although written by an Anglo-Canadian, is in direct line of descent in theme and attitude from the work of Stuart Cloete and Sarah Gertrude Millin. Modeling the book after the historical novel but setting it in a contemporary milieu, Nicholas Monsarrat here describes the imaginary British island colony of Paramaula, off the southwest coast of Africa. Dinamaula, an Oxford-educated black prince, is on his way back to the island after seven years abroad, in order to take over the chieftainship. On the same plane are a British journalist and a new, callow British civil servant. These three play the leading thematic roles in the story. The journalist becomes the villain whose spurious liberalism causes a riot, murder, and squandered fury; the Oxford-educated African becomes the dupe of both the primitive, tribal elements, and the Communists; and the callow careerist grows into a maturity symbolized by his deep appreciation of a policy of gradualism toward African independence. Monsarrat employs all the motifs of the novel of violence—misunderstanding, brutality, primitive orgies, riot, and profound mistrust of the African's capability and good will.

Monsarrat goes many steps farther than Cloete and S. G. Millin in his denunciation of misled and misleading liberal intellectuals and "humanists." His villain of the piece, the journalist, writes a story about color restriction at a hotel bar. This article leads to a flurry of both political and social protest, and ends in a riot by the natives against the British government. The journalist considers his role justified, but the point of Monsarrat's novel is that the journalist's facile criticism is responsible for the trouble in Paramaula. The journalist claims to believe in the equality of races, but Monsarrat is careful to show that in fact he believes in nothing but the exploitation of fashionable ideologies.

The view of the African as an inferior is expressed many times in the novel by several characters trying to make the journalist, Tulbach Browne, see the damage of his egalitarian propaganda. An American consul, Lou Strogoff, expresses his sympathy for the British government's plight in dealing with the Maula tribesmen: " 'Give the Maulas democracy,' he continued, 'that is, full social and political equality, and you'll have the worst mess you can think of. In the first place, they wouldn't know what to do with it; in the second, the process of finding out would be very painful and completely chaotic; and thirdly, there are just enough smart operators among the Maulas—especially here in Port Victoria—to take advantage of the sudden grant of freedom and run it as a personal racket.' " [24] And Father Schwemmer, the sympathetically portrayed priest, says: " 'It means also that we have not taught

---

[24] New York edn., 1956, p. 77. All subsequent quotations pertaining to this book have been taken from this edn.

them for long enough. It means they are simple, savage children who must remain in the nursery. It means that we, the white teachers, cannot go away from them for a long time'" (p. 157). When David, the civil servant, is asked by Browne "'Then you don't think a black man can do a white man's job?'" David replies, "'I think that may turn out to be the twentieth century's most fatuous illusion'" (p. 494). And Macmillan, the resident commander, summons Browne into his office to explain his position: "'Give an Englishman an entirely free hand, and he won't make a fool of himself; he knows enough not to abuse his freedom. Do the same thing here, and God knows what would happen. It's true of a lot of things before farming. They're just not ready to run their lives'" (p. 149).

Brown does not listen to his advisers but continues his crusade of exposing British paternalism. Monsarrat's novel expresses the folly of Browne's actions. Browne's cries for immediate freedom for the Maulas and the destruction of the color bar end in the suicide of the resident commander, the rape, murder, and castration of a young, idealistic white couple by bloodthirsty natives, and the crucifixion of a priest. And in the end, Dinamaula, the Oxford-educated prince, is exiled to England until order is restored on the island. The closing scene finds Dinamaula and David Brachen, the young civil servant, on the same plane to England. Both men admit that each, African and British, is at fault—Dinamaula for wanting independence too quickly, and being too naïve for its political complexities, and David for arrogantly dismissing the sense of hurt suffered by Africans. The novel thus ends in a justification of benevolent British imperial policy.

In addition to expounding his social and political philosophy and his use of the riot motif, and in his exploitation of the myth of the black man's sexual potency and brutality, Monsarrat shows a strong disposition toward violence. At a garden party the ladies of the diplomatic colony discuss, in titillating tones, tales of the natives' sex lives. Later, when the natives revolt, they do not merely engage in battle but take part in a lurid sexual ceremony with a captive white woman. They also draw out, with a forked wand, the entrails of a living white man; after pounding them into a paste mixed with the blood of goats, they drink the mixture and utter their tribal oaths.

If there are novels on the right—that is, novels defending the Boer or white supremacist point of view—there are also novels on the left—that is, novels championing the rights of Africans and urging a more humane view toward the color question. This distinction is not meant to suggest that these novels are necessarily politically inspired or that their dominant orientation is political. It is a distinction for clarity's sake, a point of reference that helps determine the broad pattern of novel writing in South Africa and the defined forms it has taken. One pattern lies in the use of the South African milieu as a lonely, inspiring place, a countryside whose rewards come from spiritual, unworldly triumphs. Another pattern lies in the utilization of the South African political and social tensions. These tensions arise from the composition of individual personalities, but they are not independent of, or even distant from, the broader social issues. In other words, the individual battle of personality is dwarfed by the larger conflicts of race and society in one's time. The novelists of violence tend to see these larger conflicts as inexorable and insoluble. Those on the "right" blame the condition of this violence on the speed with which African political independence has been granted. In large measure these novelists are gradualists in the sphere of political and human relations. Their novels are pleas for a slower, more conservative pace; their affection for the black man is deep-rooted, but it is an affection for the 'darkie" they have grown to regard as their personal burden. Novelists of violence on the "left" angrily demand more political rights and freedom for the Africans, and their novels reflect

the bitterness with which they view the delay in the granting
of these rights. Among these novelists on the "left" are William Plomer, Laurens van der Post, and Harry Bloom.

William Plomer was the first South African writer to create
a fictional hero (Ula Masondo) out of a migrant native laborer
in the gold mines. His novel *Turbott Wolfe* was the first work
of fiction to treat miscegenation and race relations from the
point of view of political and social protest rather than as a
moral shame—the quality with which earlier South African
writers had invested them.

Turbott Wolfe, Plomer's first novel, written when he was in
his early twenties, is the story of a young man who comes to
Africa and falls in love with a black native girl, Nhliziyombi.
Because he is inhibited by social pressures, he does not tell
her of his love. The native girl marries, and Turbott Wolfe,
in his unrequited, secret passion, sets up a trading post on the
reserve so that he may watch the girl come and go from his
store. On the reserve he meets two missionaries—one, an old
Norwegian, who, practicing separation between black and
white, manages to conduct an impersonal but efficient church;
the other, a new missionary who has come to replace the Norwegian. This new missionary, Friston, believes in equal rights
for all and declares his beliefs at every opportunity. Friston,
however, is defeated by his own passion. The girl with whom
he falls in love, a young South African white, marries an intellectual, politically active, black native. Friston, after per-
forming the marriage ceremony for them, takes an African
drug and goes mad. He runs naked into the African bush,
where he is murdered by natives.

Turbott, in despair at the failure of relationships between
members of different races, and especially disillusioned by
Friston's death, sells his store. He says good-bye to three people: a gentle English rector and his wife, and to his own native
servant. The irony of the novel is underscored in the concluding scenes: the Department of Aboriginal Protection, a

bureaucratic division for administering native problems, accuses Friston of being a Bolshevik and Wolfe as acting as a subversive element, and demands that Wolfe leave the reserve. Wolfe gains what little pleasure he can from informing the Department that he has already put his shop into the hands of an agent. But a further irony follows: the trading post is sold to a white supremacist.

Turbott Wolfe, in Plomer's words, is "a violent ejaculation, a protest, a nightmare, a phantasmagoria. . . . Its justification was that of an original sketch-book, an outburst of poetic frenzy on the part of a solitary and emotional youth . . . a picture of a world 'dominated by race fear and race hatred' and 'a revelation of savagery in a vaunted civilization.' " [25] Because he considered the novel to have been written in his immaturity, for many years Plomer refused to allow it to be reissued either in England or the United States, where several publishers were anxious to bring out a new edition.[26]

The theme of his novel has become an obsession with later South African writers, and *Turbott Wolfe* may be said to be the prototype of the modern liberal protest in fiction against *apartheid*. Here, Plomer deals with two examples of miscegenation: one the unfulfilled passion of Wolfe and the native girl he idealizes; the other the affair between the South African white girl and black radical. One affair ends in consummation; the other achieves nothing more solid than a sigh. It is significant that the white South African girl who marries her black lover is called "Eurafrica" and that she survives in Africa, while Wolfe feels bound to leave it. At the end of the novel, Wolfe's trusted servant asks him to stay and help promote 'Young Africa," the political group working for native rights in South Africa. Wolfe rejects the offer and says that the group

---

[25] *Double Lives* (London, 1943), p. 187.
[26] *Turbott Wolfe* was eventually reissued in 1965 in London and New York, with a lengthy introduction by Laurens van der Post.

was formed for personal reasons: the white South African girl organized it so that she could marry her black lover, and he, Turbott Wolfe, joined it because he wanted to feel spiritually closer to the native girl he loved. Now, he tells his servant, he can no longer stay in Africa because the illusion that his work, the improvement of conditions for natives, was motivated by a social, humanitarian conscience, has proved false. For him, interest in the native problem has been only a pretext, a means of filling the void of love within himself.

Plomer's view is radical but pessimistic. The two liberal, sensitive heroes, Wolfe and Friston, fail to achieve their desires or a sense of the fullness of their own beliefs. Both die with the taste of failure on their tongues; Wolfe dies a few days after telling his story to the "I" narrator, who by a realistic touch is referred to as "William Plomer." The novel in fact seems an indictment of Wolfe as a weak liberal, a man without the courage of his convictions. He could not declare his love for the native girl through fear of losing caste, yet ironically he is called a "nigger lover" and accused of "hobnobbing with the blacks." The tag "Chastity Wolfe," with which the natives label Turbott (because he seems to shun sexual activity), is an apt symbol: his life has been a rejection of experience, and that rejection has led to the void that encloses him. Miscegenation in *Turbott Wolfe* is not only condoned—it is encouraged and demanded as a condition of health. "Eurafrica," the union of the two races, is the novel's pervasive image.

Today, it is easy enough to understand why *Turbott Wolfe* stimulated much controversy on its first publication. And, because the novel calls for the abolition of the color bar in a violently sexual manner, the book has remained controversial Plomer's next book, *I Speak of Africa*, was less controversial but no less influential. A collection of three short novels, i appeared in London in 1927 and introduced a new kind o hero in "Ula Masondo." "Ula Masondo" is the story of a nativ who tries to adapt to Christian and Western standards and who fails because his eagerness to please cannot adapt itself to white immorality and sloth. The story is the record of another instance of failure in the relationship between black and white: the African who has loved and respected, and who has tried to imitate his white masters is brutally mistreated by them. Its hero is now found in many novels in English about Africa—the African who comes to the mines or city with love and respect for the white man and who is then abused, confused, and betrayed by white hostility.

"Black Peril," one of the other two stories in *I Speak of Africa,* also deals with the color question. This piece of fiction is an indictment of the modish, superficial woman who seduces black men because of their reputedly superior sexual virility. The story is poorly written, but it is another reflection of Plomer's concern with sex as an essential element in any comprehension of the South African scene.

"Portraits in the Nude," the third story, consists of a series of vignettes about a Boer family and the Englishman who lives with them as a paying guest. It reveals a side of Plomer that he has not often exhibited. The story is in the gentle mood of Olive Schreiner's *The Story of an African Farm*: the days pass without any sense of climax under the burning sun; the Boer women are deceived by sophisticated scoundrels from the city; the natives enter as servants, mysterious, powerful, and elusive.

Plomer is a novelist of violence because he views the South African scene as an environment of tension and repressed hostility which cannot be altered by quiet good will. It is action, and not sentiment, which affects South Africa in his fiction. I have called him a novelist on the "left" because his fiction represents an attack on the existing social and moral codes of his time.

Another writer whose work flows from the same spirit of compassionate protest as Plomer is Laurens van der Post, whose three novels show the influence of Christian socialism, Jungianism, and a personal mysticism. Van der Post is an heir to the literary tradition bequeathed by E. M. Forster, but he also reflects the influence of William Plomer and Joseph Conrad. His first novel, *In a Province* (London, 1934), dealt with two men, of different cultures and races, trying and failing to understand each other. Van Bredepoel, the white South African hero, is a sensitive, lonely man who came to a big city to participate in life. Like Turbott Wolfe, his sense of isolation engulfs him and prevents him from expressing his romantic passion. He takes a job as a shipping clerk, hoping to find in humble life the entrance to an active world. In the boarding house in which he lives, he meets a native boy, Kenon, who has also left his farmland for the big city. The novel becomes a record of the love-friendship between van Bredepoel and Kenon, and it ends like E. M. Forster's *A Passage to India* and Plomer's *Turbott Wolfe* in the flickering ideal of a *rapprochement* between alien groups.

Van Bredepoel fails to help Kenon, or at least he believes himself to have failed; he dies with the feeling that he has never been able to commit himself to another human being or cause. Shortly before his death he says of himself and Kenon: "We were brothers in misfortune and inadaptability, but I could have helped him, and I didn't. Remote from one another we passed through life like two shadows over a hill, darkening it, but not altering it at all" (p. 377).

This theme of personal and spiritual isolation is found throughout van der Post's writing. All his heroes are unmade men searching for the vital relationship which will connect them to a sense of sharing in the ocean of experience. Van der Post ties this theme of isolation to the color issue in South Africa so that the psychological journey within the individual is completed through identification with one's black brother. In *In a Province* the hero comes to maturity through accepting his commitment to the native boy; in *The Face Beside the Fire* (London, 1953) the hero accepts his role in life after a

dream in which he identifies with the white-stubbled negroid
face of an old man; in *Flamingo Feather* (London, 1955) the
hero continues his fight for racial harmony after identifying
himself in guilt with African rioters.

Van der Post's emphasis on the necessity and joy of love of
white men for black men is the symbolic counterpart of miscegenation. Sexual love rarely occurs in his novels; the passion
of friendship, of deep platonic affection, takes its place. He
substitutes symbolic and emotional identity for sexual union.
This substitution can be seen clearly in *In a Province*, when
van Bredepoel is reflecting on his failure to help Kenon:

> The picture in his mind of the still, black figure lost in the
> shadows of a backyard in Port Benjamin haunted van Bredepoel;
> it became the symbol of his failure to help the boy when he
> alone could have helped. He did not try to justify himself as
> once, to his tutor, he had justified a complete lack of interest
> in a native girl with the mere exclamation: "But, Meneer
> Broecksma, she is black!" Since those days he had moved far.
>
> (p. 145)

The girl to whom van Bredepoel is referring had caused him
anguish in his young manhood because he had felt attracted
to her. His Dutch professor had urged him to sleep with a
black woman if he desired her, but van Bredepoel had been
shocked at the suggestion.[27]

---

[27] It is interesting to compare the fictional monologue of the Dutch professor with the speech van der Post gave to the C. J. Jung Institute
and Psychological Club of Zurich in March 1954. This is the professor's advice: "'There is nothing, nothing outrageous about being
fond of a black person. I feel almost ashamed to have to say so
obvious a thing; this is the only country I know in which it is necessary
to say it. I want you to remember, in case you should one day meet
people who feel about black women as I have felt about Johanna,
that every white man who does sleep with a black woman commits a
social act of the greatest value. Every white person who sleeps with
a black person, merely by suggesting to the rest of the world that it
is possible to want to do so, is helping to break down this wicked
superstition, is helping incidentally the individual to realize an emotional richness in himself hitherto ignored'" (pp. 44-45). And in

Although van der Post has treated Communist agitation in his novels, he is more interested in the psychological lessons of the African scene than in its political and social complexes. In this sense he is a representative of the Conradian tradition, seeing Africa in terms of the deep center of a man's soul. Thus, Africa, more than a state of people, becomes a condition of man. Or as van der Post put it in *The Dark Eye in Africa*, a book in which he related his personal mythology to *Mata Kelap*, a Malayan phrase referring to a gentle person who erupts suddenly into violence, "Nevertheless, the interest of the world is compelled by events in Africa because, unconsciously, the world apprehends that Africa may hold the secret of its own lost and hidden being. . . . Let us pray therefore that we all realize that it is also ourselves we are looking at in Africa and not destroy this precious magic mirror in our rage— as so many vanished civilizations before us have destroyed theirs to their own undoing" (p. 83). Yet, if van der Post fears violence, he also sees it as an unavoidable condition. In his novels riot and violence are the beginning, not the end, of racial harmony. The violence is the necessary catharsis, the expulsion of the festering wound. In *In a Province* the native boy Kenon, who came to the white man's city out of respect and desire to seek out and identify with a new civilization, falls into the role of a dope addict and mercenary agitator. Kenon causes the riot that ends in his own death and the deaths of a noble police officer and van Bredepoel. Here, it is undoubtedly van der Post's implication that the white man and black man achieve in death what they could not achieve in life, an equality and a companionship.

---

his speech, van der Post had this to say: "The humble individuals, black and white, who have contracted a union in obedience to an urge of life in them, are perhaps unwittingly serving a cause both of history and life" (quoted in *The Dark Eye in Africa* [New York, 1955], p. 197). Van der Post's attitude to miscegenation seems to have remained consistent through the years.

In some contrast to the approach of Laurens van der Post is the novel *Episode* (London, 1956) by Harry Bloom, a novel of violence written with all the fervor of a propagandist for more humane conditions in South Africa. In this work Bloom, a South African lawyer, journalist, and dramatist, takes the mythical town of Nelstroom, neat and clean and tidy, and pits it against its nearby Location, a squalid and dirty homestead for black laborers. Few South African novelists have attempted the wide canvas Bloom draws on: the entire town and its Location are painted in detail. Yet, although everything in this novel—mood, plot, theme, and characters—is alloyed with the author's message, the propaganda is not corrosive. Bloom's intention is not to paint individual characters but a milieu of tension and violence. The chief asset of the novel is the author's grasp of atmosphere, and of the subtle discords that make inevitable the explosion of human feelings. The fuse by which the violence and riot are ignited is a simple, commonplace argument over a collar missing from a bundle of laundry. A Zulu washerwoman claims she is returning everything handed to her by her white mistress; the white lady claims the Zulu has stolen the collar. From this argument develop a series of altercations which lead ultimately to the death of hundreds of blacks, whites, and Cape Coloreds. The character types killed in, or because of, the riot (Bloom is more successful in outlining a personality than in clothing him in artful substance), include a brutal police officer who cares more for bloodshed than order, a Negro family trying to live according to the standards of upper-class whites, a flashy, vital whore, and a kindly couple who treat their black servants with love, if not equality.

In his novel Bloom criticizes most of the white liberals, and especially the representatives of the paternalistic government. Du Toit, the white superintendent who believed his natives "loved" him, is shocked into recognition of their hostility. Like the kindly white couple killed when they attempted to rescue their servant from the rampaging Location, Du Toit reveals a lack of awareness of the depths of hatred among his black neighbors. Though he sees some hope for racial harmony in South Africa, Bloom does not see its evolution without the precondition of revolution. The African hero, Mabaso, who is meant to represent the spirit of love and forgiveness, is as much a sacrifice to violence as the white superintendent. But there is this difference: Mabaso's spirit, symbolized by the Zulu phrase *Mayebuye* ["May it come"] and the refrain of a song, "Awake, black hearts/ Awake, black hearts/ Awake, black hearts/ Win Africa back," gives renewed strength and determination to his people. Violence is not condoned by Bloom but is seen as a necessary part of South African life today. Its immediate victims are the liberals, the compromisers whose pacific ideals are of themselves no longer effective in the human arena.

Many other novels of violence have been published in English, and many more are now flowing almost monthly from publishers' presses.[28] While, naturally enough, individual dif-

---

[28] Among other novels of violence are: *Pilgrim's Rest* (London, 1922), *They Seek a Country* (London, 1937), and *The City of Gold* (London, 1939), all by Francis Brett Young; and *Mittee* (London, 1951) and *Wizards' Country* (London, 1957), by Daphne Rooke. F. B. Young's South African novels treat the history of Johannesburg and the gold rush which raised that city to its plateau of wealth; in *The City of Gold* he described the events that culminated in the ill-fated Jameson raid of December 1895. In *Mittee* Daphne Rooke used the Boer struggle as the climax of her novel. Miss Rooke invested her handsome Boer hero with an irresistible, illicit passion for the Cape Colored servant of his wife. In her *Wizards' Country*, Benje, the hunchback narrator, tells of the war in 1870 between the Zulu tribe, the Tshanini, and the English. Daphne Rooke is also the author of several other novels dealing with the problems of white settlers in a hostile land and of African servants thrust into the complexities of white people's lives. Among her other novels are *A Grove of Fever Trees* (London, 1951), *A Lover for Estelle* (London, 1961), and *The Greyling* (London, 1962).

ferences of style and artistic skill separate these works from
each other, a general pattern nevertheless unites them. The
novel of violence concentrates on miscegenation; and it sees
the eruption of racial tensions as a necessary catharsis or political inevitability. Good intentions, especially those manifested by contemporary compromisers, are no palliative to the
long-nurtured resentment of the African. In these novels the
climax is usually the result of an interracial sexual or love
affair. In Plomer's *Turbott Wolfe* miscegenation is presented
as the healthy solution for an effete Western world. In David
Lytton's novel, *The Goddam White Man* (New York, 1960),
the ambitious Cape Colored hero coldly sleeps with a white
woman not only to appease his physical appetite but to feed his
sense of power. There is neither idealization nor love in his
act, and it represents the triumph of African strength over
Western sentimentality. In van der Post's novels friendship
between men is never achieved till they have accepted their
black or white brothers; no man is free of the chains of his
immaturity till he has crushed and despoiled himself of all
reserves of racial prejudice. The problem of color, as in all
South African literature, dominates these novels; other issues
remain secondary.

3

The theme of the revolution of thought, the beginning of forgiveness by both black and white, distinguishes the work
of Peter Abrahams, Dan Jacobson, Nadine Gordimer, and
Alan Paton. In their work temporary political and social defeat is secondary to man's eternal spiritual resistance to isolation by color. The rationale for this belief is neither intellectual
nor sentimental; it is spiritual. Hate contracts and dries up the
inherent spiritual powers of man; love expands them into a
glorious sea of potential experience.

Abrahams, Jacobson, Paton, and Nadine Gordimer treat the problem of adjustment in their novels in two characteristic ways. One is to bring a native into the big city, in search of the things white people possess, and to show him descending usually into crime and violence before he comes to that superior measure of understanding which obliterates his hate, resentment, and envy. The other way is to treat the relationship between white and black on the many levels in which each alternately becomes servant and master. Characteristically in the work of three of these writers, the Jew is used as a symbolic brother of the black African; each is an outcast, and thus each understands the other.

In *The Path of Thunder* (New York, 1948), Peter Abrahams' best novel to date, both these thematic methods are in evidence. The hero, a brilliant young Cape Colored, returns to his home village after seven years in Cape Town, where he has reaped a university education and high scholastic honors. He rejects the city, where the road to personal success is easier and more lucrative, for the small town, where he will take a job teaching in night school. As he steps off the train, he is assailed and beaten by two Boer farmers who object instinctively to his clean, well-dressed appearance. When they have finished insulting and beating him, Lanny lifts his suitcases and trudges down the long road to his mother's house.

In Lanny's visionary world, color makes no difference. At first, however, he resists the love he feels for a rich young white woman, but he surrenders to it when he comes to accept his own philosophy. The young Jewish observer, Isaac, describes the surrender in this manner: "To Swartz [Lanny], Sarle Villier is a girl. He is not conscious of her colour. For days, he tried to keep the fact that she was white firmly fixed in his mind. Today, in front of my eyes, she swept it aside, for she's not conscious of his colour. Yes, in front of my very eyes she swept race and colour and nationality away as though it were a filthy little cobweb. They were just a man and a woman" (p. 163).

Miscegenation in novels of adjustment and forgiveness occurs as frequently as in novels of violence. The difference lies in the author's attitude toward the act. For Abrahams, Paton, Jacobson, and Gordimer, miscegenation is a painful but necessary evolution.

In *The Path of Thunder* Abrahams treats two other incidents of miscegenation. One is the affair between the white supremacist and the black girl who rejects his lust. Abrahams' description of this affair is lurid, poorly written, and highly colored propaganda, probably for the reason that he is here dealing with a fictional type rather than a character exciting his imagination. He is more successful in his depiction of a love affair between Lanny's sister and an Englishman on a visit to South Africa. Lanny's sister Mabel is much like Abrahams' heroine in his short novel *Mine Boy* (New York, 1955): both Cape Colored girls want beautiful clothes, glamorous lives, suburban homes. They want to be "white." The Englishman, before returning home to his wife and two children, justifies his behavior by explaining that he developed his relationship with Mabel so that he could write about her. The Englishman, in effect, was taking notes on Mabel so that he could spread his gospel of equal treatment for Cape Coloreds and blacks.

The inclusion of these two subplots is evidently meant as contrast to the main plot and theme. Abrahams is examining three cases of miscegenation: one he approves of, though it ends in tragedy; the other two he either condemns or satirizes. From the point of view of craftsmanship, however, the inclusion of the three incidents makes for clumsy contrast rather than subtle counterpointing. Part of this fault lies in Abrahams' lack of expertise (at present he is much more a brilliant, discursive essayist than a novelist). Part is also due to the material with which he is dealing. Abrahams' comments become locked in the vise of his liberal views. Though more than any other South African writer he has publicly declared his intention to avoid political issues in his fiction, his novels still suffer from the evangelism of a radical propagandist. Novels of adjustment and forgiveness can be as much tracts as novels of violence.

Evidence of Love (Boston, 1961), by Dan Jacobson, a young South African writer now living in England, is another proof that miscegenation is the prime subject of South African novels. In this novel Jacobson describes the passion that drives Kenneth Makeer, a Cape Colored who can pass for white in England, to return to South Africa with his white bride. The protest which Kenneth and Isabel Last make against *apartheid* is doomed to immediate failure, but its reverberations touch off the first chord of understanding between Isabel's father and Kenneth's brother, two exponents of black and white insularity.

Miscegenation has appeared elsewhere in Jacobson's work—it is the cause of the poetic justice implied in *A Dance in the Sun* (London, 1956)—but *Evidence of Love* marks Jacobson's profoundest venture into the subject. Like Alan Paton's *Too Late the Phalarope* (New York, 1955), Jacobson's novel is told through the voice of a compassionate observer who is feeling for the first time the full implications of the tragedies engendered by *apartheid*. The use of the point-of-view technique is significant, providing as it does another instance of Jacobson's intent to emphasize the effect of love between two people of different races and colors on the closely guarded fortresses of rigid morality and social legislation, rather than the act of love itself. The general thesis of Jacobson's work is the revolution and liberation of thought engendered in observers of the communion of love.

In Jacobson's work is found also the Jew, in the role of the brother-outcast. In "The Zulu and the Zeide," the title story in his short story collection (Boston, 1959), an old Jewish man who can speak only Yiddish and a young Zulu servant who can speak only his native tongue grow to love each other. Though they cannot understand each other's words, they understand each other's gestures. The old man, when he is dying, calls for his black servant rather than for his rich son who has assimilated perfectly into the smart, bourgeois world of South Africa.

Another writer employing the Jewish motif to advantage is Nadine Gordimer, who remains one of the few internationally known South African writers still living in the Republic of South Africa.[29] Miss Gordimer is the author of three short story collections and four novels. Her work bears the air of the compassionate observer rather than the passionate protestant, and it is filled with the themes of understanding, forgiveness, and adjustment. Miss Gordimer is probably the most skillful of the writers now recording the abortive attempts of middle-class whites and poor blacks to respect each other's values. She has set down in lyric tones the plight and frustration of Johannesburg people whose psychological problems outweigh their economic ones. Her work, however, bears the uneasy patina of too-easy regard for surface detail as symbolic of the emotional state. Much of her short fiction, which has appeared regularly in *The New Yorker* magazine, so astutely avoids comment that a seeming reportorial indifference is evoked.

Nadine Gordimer and Dan Jacobson write of the same

---

[29] Many other novels treating Jewish life have been written by South Africans. Among them are *The Daughter* (New York, 1951 [*Facing North* (Johannesburg, 1949)]), by Arthur Markowitz, which describes the coming-of-age of a twenty-year-old daughter of Polish immigrants; *Johannesburg Friday* (London, 1954), by Albert Segal, an account of the lives of four members of a Jewish family on the day before *Yom Kippur*, the Day of Atonement; and *Night Winds* (New York, 1954 [*Birth of a Dark Soul* (London, 1953)]), by Brian T. Cleeve, which deals with the theme of personal revelation following a robbery in the home of a rich Jewish businessman.

milieu—Johannesburg middle-class people, most of them Jewish—but whereas Jacobson's work is filled with a social realism,
Nadine Gordimer's is filled with a lyrical objectivity. Both
writers have reluctantly (it appears) come to face the problem of color after first attempting to deal with other more
immediately personal conflicts. The commitment to the color
issue has worked its way into their fiction as their work has
become less autobiographical and more mature. In *A World
of Strangers* (New York and London, 1958), her second novel,
Nadine Gordimer made of Johannesburg a mirror in which,
as it were, the white man's reflection is his black brother. The
novel opens with a ship full of strangers on their way to
South Africa; the symbolism of the ship and the people on it
seeking fulfillment in a strange land is evident. All the pas-
sengers, who are white, are misfits, and when they land in
South Africa they secretly envy the natives. The situation is
reminiscent of a comment made by Dan Jacobson:

> Yet it remains true, too, that the happiest people one meets in the
> streets of South Africa today are the black people. I have been
> met with total incredulity when I have said this in conversation
> with people in England, but it is true, and I am not the only
> South African, black or white, who has seen it. And it is true
> for a number of reasons, only one of which we need go into
> here. The blacks are cheerful in South Africa because they are
> the majority within South Africa itself and overwhelmingly so
> within the entire continent." [30]

A World of Strangers is the record of a change of feeling
from indifferent liberalism to personal commitment on the
part of the hero, a weary young liberal publisher who feels a
sense of guilt at not really caring about anything. When Toby
arrives from England to take over the South African branch
of his family's publishing business, he is ready for the kinds

---

[30] D. Jacobson, "James Baldwin as Spokesman," in *Commentary*, XXXII
(December 1950), 500.

of revolutionary experience which he feels will excite in him a true sense of purpose. He has two affairs, one with a militant liberal and the other with a spoiled, attractive divorcée. With the militant liberal, though he agrees with her views, he feels ill-at-ease; with the divorcée, though she represents different social and political attitudes, he falls in love. Toby's personal revolution—that is, his ability to feel and to commit himself to his feelings—is effected through his friendship with an African rogue. Steven becomes for Toby the representative of freedom of feeling. Steven is joyous because he is free in spirit. When Steven is killed in an automobile accident after being ordered to leave Toby's house by the landlady (South African leases prohibit the entrance of Africans into white homes for any reason other than that of domestic service), Toby realizes he cannot go back to his easy, indifferent views. Though his business arrangements are completed, he stays on in Africa, determined to bring a closer understanding between his white and black friends. In the last scene, as Toby says good-bye to the divorcée he had once thought he loved, he realizes that she is shocked at his newly expressed beliefs. In her eyes, an African friend is equal to an African mistress, and the divorcée looks at Toby with envy and distrust as a man who has committed himself to entrance into a dark, illicit world.

The most famous and one of the earliest novels of forgiveness is Alan Paton's *Cry, the Beloved Country*. This work and *The Story of an African Farm* are the two best-known novels in English—with a South African locale—to readers outside South Africa. Ironically, though Paton's novel has spawned a host of imitations and has been highly praised as propaganda, most contemporary South African writers deny any literary indebtedness to Paton. Yet *Cry, the Beloved Country* is at least as well-written a novel as the many novels which have followed its lead. Today also, Paton's humanism is being attacked as old-fashioned and sentimental. Ezekiel Mphahlele has accused Paton of falsifying human nature because in his view

Paton divides people into good and bad and then lays on these cardboard figures a heavy liberalism and a "monumental sermon." [31] Peter Abrahams, in reviewing *South African Predicament: The Economics of Apartheid* (London, 1960) by F. P. Spooner, commented:

> In the main, social, political and economic studies on South Africa (as well as practically all the fiction) have been written by people who are not in step with the prevailing mood of the majority of white South Africans: people like Alan Paton represent a tiny fractional minority viewpoint in the broad spectrum of general white South African opinion on the problems facing that unhappy country. . . . The denunciation, unlike that of the Alan Paton minority, is not that apartheid is evil and immoral and socially wrong. They (and Mr. Spooner is one of their most intelligent spokesmen) denounce apartheid because it will not work. [32]

In *Cry, the Beloved Country* the ways of justice and God are mysterious, but in the person of Paton's central character love brings an acceptance that explains nothing while meaning all. Stephen Kumalo, a Christian Zulu minister from the hill country of Ixopo, travels to Johannesburg to rescue his sister and his son: his sister has become a whore, and his son a murderer, while Kumalo's brother has forsaken Christianity for atheism and the political force of trade unionism. Kumalo's journey is abortive, yet it is not entirely fruitless. Though the son is executed by the State, the father of the murderer and the father of the murdered son join hands in friendship. Ironically, the murdered man was a white liberal who was writing a report, "The Truth About Native Crime," at the time of his death.

The novel is at least one report on this truth about native crime. The murderer was a boy unable to resist the tempta-

---

[31] See *The African Image* (London, 1962), pp. 131-33.
[32] *New York Times Book Review* (October 22, 1961), p. 3.

tion of the big city. In the hill country he was a decent boy; in the big city he is easy prey for criminals, who exploit his ignorance and gullibility for their own ends. The first half of the novel ends with the return home of Kumalo to the hill country, where his Christian message of love still dominates.

The second half of the novel has had a profound influence on the thoughts of non-South African readers, even if its message is currently being derided by some black South African literary critics. For Paton's novel is the supreme example of the kind of novel of forgiveness which calls for the construction of love on the ruins of tragedy. The father of the murdered man comes to the humble church where Kumalo preaches in order to say good-bye before leaving for Johannesburg. Kumalo thanks him for the large donation he has given for the reconstruction of the church roof. The white man says, "I have seen a man who was in darkness till you found him. If that is what you do, I give it willingly." And as the white man leaves, each cries to the other, "Go well, go well" (p. 268). This lyric to the suffering of Africa, the portrait of the long hard road to understanding is simply, gracefully expressed in biblical rhythms.

Paton's second novel, *Too Late the Phalarope,* is another example of propaganda in fiction which succeeds in creating a biblical aura of suffering. The theme of *Too Late the Phalarope* is miscegenation; and like Jacobson, Gordimer, and Abrahams, Paton does not exploit it but tries to understand it. The hero's compulsion to destroy himself is described by his aunt, an uneducated but deeply compassionate woman. Pieter, the hero, is a police officer of split personality whose opposites do not merge until he commits the act of miscegenation that sends him to prison and sets him psychologically free. One side of him is efficient, objective, firm; the other is feminine, gentle, and self-destructive. Paton suggests that Pieter's father, an authoritarian who never exhibited any display of love for his son, is responsible for the son's emotional instability. One significant episode shows Pieter, now a successful police administrator, secretly engaging in the purchase of stamps—a re-vivification of a childhood hobby which his father called effeminate. The symbolism of the phalarope, a bird whose "sexual characteristics suffered reversals," [33] reinforces the theme.The father thinks of inviting his son to see the phalaropes with him *after* Pieter has committed the irredeemable act in South Africa of sleeping with a black woman. The phalarope is symbolic of sexual misplacement; the father's ignorance of his son's emotional needs is responsible for this sexual misplacement in Pieter.

If *Cry, the Beloved Country* has been likened to a sermon, *Too Late the Phalarope* can be likened to a lament. Pieter's aunt, in relating the tragedy, constantly reiterates the fact that she was too late in understanding the forces which controlled Pieter. She believes she could have helped avert the situation, had she known the facts. Yet the point of Paton's novel is not that Pieter could have been saved by the psychological awareness of others; it is that the South African milieu destroys those who are seeking love irrespective of color. Paton's people are not romantics but people simply open to the fact of experience. Those who accuse Paton of soft sentimentalism should look at his characterization of Stephanie. She is not represented as a heroic or vivacious woman but as a frightened animal, and Paton's attack on the Immorality Act (prohibiting cohabitation between white and non-white) is aimed at its senselessness. Pieter did not love the black girl he slept with. It was a matter of sexual, animal urgency, yet Pieter has to pay for his act with imprisonment and moral denigration.

Miscegenation in Paton's second novel brings neither violence nor bloodshed but imprisonment and shame to the accused white man. So moral an issue is miscegenation in South Africa that the father refuses to speak to his son again; Pieter's

---

[33] See Robert Ardrey, *African Genesis* (New York, 1961), p. 50.

father shuts his town house and retreats to the country. Yet miscegenation in this novel also brings understanding—not between black and white, but between three members of a white family. His wife and aunt at last appreciate the need in Pieter that drove him to his act. Pieter at last accepts his love for his wife and family, for he is now free of his festering onus.

Paton is the most important force in the literature of forgiveness and adjustment. His popularity and his integrity have made possible a receptivity to a whole new body of work that might otherwise have remained unnoticed. Undoubtedly his work is more significant as propaganda than as literature, but it should be emphasized that his writing is not without literary quality. If his talent lies in his ability to project the fervor and sentiment of his liberal views rather than in his ability to convey full-blooded human beings, it also contains much that is genuinely creative.

The history of South African literature by white South Africans shows an obsessive concern with the color question. Its exponents sooner or later become propagandists of one view or another. This concern cannot be explained merely by reason of the existing color problem in the society these writers describe. Not every novel written by an American contains a Negro character or a race-relations issue. Many American novels of the nineteenth century never mentioned the American Indians or the Negroes, and both these groups were in one degree or another major "color problems" of the time. The answer appears to lie in the moral, puritanical attitude of South African writers to their work. These writers have not yet broken from a propagandistic orientation and a moral fervor. None of their novels, with the exception perhaps of the one undisputed masterpiece, *The Story of an African Farm*, conveys to the reader a purely esthetic experience. The South African novel invariably has been a tract, and instruction—rather than esthetic appreciation—is its excuse for being.

However, two recent novels by white authors suggest that even South African literature may be changing its tune. Perhaps in every age the period of protest is followed by a resigned and often lyrical placidity. The 1940's and 1950's in American literature were patient, recuperative stages following the onslaught of the anguished cries of American writers in the 1930's. Part of the reason for the disappearance of the *cri de coeur* in South Africa is obvious—any honest book about social conditions cannot be published in South Africa today. Only history (and only a peculiar kind of history) books and manuscripts about the individual plight of the white man find their way into publishing companies. Yet if the battle for human rights has been temporarily halted, not all operations have been stilled. *Bite of Hunger* (New York, 1965), by Hilda Kuper, and *The Hawk Alone* (New York, 1965), by Jack Bennett, suggest that other kinds of lamentations are still being heard.

Jack Bennett, a young South African, writes in the manner of Hemingway, not only stylistically but thematically. His novel, *The Hawk Alone,* is a tale about the end of strength and bowing to age. Bennett's hero is a Hemingway type—the virtuous hunter who has kept to his ideals in the face of a constantly deteriorating ethical society. The hunter is profoundly isolated from his society, because his ideals, which have sustained him through life, are no longer accepted or challenged. They are simply anachronistic in an age demanding not personal heroism but social ingenuity and shrewd compromises.

A sense of loss, of spiritual isolation, also haunts the main character of Hilda Kuper's novel, *Bite of Hunger.* Hilda Kuper, a native of Southern Rhodesia but now a Professor of Anthropology at the University of California in Los Angeles, tells the tale of a young tribal princess who leaves her village in Swaziland to try for a new life in Johannesburg. Everything is against her—her family in the tribal village, and presumably the whites of Johannesburg. What impels the heroine is her desire for peace with her human friends, her wish to understand the strangers who are so hostile to her people. The author's humanistic solution to the racial problem may well be attacked for its naïveté. The heroine who lives in Swaziland has never experienced the color-bar laws of South Africa. For her, the evils of Johannesburg are myths, and the myths of Johannesburg's urban greatness are real things awaiting her. Yet granting the naïve quality of the heroine, the novel ends in an heroic act, a sacrifice worthy of those of the heroes in Alan Paton's fiction. And the heroine's willingness to continue the struggle to understand provides the book with a pathos that accompanies her feelings of hope and despair. In Bennett's novel the old "hawk" commits suicide because there is no way for him to turn: a group of South African teenagers convince him by their shallowness that his allegiance to his set of ideals is now futile. In Hilda Kuper's novel the heroine is foolish and wise: suffering awaits her, but her hopes and her energy fit her for survival. This heroine is much like the Dilsey of Faulkner's *The Sound and the Fury*. Her goodness will prevail.

Nevertheless, in spite of their slight shift of key, both *The Hawk Alone* and *Bite of Hunger* fit into the general tradition of South African literature. One is an example of what has been termed the novel of forgiveness; the other can loosely be called a novel of violence, since it deals with the matters of killing and violence in Africa. What marks a difference in the two popular novels from their predecessors is that the color question has now been woven into the fabric of the stories; the issues of racial prejudice and Christian humanism no longer trample across every page.

SIX

The Pen, the Club,
and the Sword

In modern novels about Africa, the journalist is a villain, the missionary a fool, and the police officer a decent man caught in an inescapable tragedy.[1] The most striking conclusion suggested by a review of the literature is that two of the reputed forces of progress and enlightenment—religion and journalism—fail not only to bring understanding between individuals and groups but that they cause damage and despair. The police officer, on the other hand, an oath-taker to a reputed system of repression, creates the bridge on which understanding travels to a more profound level.

These roles are not confined to any one region of Africa, and through their portraiture over the last sixty years they may be said to have assumed a tradition. The police officer is found in West Africa (*The Heart of the Matter*; *The Loved Enemy*; *The African Witch*; *Riot*), East Africa (*The Day of*

---

[1] Occasionally, but less significantly, the police officer is cast in the familiar role of the brutal sadist. These remarks, and examples, comment directly on novels written in English, but they may be taken to characterize all European and American fiction on Africa.

the Monkey), and South Africa (*Too Late the Phalarope*; *In a Province*). He is the man divided—within himself and outside of himself. His inner conflicts are parallel to the social conflicts with which he finds himself inevitably, if reluctantly, engaged. A gentle soul, he cloaks his yearnings for tenderness under the efficient performance of his duties. Essentially he is a man of feeling who is forced to dispense with these feelings in order to continue in his social and bureaucratic role. Often he is the man who appears to be afraid of success. Scobie, in *The Heart of the Matter*, is a perennially ignored man in the matter of promotion; far from feeling injustice at his situation, Scobie courts the denial of recognition. Scobie's passivity and seeming lack of ambition are manifested in all his roles in life. His marriage has evolved into a state of passionless contiguity with his wife; his extramarital affair produces a conflict which he solves by self-rejection and suicide. Yet Scobie is the one who comes closest in *The Heart of the Matter* to caring about the African and to identifying with him. The other Englishmen and foreigners are too much involved in their petty affairs to think of the African as more than a servant or nuisance. Scobie, however, has developed a friendship with his native boy Ali that wipes out the color bar by making it irrelevant in the sphere of human love. Ironically, Scobie is responsible for the murder of his native boy, and it is in the recognition of his guilt—personal and racial—that Scobie is able to rise out of his moral indifference.

In *The Heart of the Matter* Graham Greene was writing on the many questions of love rather than on the color question, but it is significant that he chose a police officer as his representative of racial compassion. Scobie, committed to one side, is unable to ignore the rights of the other side. In that double view, that inability brutally or cleanly to reject what is inopportune, lies first the cause of Scobie's spiritual despair, and second, the cause of his physical death. Yet Scobie's physical death is a triumph of will; the groping that ends in suicide is not a dirge but a hymn to love.

The hero of Alan Paton's *Too Late the Phalarope* is another complex, gentle, divided police officer who suffers a painful enlightenment as a result of yielding to his compassion. Like Scobie, Pieter is disinterested in the color question on its academic, social, and political levels, but he is forced to face it on a personal level. Pieter, an officer sworn to uphold the South African law of *apartheid* and to apprehend anyone who contravenes it, is dismissed from service and imprisoned for his act of miscegenation. Significantly, Paton chose a police officer to create the first small break in the wall of human animosity between black and white.

The police officers in *The Loved Enemy, The Day of the Monkey,* and *Riot* are similar characters. Their round of duties forces on them a burden of conscience that other white inhabitants of Africa repress. They are the representatives of a tradition in which human morality triumphs over social order. They are not leaders who have sought their burden, but men seized by circumstances into the act of heroism. This kind of police officer, fulfilling his duties while at the same time suffering with his victim, is idealized in Laurens van der Post's *In a Province*. A police colonel risks his life in order to avoid a riot between black and white. This man, who could have stayed behind police lines, walks instead into a clearing to talk to three potential revolutionaries and thus exposes himself to enemy fire. One man who observes that action thinks, "that there was something infinitely heroic about his action, that this obscure Colonel of police in an obscure country village had suddenly become great, not because of anything attaching to his own life, but because he placed himself like a bridge between the conception and execution of a duty that was greater than himself" (p. 323). Minutes later, when the Colonel has been killed, the same observer:

> . . . felt an immense pity for the Colonel. He admired his rigorous conception of duty, which had lifted him slowly into place,

like a bridge over a gulf, in that last moment before his death. He admired his determination to be just to both white and black. It seemed to him there was some compensation for the Colonel in the way he had died.   (p. 337)

It is instructive to compare the heroic-compassionate role assigned to police officers with that assigned to most "liberals" or understanding government officials in the same kind of novel. In almost all cases the government official (beyond the rank of the minor police officer) who appreciates the complexities of African administration is weakened by his insights. The blind devotion to a cause that makes for efficient rapacity is missing, but in its place is a tolerance that has no effective force. Roper-Traherne and Humphreys in *Honey for Tomorrow*, Du Toit in *Episode*, Bewsher in *An American Visitor*, Robert in *The Walled City*, Macmillan in *The Tribe That Lost Its Head*, and Scobie's superiors in *The Heart of the Matter* are all people who believe they are bringing enlightenment to Africa. They are all individuals who are kind and just in their personal relationships. Yet invariably these individuals are frustrated by events. The black man turns on them, rejecting their offer of tolerance and promise of freedom. At the end of the novels all of these men are spent; their lives have ended in waste rather than being begun in tragedy. They have milked dry their compassion and are afraid to go beyond the shed of beliefs they have created. Unlike the lowly police officers who have ventured into a new experience, these men have been compromised by their positions into anachronisms. Comparison between the depiction of the police officer and the government official in English-language novels about Africa shows that novelists have concentrated heroism upon individuals not encumbered with success or rank.

If the police officer is often the hero of modern novels in English about Africa, the journalist is always the villain. Either

he is a purposeful liar or a fervent propagandist, but in both
cases he causes great damage and mischief. English writers
on Africa have exhibited this attitude to journalists as early
as the time of John Buchan's *Prester John* (1910), in which
a correspondent for *The Times* reports inaccurately nearly
every incident in the "Kaffir Rising," and where he is described
as a "picturesque historian" (p. 303). Even in the one novel
by an Englishman, *Sea Never Dry* (London, 1958) by Anthony
Smith, in which African newspapers and newspapermen are
treated sympathetically, the African journalist is admitted to
be careless of facts. In general it may be said that the English,
American and African journalists are all tools of violence and
misunderstanding in the novels about Africa in which they
appear. More sympathy is extended to African journalists than
to their English or American counterparts, but all newspapermen are treated as distorters of fact.

The most violent attack on newspapermen is contained in
Nicholas Monsarrat's *The Tribe That Lost Its Head*. Here a
journalist's irresponsibility is almost wholly responsible for the
unnecessary bloodshed in a British-ruled African colony. Although this newspaperman, Tulbach Browne, is repeatedly
warned about his potentially evil influence, this does not deter
him from rushing blindly to create a story out of a supposed
act of color discrimination at a hotel bar in the colony. That
the journalist has misrepresented the facts in no way inhibits
the success of the story in inciting Africans to riot. The resident
commander of the colony pleads with the journalist to discon-
tinue, until the situation is calmer, his blatant articles urging
immediate independence. When the journalist refuses, the
government officer breaks into a tirade:

> "You don't know what you're stirring up, you don't know what
> you're talking about. You've jumped into this thing like a whore
> at a christening. If you write about the Maulas as though they
> could take charge of their own affairs tomorrow, if you talk to
> them on those lines, if you try to persuade them that they can

do without *us* . . . it'll be the worst day's work you've ever
done."   (p. 150)

The journalist accomplishes his day's work: a riot breaks
out in which hundreds of whites and blacks are killed. That
the journalist's lack of respect for facts and for people, that his
love of fame and sensation, and that his need to be in the
public eye in England and the United States are responsible
for his actions is made abundantly clear throughout the novel.
Browne wants a story, he does not want the truth.

Journalists of the stamp of Browne are found in many other
novels in English about Africa. The trouble in *Picnic at
Porokorro* (London, 1961), by Hugo Charteris, is started by a
journalist who sacrifices himself before the altar of righteous
indignation rather than that of objective reporting. In Graham
Greene's *A Burnt-Out Case* a man's desire to find anonymity
and a new life is thwarted by a famous journalist on the hunt
for good newspaper copy. The journalist's meddling is also
responsible in part for the death of this man, Querry. Greene's
contempt for journalism is manifested almost immediately in
the novel. Querry, a famous architect who has run away to a
place where no one will know him, is recognized by a woman
who remembers seeing his face in an issue of *Time* magazine.
Her recognition paves the way for Parkinson, an English
journalist no less insensitive than Monsarrat's Tulbach Browne.
Parkinson writes a foolish story about Querry as a saint who
has come to the Congo in order to devote his services to the
construction of a leprosery. Parkinson's story is as sentimental
as it is false, but these defects do not hinder it from achieving
world coverage. Greene satirizes Parkinson's pomposity and
pretentiousness in many ways, but he always returns to the
forefront of his attack—to the overweening, blind ambition of
the journalist which allows him to dismiss facts that stand in
the way of his own success. Parkinson begins his story of the
discovery of Querry in Africa with these words: ". . . three

weeks by boat to reach this wild territory. Struck down after seven days by the bites of tsetse flies and mosquitoes I was carried ashore unconscious. Where once Stanley battled his way with Maxim guns, another fight is being waged—this time in the cause of the African—against the deadly infection of leprosy" (p. 128). On learning that a doctor knows his story is a fabrication, Parkinson retorts:

> "Tell him it's more true than the truth. . . . It's a page of modern history. Do you really believe Caesar said, '*Et tu, Brute*'? It's what he ought to have said and someone on the spot—old Herodotus, no, he was the Greek, wasn't he, it must have been someone else, Suetonius perhaps, spotted what was needed. The truth is always forgotten. Pitt on his deathbed asked for Bellamy's Pork Pies, but history altered that."   (p. 128)

Parkinson, no less than Tulbach Browne, is not a harmless go-getter. His stories create a tension that explodes into the death of Querry and the failure of his spiritual quest.

Less virulent portraits of journalists are found in several contemporary English satires, which depict newspapermen as facile scribblers bent on pinpointing an "angle" of the truth rather than the whole of it. In novels about Africa in the twentieth century three important English satirists have taken a swipe at newspapermen. Joyce Cary characterized the journalist in *An American Visitor* as an American woman who comes to Africa seeking the promised primitive land she had read about in Emerson and Thoreau. Marie Hasluck's idyllic philosophy is indeed fuzzy, but the author invests it with the charm of sweet ignorance. Evelyn Waugh, in contrast, pours ridicule on his newspaper correspondents in *Scoop*. This novel is a roar against the nonsensities and inevitable nonsequiturs of current journalism. An American journalist sent to Africa to cover a revolution there sits in his hotel room and types his memoirs of high life in London and the United States, a literary task that consists mainly of his dropping the names of famous people he has rubbed shoulders with at fashionable dinner parties and in hotel bars. The American journalist never once bothers to go out into the street to observe the African scene; he prefers that his mind be uncluttered by facts. The satire is further exploited in Waugh's hero John Boot, who, sent to Africa by a case of mistaken identity, gains his "scoop" through a combination of ignorance topped by gullibility.

Waugh's attack on newspapers and newspapermen is contained in other novels—he makes fun of them in *Vile Bodies, Black Mischief,* and *The Loved One,* among others—and journalists, whether in Africa or England, were evidently one of his *bêtes noires.*

Another satirist who finds newspapermen a bitter comic pill is Winifred Holtby, whose *Mandoa! Mandoa!* presented an "enterprising" correspondent who immediately begins collecting opinions on the "catastrophe" of a reported kidnapping without once verifying the story.

The most sympathetic novel—and the only one revolving entirely around a newspaper office in Africa—is *Sea Never Dry* by Anthony Smith, an English journalist and former editor of the monthly periodical *Drum* (Nigerian edn.).[2] This novel concerns the growth and death of a newspaper in Nigeria. In its short life, it employs circulation techniques familiar to Western readers: a beauty contest, crossword puzzles, advice to the lovelorn, and "People's Points," a feature that deals with important issues in inflamed language yet with abysmal superficiality. The comedy in Smith's novel often centers upon the

---

[2] Several books by the English journalist J. M. Stuart-Young have given an amusing and sympathetic picture of newspaper life in West Africa, but these are not novels. Among Stuart-Young's books are *The Coaster at Home* (London, 1916) and *Chits from West Africa* (London, 1923).

inflated language used in the paper to describe mundane or unpleasant occurrences. When thieves break into the post office, the paper gives the incident front-page prominence:

> Now we have in our town a post office, resplendent and big. It is a fitting edifice to enrich a nation. But is it fitting that thieves, blackguards, villains, footpads, knaves and brigands, should be able to walk in at their leisure and at their will? Is it right that the forces of law and order are nothing but monkey-bluff?
>
> (p. 79)

Although the paper is eventually killed off by a combination of libel suits, political opposition, and lack of funds, during its circulation it creates for its owners, employees, and readers a sense of exciting participation in local and national events. This sense of participation is not achieved without purposeful exaggeration of the facts: Smith's journalists see a news story as the means of stimulating lively controversy and not as a medium for reflective objectivity. This approach is defended by way of the mental interpolation of one of the newsmen, Ugo, concerning a fellow reporter, Daniel:

> Like many other journalists, he [Daniel] often stretched a good point so far that the facts no longer fitted it, and several of his remarks about Europeans had been overstretched. But Ugo, who always tried to see the other side of things, knew that Daniel was right. In spite of the apparent altruism of Europeans in West Africa, in spite of the missionaries and the schools and in spite of the desire to grant self-government to the Africans, the whites, who live along the Coast, have chalked up quite a lot against themselves in their time.
>
> (p. 88)

Another journalist who offers the same justification for his editorial slanting of straightforward facts in a news story is Amusa Sango of *People of the City*. Sango, grieving over the murder of a good friend by a Syrian, utilizes the story of that murder for an editorial attack on the Syrian and Lebanese "menace." Sango recalls the fact that most of the wealth,

especially that coming from retail trade, is in the hands of
Syrians. When Sango is released from his job because of pres-
sure by the Syrian elements, he endeavors to justify his reportorial attack by maintaining that it consisted of no more
and no less than the truth. The significant feature here is not
the validity of Sango's statement, but the relevance and suit-
ability of his remarks in relation to the incident in question.

This tendency to see in every story, short or long, a means
of editorializing on larger and more profound issues is reflected in most novels on Africa whenever African journalists
enter the scene. English novelists writing on African newsmen
often convey their apparent shock at this journalistic license.
John Wyllie in *Riot* presents a scathing portrait of Marcus
Aurelius, the pseudonym of the West African journalist who
spreads lies and exaggerations in his propaganda campaign to
rouse his countrymen to revolution against the "white imperialists." In *The Walled City* Elspeth Huxley shows the transition
of a mission-educated African boy from gentle submissiveness
into rabid nationalism—into a propagator of violence. In
symbolic proof of the African's change, Elspeth Huxley casts
him in the role of a journalist who writes a newspaper story
that results in the destruction of the one possible equitable
solution in a West African community. In *Into Strange Country* Carol Christian, an English resident in Nigeria, has her
main character express these views on Nigerian newspapermen: "I saw that, with such nerve, he could only be a newspaperman" (p. 27); "Why do they go on printing such rub-
bish? Surely there are one or two educated people by now.
Don't be an architect, Felicia, be a newspaperwoman, and stop
these half-baked schoolboys with undigested vocabulary lists
from earning a living in this way. It's a roaring scandal"
(p. 80); "That's not reporting. . . . It's rabble-rousing, inciting
to riot. Talk about 'innocent blood.' There will be more, and on
his head. What does he hope to gain? The end of British rule.
More likely, British chaos" (p. 122).

Carol Christian's main character's comments are not those of a hostile but of a friendly critic, and they show again the incredulity of British critics at the double role of reporter-propagandist played by African journalists. Even an English-woman married to a Nigerian in the novel says, "Don't ever have a journalist for a brother-in-law, Ellen. We are so ashamed of some of the things he [her journalist brother-in-law] says" (p. 112).

If, however, English writers seem shocked at the behavior of African journalists, for their part African writers seem prone to "explain" the phenomenon as part of the legacy of Western imperialism. In their novels, newspapermen wreak damage by their nonobjective approach to their work, but their activities are defended, or at least rationalized. Sango in *People of the City* and Daniel in *Sea Never Dry* excuse their exaggerations as a reaction to the propaganda forced on Africans for decades by Westerners. The newspaper becomes for the African the symbol of freedom, but a protestant freedom not yet secure in its reality. That this fictional representation is true to the realities of West African journalism is pointed in a study in recent years of conditions in Ghana before its independence:

> They [broadcasting and journalism] were deliberately and most effectively used to reduce the image of the European to life-size, and to enhance the African self-image correspondingly. If the African trumpet was sometimes blown in what appeared a rather loud and shrill manner, it is as well to pause before judging and to remember that the still small voices of European superiority had been heard whispering for so long and so insistently, that its message had become deeply engraved in the minds of the listeners, and therefore a great effort was required to counteract it." [3]

In the world of fact, however, the situation has become anachronistic. African journalists, no longer geared single-

---

[3] Gustav Jahoda, *White Man* (London, 1961), p. 106.

mindedly to promoting nationalism, are nevertheless constantly subjected to rebuke or criticism by journalists of other
lands. A comparatively recent newspaper article announced
an appeal to the world's leading newspaper editors for "educating journalists in the emerging nations of Africa to higher
skills and standards of objectivity in reporting the news." [4]
Implicit in this plea is due recognition of the increasing importance of African states in the world scene, an acknowledg-
ment that will undoubtedly have an impact upon African
journalists and the fictional representations of creative writers.
In future years the African newspaperman—and even the English journalist—may be cast in heroic or at least praiseworthy
roles. At present in modern literature in English about Africa
they are seen as exploiters of propaganda—on the one hand for
nationalism and glory, on the other for money and success.

Like the journalist, the missionary is enthusiastic, and his
enthusiasm, as seen in modern English-language novels about
Africa, is deleterious to his environment. A large body of work
by English, African, and South African writers depicts the
missionary as a fool wreaking damage wherever his best intentions get a chance to display themselves, but few novelists
see him as a self-seeking knave. Curiously, the missionary
comes off best in African-setting novels by Americans and
about American missionaries. The missionary has also had
apologists in three major English writers of the twentieth century, Graham Greene, Joyce Cary, and Evelyn Waugh.

The tradition in fiction of attacking the missionary is at
least sixty years old. One of the earliest modern influences was
Mary Kingsley, whose books had a profound effect on the
attitude of many writers. Mary Kingsley asserted that West

---

[4] Thomas R. Bransten, "Western Editors Hear Plea for Aiding Press
in Africa," in *New York Herald Tribune* (Paris edn.; May 16, 1962),
p. 3.

African missionaries produced "incalculable" evil, and that
their influence led to the British policy of eliminating native
states. She also laid the blame for British military repression
on the "exaggerated" reports of tribal cruelty and immorality
written by missionaries in order to horrify the British public
into subscribing to the government's policy of force. The British novelist Marguerite Steen, in the introduction to her novel
Twilight on the Floods (London, 1949), said that most traders
went along with Mary Kingsley's claim—in *West African
Studies* (London, 1899)—that the missionaries' evangelical
horror at the African scene was the prime cause of the full-
scale Ashanti War (in what is now Ghana).

Mary Kingsley's attitude is paralleled by that expressed by
one of her contemporaries, Mary Gaunt, who in *Alone in West
Africa* had this to say: "Frankly my sympathies are not as a
rule with the missionary, certainly not with the African missionary. I have not learned to understand spiritual misery, and
of material misery there is none in Africa to be compared with
the unutterable woe one meets at every turn in an English
city" (p. 225).

Missionaries were also attacked by Conrad in *Heart of Darkness*, in his ironic use of the word "pilgrims" to describe those
bringing, not enlightenment, but exploitation to Africa, and
in his description of Brussels as a "white-domed sepulchral
city" where traders and missionaries begin their trek into the
heart of Africa.

Even Olive Schreiner (in *The Story of an African Farm*)
implied an attack on the missionary system for allowing the
kindly German preacher to be destroyed so easily by his companions; a more open attack may be seen in her depiction of
Bonaparte Blenkins, the opportunist who saw his way to success through the hypocritical pretense of playing a preacher
and mouthing a missionary's dogma. John Buchan, in *Prester
John*, offers a concluding chapter in which he tells the reader
what happened to those who took part in the Great Uprising

of the Kaffirs against the British. One of them, Aitken, a diamond merchant and ex-soldier, became rich and

> . . . laid down a big fund for the education and amelioration of the native races, and the first fruit of it was the establishment at Blaauwildebeestefontein itself of a great native college. It was no factory for making missionaries and black teachers, but an institution for giving the Kaffirs the kind of training which fits them to be good citizens of the state.   (p. 373)

In all these early attacks on the missionary, the authors concentrate mainly on the missionary as a dupe of the British government or of his own blind dogma. Richard Wright summed up the African's point of view on this kind of missionary as follows:

> The more I reflected upon the work of the missionary, the more stunned I became. They had, prodded by their own neurotic drives, waded in and wrecked an entire philosophy of existence of a people without replacing it, without even knowing what they had been doing. Racial pretensions had kept them from sharing intimately the lives of the people they had wanted to lift up. . . . What would happen when the native began to realize all of this clearly? [5]

The attack on missionaries in later novels, however, concentrates on a different evil. That evil is implied in Buchan's sarcastic comment about the missionary's wrong kind of teaching, a facet which was to become the major reason for the novelists' view of missionaries as troublemakers. For most twentieth-century novelists see the missionary as a teacher whose training ill-equips him and the African he is teaching for any role in modern African affairs. White supremacist or *apartheid* sympathizers among the novelists, like Sarah Gertrude Millin, present the missionary as a busybody whose teachings destroy himself and influence no other. Most other novelists see the

---

[5] *Black Power,* p. 152.

missionary as responsible for creating out of the African a compliant laborer with a sense of his own inferiority. A third group of novelists presents the missionary as a sincere proselytizer caught in the dilemma of educating the African to the point where he must turn on his teacher in a burst of independence. All these portraits afford unsympathetic criticism, although they may at times be tempered with compassion for the plight of the missionary.

Thus, the attack on the missionary in modern English fiction about Africa may be said to fall into three patterns. The first pattern draws him in the shape of a blind dogmatist or a weakling unable to stand up to the onslaught of the reality of Africa. This type of missionary is found in Francis Brett Young's *The Crescent Moon,* C. S. Forester's *The African Queen,* and William Plomer's *Turbott Wolfe.* In *The Crescent Moon* the missionary arrives in Africa full of idealism and optimism; he believes he can raise the African from his low level to a superior moral order of life. However, the missionary is soon reduced to the state of a wounded animal, crawling on all fours to a jungle fire to stop a primitive orgy in which his enemy, a German coffee planter, and many Africans are taking part. When the missionary returns from this encounter, in which he has proved himself a failure, he collapses and suffers a nervous breakdown which keeps him spiritually and physically ill for months. Young, in the guise of narrator, comments on the situation in this manner:

> One gasps at the criminal, self-sufficient ignorance of the people that sent him to Central Africa, at the innocence of the man himself, who felt that he was in a position to go; for forlorner hope it would be impossible to imagine. Here . . . there was no shadow of an attempt at adjustment. . . . I wouldn't mind betting he went there in a collar buttoned at the back and a black coat with flapping skirts. To Equatorial Africa. I've seen it. . . . Nor was that the only way in which I imagine his hope forlorn. He had gone there with the wrong sort of religion: with the

wrong brand, if you like, of Christianity. You can't replace a
fine exciting business of midnight n'gomas and dancing ceremonies by a sober teaching of Christian ethics without any exciting ritual attached. (p. 15)

Another missionary full of optimism and hope whose life is
destroyed when his African charges desert him and burn his
station on the eve of World War I is found in C. S. Forester's
The African Queen. In Plomer's *Turbott Wolfe* an American
Baptist missionary indulges in the folly of exchanging his
black suit for an African's loincloth, to prove all are equal
under the sun. Later, the Baptist goes mad.

The missionary as weakling is seen most plainly in the
novels of Sarah Gertrude Millin. In *God's Stepchildren, The
Herr Witchdoctor*, and *The Burning Sun* the heroes are missionaries who arrive in Africa ready to preach the Christian
notion of equality before God. In all three cases the missionary
ends up a pathetic, spiritually isolated man. One of them, the
Reverend Andrew Flood, dies in a dirty hut, not even respected by the Hottentots for whom he has sacrificed his life.
Another, Johannes van der Kemp, is a wasted soul, still burning inside himself and unable to find spiritual peace. The
third, Barry Lindsell, is on the road to spiritual despair, having been deserted by his few African converts. One of them
before leaving had said: "I don't say that many missionaries
are not very good. But I don't like it when they want to serve
God through *us*. Why should our souls be their workshop—
even their playground?" [6]

In her autobiographical volume *The Measure of My Days*
S. G. Millin gives this key to her view of missionary work:

Of all people, however, the natives of South Africa have always
disliked most the negrophilist missionaries. I have written a
book, *The Burning Man*, in which a missionary goes from tribe
to tribe only to be called Nyengana, he who steals in. The book

---

[6] *The Herr Witchdoctor*, p. 133.

is based on fact. To this day, the natives are burning down mission churches. I have asked them why. They say they don't like to be treated as children. I don't know if they mean it. I don't know how we can save both themselves and us.   (p. 270)

This attitude is more extreme than that of most writers in English on Africa, but it is part of a general pattern. In addition, S. G. Millin reflects a strong bias against German missionaries. Wherever they appear in her novels, especially in *The Herr Witchdoctor,* they are undercover agents for the German government. One of them in *The Herr Witchdoctor* is the leader of a Nazi movement working secretly with witchdoctors in Southwest Africa to foment a revolution that will bring Southwest Africa into World War II on the side of Germany. An African, explaining the incredible evil of a witchdoctor, blames this condition on German missionaries: "Even Popanyane might not have been so wicked but for the German missionaries. It is since these missionaries have come to our reserve that evil has spread among us, that people have begun to wish for what they cannot get and to hate one another and to kill one another" (p. 238).

The second type of missionary found in modern English novels about Africa—the blind dogmatist—is the Christian who unwittingly uses Christianity to instill a sense of inferiority in the African native. Such missionaries appear in many novels, and the reaction they cause among the Africans is extreme and bitter. In Elspeth Huxley's *A Thing to Love* the evolution into a Mau-Mau terrorist of Gitau is credited to his disgust with Christian missionaries:

He had intended to love and honour Europeans and by patience to win their respect. He had believed in Aggrey's parable about a piano's black and white keys. . . . He couldn't remember exactly when he began to see that he was being taken in by a gigantic fraud, that the Europeans were using their religion as a medicine to confuse his senses and blind his eyes. Perhaps it was when a new master came, an African, who pointed out that most of the Europeans were not Christian at all, but paid missionaries to tell these lies to Africans, so as to keep them harnessed to the yoke like oxen, without asking why. (p. 103)

Allied with this novelist's view is the criticism of Christianity as a religion lacking vitality. This is the excuse the African intellectual in *The Herr Witchdoctor* gave when he left the Christian Church to join a Fascist movement that had both a shibboleth and an immediate purpose. This criticism of Christianity is not restricted to its role in Africa, but is part of the larger attack hurled upon it for its decay into a static philosophy. D. H. Lawrence in *The Man Who Died* called for a return to the kind of Christianity symbolized by a fighting cock and an aggressive spirit of love. William Plomer, who includes several kinds of missionaries in *Turbott Wolfe,* summarizes through the narrator the continuing tradition of this attack on Christianity as a robber of the human spirit:

She was a fine rare savage, of a type you will find nowhere now: it has been killed by the missions, the poor whites and the towns. There was a chance, at the time when those blacks were first taught to stop fighting, there was a chance then to build up a new Christianity. The right man could have built their new Jerusalem. I have seen not a little of the natives, and I have immense faith in their character. But it is too late now. The missionaries brought them the sacrament, but I could give you more than one instance where they brought them syphilis too. They took everything from the natives—all those vague mysterious savage ways of mind on which their lives were conducted, often very honorably and even nobly, certainly with method, and what on earth did they give them instead? Example? No.
(pp. 55-56)

The third type of attack on the missionary is the most complimentary. It concedes that the missionary has fulfilled a useful role in educating the African to more modern concepts of life, but with that concession comes an acceptance of the missionary's expendability. The missionary's role as instructor comes to an end when the African becomes independent, and independence, as shown in these novels, means a slap at and rejection of the paternalistic figure. Such a missionary is found in Father Anselm in *The Walled City* by Elspeth Huxley, and such a divorce of feeling is experienced by the African Benjamin and his white Christian missionary teacher. Benjamin, who had idealized and believed in Father Anselm, finds himself in the dilemma of having to turn upon the man who has made his education possible. As Benjamin enters college and the world of journalism, he becomes more aware of white prejudice, and he finds that Christianity offers no immediate, practical way of combating this prejudice.

The attack on missionaries, whether by British, South African, African, or American (though it must be emphasized that the Americans are least critical), centers on the unfinished state in which the missionaries leave the African. The mission-boy African in these novels idealizes his minister, and he desires fervently to follow the peaceful, humble ways of Christian behavior. But education brings to the African a sense of the wrongs he has suffered, including the hypocritical repressions by the Church. The African in a state of anger and rebellion turns on the missionary both personally and socially. Out of such materials the drama is made. Most novelists see the tragedy—that is, the inescapable rupture between teacher and student, older man and boy, the idealized figure and the adolescent—in terms of pity for the minister, but their sympathy is reserved for the African who must burn his bridges behind him before he can build stronger foundations underneath himself.

Corresponding with this personal drama between black and white is the social drama. The mission boy and the missionary are attacked by their neighbors for their attempts at creating understanding. The strongest attack is found in novels by South Africans, who see the missionary as a mischievous sentimentalist, but the attack is not limited merely to the region of *apartheid*. The attitude of one of Doris Lessing's characters in *The Grass Is Singing*, the action of which is set in Rhodesia, is distinguished in this manner: "'Mission Boy,' he replied. 'The only decent one I've ever had.' Like most South Africans, Dick did not like mission boys, they 'knew too much.' And in any case they should not be taught to read and write: they should be taught the dignity of labor and general usefulness to the white man" (p. 180). A character in Gerald Hanley's *Drinkers of Darkness*, the action of which is set in East Africa, says, "'Samuel, eh?' The policeman was right in, sniffing. 'That's a mission boy, I'll bet. . . . The mission boy is the curse of the country'" (p. 248). Mission-school education is blamed for the arrogant, self-assertive behavior of the African hero of Robert Lait's *Honey for Tomorrow*, the action of which is also set in East Africa. Richard Wright, who in *Black Power* recorded his impressions of a tour through Ghana, commented here on this love-hate between mission boy and missionary:

> Over and over again I found that same reaction: the Gold Coast African loved the white missionaries as long as he thought of them in the category of their teaching him to read and write, but when the same reading and writing brought home to him a knowledge of what the British had done to him, a knowledge of how his country and his culture had been shattered and exploited, he felt a rising tinge of resentment against the missionaries. Unwittingly, the missionaries had placed themselves in a strange position, a delicate position in the minds of the African people. Toward the European missionaries the African held the somewhat ambivalent attitude of love and hate he held toward almost everything Western.   (p. 149)

Missionaries have been defended, of course, in literature by English writers about Africa. The most famous example is Alan Paton's *Cry, the Beloved Country*, but significantly the major figure of this novel has been criticized as being too good, too Christian, too forgiving, and too soft to be true to the complexities of human personality. Another example is Harry Bloom's Zulu Christian minister in *Episode,* who tries to drown the black upsurge of hate in the native Location in a sea of Christian philosophy. Both these missionaries are, however, African, rather than European or white. The few European or white missionaries presented with any degree of heroism, minor though it be, are those depicted by American authors or as American characters; the Catholic emissary is also treated sympathetically by Graham Greene and Evelyn Waugh.

Among the worthy missionaries are three heroines, to be found in *Rachel Cade,* the *White Witch Doctor* (New York, 1950), and in Laura Woodbury of *Beyond the Hungry Country.* In *Rachel Cade* (New York, 1956), by Charles Mercer, a missionary nurse defies what she views as primitive superstition and prepares the African mind for the Christian faith. Louise A. Stinetorf, an American missionary who worked in the Belgian Congo, describes in *White Witch Doctor* the successful life of an American medical missionary in the Belgian Congo. In *Beyond the Hungry Country* (New York, 1954) Miss Stinetorf narrates the story of an African-born child of American missionaries who returns to Africa as an agricultural missionary after an unhappy experience as a student in the United States. Another American missionary, Esther S. Warner, wrote one novel, *The Silk-Cotton Tree,* and one fictionalized biography, *Seven Days to Lomaland,* in which American missionaries were invested with charm and virtue. The British writer John Wyllie made of the American missionary character in his novel *Riot* one of the two human bridges spanning the gap of racial misunderstanding.

Two writers whose Catholicism has played a large part in defining their attitudes have generally presented a sympathetic portrait of the missionary: Evelyn Waugh and Graham Greene. Evelyn Waugh, who satirized almost everything in his novels about Africa, paid respect to the Catholic missionary at Marodi in *Black Mischief* as the only man who had the inner strength to resist panic when the land was threatened. In *They Were Still Dancing* [7] Waugh commented: "In reaction from the proselytizing fervour of fifty years ago, there is at the moment a good deal of distrust of foreign missions. Many officials in unofficial moments will confess that if they had their way they would like to clear all the missionaries out of the country; many private persons told me that they would never engage a 'mission boy' as a servant—they were always dishonest and often insolent" (p. 272). Waugh himself remained isolated from this stream of opinion, and during a period when his writing was at its most brilliantly cynical, he composed this idyllic picture of a mission station:

> We went out together to luncheon at Kokonjiro, a convent of native girls presided over by two European nuns and a woman doctor. They wear habits and live by strict rule; here they are trained as nurses and schoolteachers. At the convent they manage a small farm and hospital, and in recreation time do skilled needlework. It does not sound very remarkable to a reader in Europe; it is astounding in Central Africa—this little island of order and sweetness in an ocean of rank barbarity; all round it for hundreds of miles lie gross jungle, bush and forest, haunted by devils and the fear of darkness, where human life merges into the cruel, automatic life of the animals; here they were singing the office just as they had been sung in Europe when the missions were little radiant points of learning and decency in a pagan wilderness. [8]

In *A Burnt-Out Case* Graham Greene draws several scathing portraits of Catholic missionaries. One of them shows a Father Thomas as a pious hypocrite partly responsible for the destruction of the hero-pilgrim. Yet in this book Greene also draws the portrait of a Catholic missionary who represents his

---

[7] British edn.: *Remote People* (London, 1931).
[8] *They Were Still Dancing*, p. 276.

calling at its highest level. Father Joseph is a good priest aware of people's errors: he does not sentimentalize or rationalize them. And he almost succeeds in his mission with Querry. If he fails, it does not mean an indictment by Greene of the missionary, but a bewildered lament by the author at the mysterious complications of human endeavor. As long ago as 1936, in *Journey Without Maps,* Greene displayed his antagonism to the "great deal of nonsense" that has "been written about missionaries" (p. 91). In this early travel book Greene compared a mission of nuns to a band of angels.

Joyce Cary also presents a series of flattering portraits of missionaries in his five novels about Nigeria, but while Cary's missionaries are sincere and hardworking they always conclude their stay in Africa confused and frustrated by events. Cary himself admitted that most people misunderstood where his sympathy lay in his first novel, *Aissa Saved,* largely about missionaries.[9]

Although there are exceptions, the general portrait of the missionary in modern novels in English about Africa is that of a confused, idealistic man often forced by circumstances into acting the fool. The missionary, through his sympathetic, Christian instruction, provides the key to enlightened Western ideas of progress, but he himself has not yet crossed the threshold of African allegiances. This is the unavoidable conflict from which the tragedy of ruptured love springs, and in its depiction most novelists reveal their complex of reactions: sympathy, pity, and painful protest.

In addition to the journalist, missionary, and police officer, the anthropologist and humanitarian come in for their share of satire and criticism in modern novels in English about Africa. Especially ridiculed are the research workers who

---

[9] Cary, "My First Novel," in *The Listener,* XLIX, No. 1259 (April 16, 1953), 637.

come to the supposedly "Dark Continent" to discover its exotic, arcane secrets and write a book about them. Such characters are found in *Scoop* and *Mandoa! Mandoa!* The humanitarians who come to Africa to prove, after research of a few weeks in a tribal community, that Africa has an equality with other civilizations are also found amusing, and satire of them is found in *Jagua Nana* by Cyprian Ekwensi, where an Englishman busily engages in note-taking without much comprehension of what is going on about him, and in *The Path of Thunder* by Peter Abrahams, where an Englishman has a sexual affair with a Cape Colored girl in order to gain first-hand "material" for his book in favor of racial equality. The quasi-intellectual is ridiculed in van der Post's *In a Province*, when a long-winded doctor of philosophy asserts that "Christ was black! My scholastic endeavours have convinced me that on this point there can't be any doubt, no doubt at all. I have it on the highest authority, the authority of the great Tertullian himself" (p. 158).

Like the journalist and missionary in modern fiction about Africa, the anthropologist and humanitarian find their chosen profession brought under intense and often fierce scrutiny. This may be one of the inevitable repercussions that stems from and reflects a shifting society, where the traditional and the outworn are shed for the new and the venturesome.

SEVEN

Neo-African Literature:
Mirror and Reality

Although South Africa has produced two waves of native black literary achievements in the twentieth century, much of this output has remained isolated from the stream of world culture. Among the representative novels in the Zulu, Sesuto, Bechuana, Cewa, and Xhosa languages are Thomas Mofolo's *Moeti oa Bochabela*,[1] and *Chaka* (Morija, Basutoland [Sesuto Book Depot], 1925);[2] John L. Dube's *U-Shembe* (Maritzburg, South Africa, 1936); R. R. R. Dhlomo's *Dingane ka Senzangakhona* (Maritzburg, South Africa, 1935); and Samuel Y. Ntara's *Headman's Enterprise*.[3]

---

[1] *The Traveller of the East,* tr. by H. Ashton (London, 1934). Mofolo has also been translated into German, in *Chaka der Zulu* (Zurich, 1953).

[2] Tr. by F. H. Dutton (London, 1931).

[3] British edn.: London, 1949. An excellent introductory reading list of native African literature, although somewhat dated, is to be found in the pamphlet "Approaches to African Literature," written and compiled by Janheinz Jahn and John Ramsaran (Ibadan, Nigeria, 1959). A much more extensive bibliography is Janheinz Jahn's *A Bibliography of Neo-African Literature* (New York, 1965). An excellent anthology, with critical apparatus of scope and depth, of various genres is to be found in *Introduction to African Literature,* ed. by Ulli Beier (Evanston, Illinois, 1967).

Only two African writers have, until the recent decade, consciously tried to bridge the gap between the African and English literary traditions. One of them, Thomas Mofolo, attempted to please his missionary teachers and friends with his fictional version of the great chieftain, Chaka, but his manuscript was denied publication for more than twenty years because the missionaries were shocked by its tales of native violence and brutality. Mofolo's novel, *Chaka*, has been called the "first African novel" by the German scholar Janheinz Jahn. In the judgment of most literary critics, it is the major achievement in early South African native literature.

Chaka is the historical figure who developed a small band of Ifenilenja tribesmen into a vast army of 400,000 men—who were undefeated at his death and whose sovereignty extended over South and Central Africa. Englishmen have called him the "Black Napoleon" of Africa, a savage and a devil; and in contradistinction, he has been described by Léopold Senghor as an exceptional leader and "the creator of the words of life."

Mofolo, a Basutoland native whose parents were Christian and who was educated at mission schools, presents many sides of Chaka. In Mofolo's novel it is Chaka who brings splendor and glory to his Bantu people; yet he is a man who is in league with the Devil. As Mofolo presents him, Chaka achieves his strength through the use of several potions, all of them coming from witchdoctors and witchwomen. As a child, he is given a medicine which enables him to kill a lion. Later he is licked by a snake as he stands in a river; the strength of this "potion" enables Chaka to kill a hyena. Yet it is this last act of strength that presages Chaka's destruction as well as his triumphs. For Chaka's father is now so fearful of his son's potency that he plots with another son to murder him. Although Chaka escapes, this plot makes him disillusioned with mankind, and when he is again visited by a supernatural spirit he chooses the role of Faust. For unlimited power he sells his soul.

Chaka is both Marlowe's Tamburlaine and Milton's Satan. Having once embarked on violence, he cannot stop. In the course of his lifetime he murders his mother, his brothers, his sweetheart, thousands of enemies, and, like the emperor Caligula, he tortures scores of innocent victims to satisfy his increasingly jaded palate. Finally, when he has conquered all and fears boredom, he is murdered by his own brothers.

To a modern audience, Chaka, possessing as he does the traditional outlines of a Faust and a Tamburlaine, has the attributes of an existentialist hero. Mofolo, a devout Christian, thought he was exposing sorcery and evil in his presentation of Chaka. Unfortunately the missionaries who controlled the printing presses in Morija, Basutoland, where the Paris Evangelical Mission had its headquarters, saw the scenes of witchcraft literally, and, judging the book a return to pagan horrors and exoticism, they were able to prevent its publication. The novel was finally published in the original Southern Sotho language and later translated into English; it has now been reissued in at least two new English editions.

Although an increasing interest in Mofolo has been evidenced by critics, it has taken a long time for Westerners to come to grips with the profundity of Mofolo's work and appreciate its visionary character. In his masterpiece *Chaka*, as well as in his own life, Mofolo attempted to reconcile Christianity with the African traditions of his ancestors. Mofolo was highly critical of Chaka's magic, and his novel is in part a defense of Christian humanism. Mofolo's disillusionment with the practices of Christian laymen and preachers, after his initial trust in Christian missionaries and their programs, are the themes that were to become pervasive throughout later African literature.[4]

---

[4] Mofolo's life story is also a record of disillusionment. A Christian mission employee, he later became a successful businessman and farmer. His farm was taken from him when the new color-bar laws were passed, and when he died in 1948 he was a poor and exhausted man.

Solomon T. Plaatje, a Bechuana, also attempted to cross traditional lines: he wrote in English and Sechuana, and translated five of Shakespeare's plays into Sechuana. Plaatje wrote and edited a weekly English and Sechuana newspaper, *Karanta ea Becoana,* for seven years and a Sechuana newspaper, *Tsala ea Batho* (The People's Friend) in 1910 at Kimberley, South Africa. Plaatje's novel, *Mhudi: An Epic of South African Native Life a Hundred Years Ago,* written at least ten years before its publication by Lovedale Press in South Africa in 1930,[5] is an attempt at blending African folk material with individually realized characters in the Western novelistic tradition; the result has been both admired and denigrated by commentators.

Plaatje's story of the two Bechuana natives who survive a raid by a warring Zulu tribe, fall in love (one episode describes the admiration which the hero inspires in his female companion when he subdues a lion by wrenching its tail), and triumph over the mistreatment they endure from the Boers whom they have aided, is leavened by humor and a sense of proportion. Although the novel contains idyllic scenes of native life, the hero Ra-Thaga, and Mhudi, who becomes his wife, are not sentimental Noble Savages but peaceful citizens forced to accept the harshness of the invading white world. The political theme of Boer cruelty is present but not overwhelming; the speech by the dying, defeated Matabele warrior Mzilikazi is dramatically prophetic as he describes the coming Boer ingratitude for the aid of the Bechuana tribe. Yet Plaatje's comments on the Boer attitude are not obtrusive even when they are bitter, and they reflect a wit that bites deeper than surface humanitarianism. His aphorisms still have a power today: "The Boers were God's chosen people, so they argued . . . they remonstrated . . . and held it unnatural to reward a Kafir [*sic*] for anything he did as liberally as if he were a baptized Christian"; and "The Boers, a race of proverbial Bible readers . . . profess Christianity to the point of bigotry." [6]

---

[5] See Ezekiel Mphahlele, *The African Image,* p. 174.
[6] Plaatje, p. 221.

Plaatje is not highly regarded by his fellow African writers today, nor is Amos Tutuola, another African whose work has been accepted by Western audiences. Tutuola, the author of some five books, writes highly symbolic folk tales in an English whose idiom sounds strange to British and American readers. His work has achieved great success in the United States, Great Britain, and France (in the original, and in translation), yet Africans have almost unanimously dismissed him as a trickster. When the journalist in Anthony Smith's *Sea Never Dry* speaks of an African writer "maltreating the 'colonial language,'" the association seems clearly to refer to Tutuola:

> Daniel said bluntly that he despised him. So, he added, did all sensible people because his simple style and inadequate spelling was letting Africa down. Daniel said he could write such tales any time he wanted, for everyone knew them. Only this man had been fool enough to try and sell them. As for the strange English, he himself had no objections to spelling words differently and maltreating the "colonial language," but he liked to see it done deliberately and not by mistake.   (p. 85)

Ignorance of Plaatje and the antagonism to Tutuola are especially significant because they constitute an ironic comment in current literary criticism about literature on Africa. Several white and black critics have suggested—the most prominent among them, Janheinz Jahn—that a major novel about Africa will have to be written by a black African, since only a black African can know what is truly going on in the heart of a black man. Such a claim may seem disproportionate if not hyperbolic to an observer removed from the scene, but in the current hysteria of black nationalism and the riding of this band wagon by liberal white supporters, the contention must be treated seriously.

The essential means of refuting such a theory should lie in the literature that has already been written; the literature in which black natives have been described by white authors, and here it is particularly instructive to look at those novels which attempt to capture the "native mind." Unfortunately most of these novels do not provide much support to a counterclaim that white writers can grasp the mind of black Africans. The early novels of native life were influenced by the work of Havelock Ellis and Sir James Frazer, whose *The Golden Bough* made obligatory a reassessment of the meaning of the word "civilization." But in spite of their serious intent and respect for African customs, the novelists interpreting the "savage" mind often painted irrelevant pictures. Edgar Wallace treated the native patronizingly; Rider Haggard and Bertram Mitford idealized him out of existence. In the 1930's a number of fictional studies appeared which attempted to show the life of native tribes before the Europeans arrived in Africa. Among the first were *The Leopard Priestess*, by Robert Rattray, and *People of the Small Arrow*, by Jack H. Driberg. Driberg's book reads like nonfiction, but Rattray's novel has a romantic air, and in its depiction of an ill-fated romance it is a kind of African *Romeo and Juliet*.

In *The Leopard Priestess* Opoku, "The Hunter," and Amalagane, "Most Beautiful," cannot admit their love because Amalagane, as a priestess of the Pentia shrine and an uncircumcised virgin, is forbidden to lie with a man. The lovers are also forbidden consummation of their love because in the Leopard fetish cult, to which they belong, all members are considered part of one family. Thus, when the passions of the two lovers override all other considerations, they are considered guilty of incest. The lovers' punishment is a death as poetic as that meted out to Romeo and Juliet. The story, which is based on fact and was told to Rattray by his African friends, represents the closest approach of its time of a white man to write a novel of African life. Rattray, the author of several anthropological studies about African civilization and a resident of West Africa for twenty-five years, was in love with the past of his adopted continent, and his novel is a valid evocation of a period which was fast disappearing. Yet, although his portrayal of African customs and ceremonies is accurate and detailed, he nonetheless invested his two main characters with a romantic European attitude.

In the 1940's two more novels by English writers appeared, and in these the setting was Africa immediately prior to the intrusion of European settlers. These were Elspeth Huxley's first novel, *Red Strangers*, written in a spare style approximating a documentary, and C. S. Forester's *The Sky and the Forest*, which imparts a highly stylized and romantic view of native life. In commenting on the difficulty which lay before her, Elspeth Huxley wrote in her foreword to *Red Strangers*:

> I am well aware that no person of one race or culture can truly interpret events from the angle of individuals belonging to a totally different race and culture. The old Kikuyu men, that rapidly dwindling number who remember life as it was lived before British rule, cannot present their point of view to us because they cannot express it in terms which we can understand. The young educated man—educated in our purely literary sense of the word—uses the thought tracks of the European; he is scarcely more able than his European teacher to interpret the feelings and outlook of the generation to whom the processes of European thought were always alien. It was the consideration that within a few years none will survive of those who can remember the way of life that existed before the white man came, that led me to make the experiment of the book. (p. viii)

Both Elspeth Huxley's and C. S. Forester's novels end with the defeat of African civilization before the onslaught of the European invasion: Elspeth Huxley's natives assimilate themselves, while Forester's Africans are annihilated by Belgian soldiers. It is revealing to compare these books, vis-à-vis their respective portrayals of black Africans, with the group of Nigerian novels published in the 1950's, all of which center upon the same milieu and period—that is, the period just before the arrival of the white man in Africa, when African civilization had developed a mature, stable order of life. The view of the black man presented in Huxley and Forester is more idealized than that found in the novels of Cyprian Ekwensi, Chinua Achebe, and T. M. Aluko. In more recent novels by white writers, however, a rather more objective picture is given of the black man's way of life in Africa before the social, political, or military invasion of Europeans. Two novels by Englishmen published in 1961, for instance—*A Man in a Mirror,* by Richard Llewellyn, and *The Brothers M,* by Tom Stacey—need no apology for their authors' understanding of the minds of their African characters.

The question of reaching the mind of the black African, of appraising his country, might be better examined by turning for a moment from Africa to larger continents of thought. Doris Lessing said in *Going Home,* "I never did believe it to be true that one has to live in a country to understand what is happening in it. I believe it even less now" (p. 105). Indeed it is perfectly true that men who have never traveled to Africa have written profoundly of its peoples and its atmospheres, as is evidenced by George Bernard Shaw's witty commentary in *The Adventures of the Black Girl in Her Search for God* (London, 1932), by Robert Shaw's psychoanalytic observations in *The Sun Doctor,* and by Saul Bellow's symbolic interpretation in *Henderson the Rain King.* And Victor Stafford Reid, a Jamaican Negro who had never lived in Kenya, was able to capture brilliantly the mind of a Mau-Mau warrior in *The Leopard* (London, 1958). Reid's achievement had less to do with Négritude, an immanent African spirit in all Negroes, than with artistic ability.

Janheinz Jahn in *Muntu* (Dusseldorf, 1958),[7] a study of the African spirit and ethic, claims that fiction written by Africans in English is not English literature, and that "literary scholars

---

[7] Tr. from the German by Marjorie Grene (London, 1961).

have not yet foreseen the rise of an independent modern
African literature based on its own traditions" (p. 155).[8] Jahn
classifies literature in English by African writers under two
categories. The first comprises the "literature of tutelage," or
works in a European style and language that promote European ideals at the expense of African culture, and in which "the
author is practicing a foreign language, follows foreign models
and expresses his thanks to his teachers" (p. 210). The second
consists of the "literature of emancipation," which crosses into
what Jahn calls "Neo-African literature." Jahn goes on to say
that "Africans could become 'Black Europeans' if they wished.
But they do not want to do so, as their representatives unanimously insist. Nor do they wish to preserve its [Africa's] basic
conceptions, of which they have become conscious in their
contact with other cultures" (p. 239). Yet for the purposes of
a critical assessment of modern fiction about Africa, it is difficult to detect the presence of a specifically "Neo-African" development or trend. The opposite seems to be the case. African
writers have followed European models at the very moment
they assail them. The ideal would be the state Jahn suggests—
an African literature that is meaningful to both African and
non-African eyes and ears. Perhaps in the work of the younger
and newer writers—the Nigerians, Achebe, Soyinka, and J. P.
Clark, and in that of the young South African writers, Richard
Rive, Lewis Nkosi, Dennis Brutus, and Ezekiel Mphahlele—this
new literature will burgeon. Certainly it is beginning to evolve.

---

[8] This and subsequent extracts from *Muntu* have been taken from the
London edn.

Selected Reading List of
Modern African Literature
through 1966

I. Bibliographies

Bridgman, John, and David E. Clark. *German Africa: A Select Annotated Bibliography*. Palo Alto, Calif., 1965 (Hoover Institution on War, Revolution and Peace).

Hoover Institution Bibliographical Series: XIV, *United States and Canadian Publications on Africa in 1961* [ditto in 1962]; XVI, *Africa South of the Sahara*.

Jahn, Janheinz. *A Bibliography of Neo-African Literature: From Africa, America, and the Caribbean*. New York, London, 1965.

Jahn, Janheinz, and John Ramsaran. *Approaches to African Literature*. Ibadan, 1959.

Northwestern University Library, *Catalog of the African Collection*. Evanston, Ill., 1962 ff.

Whyte, Morag. *Bibliography of the Works of S. G. Millin*. Johannesburg, n. d.

Work, Monroe N. *A Bibliography of the Negro in Africa and America*. New York, 1965.

II. The Literature

Dates and places of publication are given for all books. In selected cases where difficulty in locating the publisher might occur, the publisher is given. Country of origin is listed for African writers in parentheses next to their names. Most authors are listed under their actual name (when available), and cross-referenced under their chief pseudonym. Description of genre is given by means of abbreviation, at end of entry.

Genre Abbreviations		*Other Abbreviations*	
a	autobiography	Afr.	African
b	biography	Am.	American
cb	children's book	Brit.	British
d	drama	ed., eds.	edited by, editor(s)
e	essay	edn.	edition
h	history	Eng.	English
m	memoir, reminiscence	illus.	illustrated (by)
n	novel	n.d.	no date
p	poetry	repr.	reprint(ed)
s	short stories	rev.	revised
t	travel or topography	tr.	translated (by)

A. AFRICAN WRITERS

1. West Africa

Achebe, Chinua (Nigeria)
Things Fall Apart. London, 1958 (n); *No Longer at Ease*. London, 1960 (n); *Arrow of God*. London, 1964 (n); *A Man of the People*. London, 1966 (n).

Aidoo, Christina Ama Ata (Nigeria)
The Dilemma of a Ghost. London, 1965 (n).

Akpan, N. U. (Nigeria)
The Wooden Gong. London, 1965 (n).

Aluko, T. M. (Nigeria)
One Man, One Wife. Lagos, 1959 (repr. London, 1964, as *One Man, One Matchet*) (n).

Beti, Mongo (pseud. of Alexandre Biyidi) (Cameroon)
(under pseud. of Eza Boto) *Ville cruelle*. Paris, 1954 (n); *Le pauvre Christ de Bomba*. Paris, 1956 (n); *Mission terminée*. Paris, 1957. Tr. Peter Green as *Mission Accomplished*. New York, 1958 (Brit. edn., *Mission to Kala*) (n); *Le roi mira-*

culé. Paris, 1958. Tr. Peter Green as *King Lazarus.* London, 1961 (n).

Clark, John Pepper (Nigeria)
Song of a Goat. Ibadan: Mbari, Northwestern Univ. Pr.,* 1962 (d); *Poems.* Ibadan: Mbari, Northwestern Univ. Pr., 1962 (p); *America, Their America.* London, 1964 (m); *Three Plays.* London, 1964 (d); *A Reed in the Tide.* London, 1965 (p).

Conton, William (Sierra Leone)
The African. Boston, 1960 (n).

Dadié, Bernard Binlin (Ivory Coast)
Afrique debout. Paris, 1950 (p); *Légendes africaines.* Paris, 1954 (s); *Le pagne noir.* Paris, 1955 (s); *Climbié.* Paris, 1956 (n); *La ronde des jours.* Paris, 1956 (p); *Un nègre à Paris.* Paris, 1959 (n).

Damas, Léon (French Guiana, South America)
African Songs. Mbari, Northwestern Univ. Pr., 1963.

Danquah, Joseph Boakye (Ghana)
The Third Woman. London, 1943 (d).

Diop, Birago (Senegal)
Les contes d'Amadou Koumba. Paris, 1947. Tr. Dorothy S. Blair as *Tales of Amadou Koumba.* London, 1966 (s); *Les nouveaux contes d'Amadou Koumba.* Paris, 1958 (s); *Leurres et lueurs.* Paris, 1960 (p); *Contes et lavanes.* Paris, 1963 (s).

Diop, David (Senegal)
Coups de pilon. Paris, 1956 (p).

Dipoko, Mbella Sonne (Cameroon)
A Few Nights and Days. London, 1966 (n).

Easmon, Sarif (Sierra Leone)
Dear Parent and Ogre. London, 1964 (d).

Egbuna, Obi B. (Nigeria)
Wind Versus Polygamy. London, 1956 (n); *The Anthill.* London, 1966 (d).

---

* Mbari Publications' books of Ibadan, Nigeria, are distributed in the United States by Northwestern Univ. Pr., Evanston, Ill.

Ekwensi, Cyprian (Nigeria)
    The Leopard's Claw. London, 1950 (s); *People of the City.*
    London, 1954, rev. 1963 (n); *The Drummer Boy.* London,
    1960 (cb); *The Passport of Mallam Ilia.* London, 1960 (cb);
    Jagua Nana. London, 1961 (n); *Burning Grass: A Story of
    the Fulani of Northern Nigeria.* London, 1962 (n); *An Afri-
    can Night's Entertainment.* Lagos, 1962 (s); *Beautiful Feath-
    ers.* London, 1963 (n); *Lokotown.* London, 1966 (s); *Iska.*
    London, 1966 (n).

Ike, Vincent Chikwuemeka (Nigeria)
    Toads for Supper. London, 1965 (n, a).

Kane, Cheikh Hamidou (Senegal)
    L'aventure ambiguë. Paris, 1961. Tr. Katherine Woods as *Am-
    biguous Adventure.* New York, 1963 (n).

Ladipo, Duro (Nigeria)
    *Three Yoruba Plays: Oba Koso (The King Does Not Hang);
    Oba Moro (The Ghost Catcher); Oba Waja (The King Is
    Dead).* Mbari, Northwestern Univ. Pr., 1966 (Yoruba folk
    operas).

Laye, Camera (Guinea)
    L'enfant noir. Paris, 1953. Tr. James Kirkup et al. as *The Dark
    Child.* New York, 1954 (n); *Le regard du roi.* Paris, 1954. Tr.
    James Kirkup as *The Radiance of the King.* London, 1956 (n).

Maran, René (Martinique, West Indies)
    Batouala. Paris, 1921. Tr. Adele Szold Seltzer. New York, 1922
    (n); *Le Tchad de Sable et d'Or.* Paris, c. 1930 (e, t); *Le
    livre de la brousse.* Paris, 1934 (n); *Bacouya, le cynocephale.*
    Paris, 1953 (n).

Munonye, John (Nigeria)
    The Only Son. London, 1966 (n).

Niane, D. T. (Guinea)
    Sundiata: An Epic of Old Mali. Tr. G. D. Pickett. London,
    1965 (p).

Nicol, Abioseh (Dr. Davidson Nicol) (Sierra Leone)
    Two African Tales. London, 1965 (s); *The Truly Married
    Woman.* London, 1965 (s).

Nwankwo, Nkem (Nigeria)
Danda. London, 1964 (n).

Nwanodi, Okogbule Glory (Nigeria)
Icheke. Mbari, Northwestern Univ. Pr., 1965 (p).

Nzekwu, Onuora (Nigeria)
Wand of Noble Wood. London, 1961 (n); *Blade Among the Boys*. London, 1962 (n); *Highlife for Lizards*. London, 1965 (n).

Okara, Gabriel (Nigeria)
The Voice. London, 1964 (n).

Okigbo, Christopher (Nigeria)
Heavensgate. Mbari, Northwestern Univ. Pr., 1963 (p); *Limits*. Mbari, Northwestern Univ. Pr., 1964 (p).

Ousmane, Sembene (Senegal)
Le docker noir. Paris, 1956 (n); *O pays, mon beau peuple!* Paris, 1957 (n); *Les bouts de bois de Dieu*. Paris, 1960. Tr. Francis Price as *God's Bits of Wood*. New York, 1962 (n); *Voltaïque*. Paris, 1962 (s); *L'harmattan*. Paris, 1964 (n).

Peters, Lenrie (Gambia)
Poems. Mbari, Northwestern Univ. Pr., 1965 (p).

Sam, Gilbert (Ghana)
A Christmastide Tragedy. Accra, Ghana: Gillisam Publishing Syndicate, 1956 (s); *Who Killed Inspector Kwasi Minta?* Accra: Gillisam Publishing Syndicate, 1956 (s); *Love in the Grave*. Accra: Gillisam Publishing Syndicate, 1959 (n).

Segre, André (Portuguese W. Afr.)
Mahogany. London, 1948 (n).

Selormey, Francis (Ghanaian Togoland)
The Narrow Path. London, 1966 (n, a).

Senghor, Léopold Sédar (Senegal)
Poèmes. Paris, 1964 (p); *Selected Poems*. Tr. John Reed and Clive Wake. New York, 1964 (p).

Socé, Ousmane (Senegal)
Karim. Paris, 1935 (n); *Mirages de Paris*. Paris, 1956 (n, p); *Contes et légendes d'Afrique noire*. Paris, 1962 (s); *Rythmes du khalam*. Paris, 1962 (p).

Soyinka, Wole (Nigeria)
  A Dance of the Forests. London, 1963 (d); *The Lion and the Jewel.* London, 1963 (d); *Three Plays: The Swamp-Dwellers. The Trials of Brother Jero. The Strong Breed.* Mbari, Northwestern Univ. Pr., 1963 (d); *Five Plays* (includes all five of the above-mentioned plays). London, 1965 (d); *The Interpreters.* London, 1965 (n); *The Road.* Ibadan, London [Oxford Univ. Pr.], 1965 (d).

Tutuola, Amos (Nigeria)
  The Palm-Wine Drinkard and His Dead Palm-Wine Tapster in the Dead's Town. London, 1952, New York, 1953 (n); *My Life in the Bush of Ghosts.* New York, London, 1954 (n); *Simbi and the Satyr of the Dark Jungle.* London, 1956 (n); *The Brave African Huntress.* London, 1958 (n); *Feather Woman of the Jungle.* London, 1962 (n).

Williams, George Awoonor (Ghana)
  Rediscovery and Other Poems. Mbari, Northwestern Univ. Pr., 1965 (p).

2. Central Africa

Kagame, Alexis (Rwanda)
  La divine pastorale. Tr. (into French) Alexis Kagame. Brussels, 1952-1955. 2 vols. (p).

Malonga, Jean (Congo)
  Coeur d'Aryenne. Paris, 1954 (n); *La légende de M'Pfoumou Ma Mazono.* Paris, 1954 (n).

Tchicaya U Tam'si, Gérald Félix (Congo)
  Le mauvais sang. Paris, 1955 (p); *Feu de brousse.* Paris, 1957. Tr. Sangodare Akanji as *Brush Fire.* Mbari, Northwestern Univ. Pr., 1964 (p); *A triche-coeur.* Paris, 1958 (p); *Epitomé.* Tunis: Société Nationale d'Edition et de Diffusion, 1962 (p).

3. East Africa

Gatheru, Mugo (Kenya)
  A Child of Two Worlds. London, 1965 (a).

Kachingwe, Aubrey (Malawi)
No Easy Task. London, 1965 (n).

Ngugi, James (Kenya)
Weep Not, Child. London, 1964 (n); *The River Between.*
London, 1965 (n).

Ntari, Samuel Yosia (Malawi)
Man of Africa. Tr. Cullen Young. London: Religious Tract
Society, 1934 (n); *Headman's Enterprise.* Ed. Cullen Young.
London: Lutterworth Pr., 1949 (Eng. version) (n).

Nyabongo, (Prince) Akiki K. (Uganda)
Story of an African Chief. New York, 1935 (a).

Rabéarivelo, Jean-Joseph (Malagasy)
24 Poems. Tr. Gerald Moore and Ulli Beier. Mbari, Northwestern Univ. Pr., 1962 (Eng. version) (p).

Ranaivo, Flavien (Malagasy)
Mes chansons de toujours. Paris, 1955 (p).

4. South Africa

Abrahams, Peter
Dark Testament. London, 1942 (s); *Song of the City.* London, 1946 (n); *Mine Boy.* London, 1946 (n); *The Path of
Thunder.* New York, 1948 (n); *Wild Conquest.* New York,
1950 (n); *Return to Goli.* London, 1953 (e); *Tell Freedom.*
London, 1954 (a); *A Wreath for Udomo.* New York, London,
1956 (n); *A Night of Their Own.* London, 1965 (n).

Barnby, Henry George
Poems, 1938 to 1945: From Balgowan to Bologna. Durban,
S. Afr., 1945 (p).

Barwin, Victor
*Millionaires and Tatterdemalions: Stories of Jewish Life in
South Africa.* London, 1952 (s).

Bennett, Jack
Jamie. Boston, 1963 (n); *Mister Fisherman.* Boston, 1965 (n);
The Hawk Alone. Boston, 1966 (n); *Ocean Road.* London,
1966 (n).

Bloom, Harry
 Episode. London, 1956 (n); *Whittaker's Wife*. London, 1962
 (n).

Bosman, Elizabeth J. (pseud.: Marie Linde)
 Among Privileged People. London, 1927 (n) (Afrikaner life).

Brutus, Dennis (Southern Rhodesia)
 Sirens, Knuckles, Boots. Mbari, Northwestern Univ. Pr., 1964
 (p).

Campbell, Roy (Ignatius Roy Dunnachie Campbell)
 Selective list: *The Flaming Terrapin*. London, 1924 (p); *The
 Wayzgoose, a South African Satire*. London, 1928 (p);
 Adamastor. London, 1930 (p); *The Gum Trees*. London,
 1930 (p); *Poems*. Paris, 1930; *The Georgiad: A Satirical
 Fancy in Verse*. London, 1931; *Pomegranates*. London, 1932
 (p); *Flowering Reeds*. London, 1933 (p); *Broken Record*.
 London, 1934 (m); *Mithraic Emblems*. London, 1936 (p);
 Flowering Rifle. London, 1939 (p); *Sons of the Mistral*. Lon-
 don, 1941 (p); *Talking Bronco*. London, 1946 (p); *Collected
 Poems*. London. Vol. I, 1949 (Vol. II, 1957; Vol. III [transla-
 tions], 1960); *Light on a Dark Horse, 1901-1935*. London,
 1951 (a); *The Mamba's Precipice*. London, 1953 (cb); *Poems*,
 ed. and with Introd. by Uys Krige. Cape Town, 1960.

Cleeve, Brian T.
 Portrait of My City. London, 1952 (n); *Birth of a Dark Soul*.
 London, 1954 (Am. edn., *Night Winds*, Boston) (n).

Cloete, Stuart.
 Turning Wheels. London, 1937 (n); *Watch for the Dawn*.
 Boston, 1939 (n); *The Hill of Doves*. Boston, 1941 (n); *The
 Young Men and the Old*. Boston, 1941 (p); *Congo Song*.
 Boston, 1943 (n); *African Portraits*. London, 1946 (b of Paul
 Kruger, Cecil Rhodes, and Lobengula, Last King of the Mata-
 bele); *The Curve and the Tusk: A Novel of Change among
 Elephants and Men*. Boston, 1952 (n); *The African Giant*.
 Illus. Rehna Cloete. Boston, 1955 (t, m); *Mamba*. Boston,
 1956 (n); *The Mask*. Boston, 1957 (n); *The Soldiers' Peaches*.
 Boston, 1959 (s); *The Fiercest Heart*. Boston, 1960 (n);
 Rags of Glory. New York, 1963 (n).

Cope, Jack
The Fair House. London, 1955 (n); *The Road to Ysterberg.*
London, 1957 (n); *The Golden Oriole.* London, 1958 (n);
Albino. London, 1964 (n).

De Graft, J.
Sons and Daughters. London, 1965 (d).

Freedman, Marian
The Slap. London, 1962 (n).

Fula, Arthur Nuthall
Johannie giet die beeld. Johannesburg: Afrikaanse Pers-Boek-
handel, 1954 (n); *Met erbarming, o Here.* Johannesburg:
Afrikaanse Pers-Boekhandel, 1957 (n).

Glanville, Ernest
Selective list: *Tales from the Veld.* London, 1897 (s); *A
Beautiful Rebel.* London, 1902, repr. 1921 (n); *The Diamond
Seekers.* London, 1903 (n); *Tyopa.* London, 1920 (n); *Claw
and Fang.* London, 1923 (s); *The Hunter: A Story of Bush-
man Life.* London, 1926 (n).

Gordimer, Nadine
"The First Circle," in *Six One-Act Plays.* Pretoria, S. Afr.,
1949, pp. 47-70 (d); *Face to Face.* Johannesburg: Silver Leaf
Books, 1949 (s); *The Soft Voice of the Serpent.* London,
1952 (s); *The Lying Years.* London, 1953 (n); *Six Feet of
the Country.* London, 1956 (s); *A World of Strangers.* London, 1958 (n); *Friday's Footprints.* London, 1960 (s); *Occasion for Loving.* London, 1963 (n); *The Late Bourgeois
World.* London, 1966 (n).

Hutchinson, Alfred
Road to Ghana. London, 1960 (a, n); *The Rain Killers.* London, 1964 (d).

Jabavu, Noni
Drawn in Colour: African Contrasts. London, 1960 (a, s);
The Ochre People. London, 1963 (a, s).

Jacobson, Dan
The Trap. London, 1955 (n); *The Price of Diamonds.* London, 1955 (n); *A Dance in the Sun.* London, 1956 (n); *A*

Long Way from Home. London, 1958 (s); *The Zulu and the Zeide.* Boston, 1959 (s); *No Further West.* London, 1959 (e); *Evidence of Love.* Boston, 1961 (n); *Time of Arrival.* London, 1963 (e); *Beggar My Neighbour.* London, 1964 (s); *The Beginners.* London, 1966 (n).

Knight, Brigid
  See Sinclair, K. H.

Kuper, Hilda (Southern Rhodesia)
  Bite of Hunger. New York, 1965 (n).

La Guma, Alex
  A Walk in the Night. Mbari, Northwestern Univ. Pr., 1962 (n); *And a Threefold Cord.* London, 1965 (n) [Berlin, 1964].

Lanham, Peter
  See Parker, C. J. L.

Lessing, Doris (Southern Rhodesia)
  The Grass Is Singing. London, 1950 (n); *This Was the Old Chief's Country.* London, 1951 (s); *Martha Quest* (Vol. 1 of "Children of Violence" series). London, 1952 (n); *Five Short Novels: A Home for the Highland Cattle, The Other Woman, Eldorado, The Antheap, Hunger.* London, 1953 (n); *A Proper Marriage* (Vol. 2 of "Children of Violence" series). London, 1954 (n); *Retreat to Innocence.* London, 1956 (n); *The Habit of Loving.* London, 1957 (s); *Going Home.* London, 1957 (m); *A Ripple from the Storm* (Vol. 3 of "Children of Violence" series). London, 1958 (n); *Fourteen Poems.* Northwood, Middlesex: Scorpion Pr., 1959 (p); *In Pursuit of the English: A Documentary.* London, 1960 (a); *The Golden Notebook.* London, 1962 (n); *Play with a Tiger.* London, 1962 (d); *A Man and Two Women.* London, 1963 (s); *Landlocked* (Vol. 4 of "Children of Violence" series). London, 1964 (n); *African Stories.* London, 1964 (s) ["Children of Violence," a planned series of 5 novels, has appeared in the United States in 2 vols.: *Martha Quest* and *A Proper Marriage.* New York, 1965; *A Ripple from the Storm* and *Landlocked.* New York, 1966].

Lewis, Ethelreda
  The Flying Emerald. London, 1925 (n); *Mantis.* London, 1926 (n).

Linde, Marie
    See Bosman, Elizabeth J.

Livingstone, Douglas
    Sjambok and Other Poems from Africa. London, 1965 (p).

Lyttle, David
    The Goddam White Man. London, 1961 (n).

Markowitz, Arthur
    The Daughter. New York, 1951 (n) [*Facing North.* Johannesburg, 1949].

Matshikiza, Tod
    Chocolates for My Wife. London, 1961 (d).

Millin, Sarah Gertrude
    Note: All the undermentioned works were originally published in London. *The Dark River.* 1919 (n); *Middle-Class.* 1921. (n); *Adam's Rest.* 1922 (n); *The Jordans.* 1923 (n); *God's Step-Children.* 1924, rev. 1951 (Am. edn., *God's Stepchildren*) (n); *Mary Glenn.* 1925 (n); *An Artist in the Family.* 1928 (n); *The Coming of the Lord.* 1928 (n); *The Fiddler.* 1929 (n); *Men on a Voyage.* 1930 (e); *The Sons of Mrs. Aab.* 1931 (n); *Rhodes.* 1933, rev. 1952 (b); *The South Africans.* 1941 (e, h); *Three Men Die.* 1934 (n); *General Smuts.* 1936 (b); *What Hath a Man?* 1938 (n); *The Herr Witchdoctor.* 1941 (Am. edn., *The Dark Gods*) (n); *The Night Is Long.* 1941 (a); *South Africa.* 1941 (e); *King of the Bastards.* 1950 (n); *The People of South Africa.* 1951 (rev. edn. of *The South Africans*) (e, h); *The Burning Man.* 1952 (n); *The Measure of My Days.* 1955 (a); *The Wizard Bird.* 1962 (n).

Modisane, Bloke (pseud. of William Modisane)
    Blame Me on History. London, 1963 (s).

Mofolo, Thomas (Basutoland)
    Moeti oa bochabela. Morija, Basutoland: Morija Sesuto Book Depot, 1912. Tr. H. Ashton, from Southern Sotho, as *The Traveller of the East.* London, 1934 (n); *Chaka.* Morija, Basutoland; Morija Sesuto Book Depot, 1925 (Eng. version, London, 1931, repr. 1949, 1960) (n).

Mopeli-Paulus, Attwell Sidwell (Basutoland)
    (with Peter Lanham) *Blanket Boy's Moon.* London, New York,

1953 (n); (with Miriam Basner) *Turn to the Dark*. London, 1956 (n).

Mphahlele, Ezekiel
Man Must Live. Cape Town, 1947 (s); *Down Second Avenue*. London, 1959 (a); *The Living and Dead*. Ibadan, 1961 (s); *The African Image*. London, 1962 (e, c).

Muir, Daphne (Daphne de Waal Muir)
Soldiers Immortal. Cape Town and Oxford, 1917 (p); *A Virtuous Woman*. London, 1929 (n); *The Lost Crusade*. London, 1930 (n); *The Secret Bird*. London, 1930 (n); *Very Heaven*. London, 1934 (n).

Nkosi, Lewis
The Rhythm of Violence. London, 1964 (d); *Home and Exile*. London, 1965 (a).

Noble, Alexander
The Boy with a Flute. London, 1962 (n).

Parker, C. J. L. (pseud.: Peter Lanham)
(with A. S. Mopeli-Paulus) *Blanket Boy's Moon*. London, 1953 (n) (based on an original story by A. S. Mopeli-Paulus).

Paton, Alan
Cry, the Beloved Country. London, 1948 (n); *Too Late the Phalarope*. London, 1953 (n); *The Land and People of South Africa*. Philadelphia, 1955 (e); *Hope for South Africa*. London, 1958 (e); *Debbie, Go Home*. London, 1961 (Am. edn., *Tales from a Troubled Land*) (s); *Hofmeyr*. London, 1965 (b).

Plaatje, Solomon T.
Mhudi, An Epic of South African Life a Hundred Years Ago. Lovedale, S. Afr.: Lovedale Pr., 1930 (n).

Plomer, William
Turbott Wolfe. London, 1926, repr. 1965, with Introd. by Laurens van der Post (n); *I Speak of Africa*. London, 1927 (7s, 3n, 2 plays for puppets); *Cecil Rhodes*. London, 1933 (b); *Double Lives*. London, 1943 (a); *Four Countries*. London, 1949 (s).

Rive, Richard
Emergency. London, 1964 (n).

Rooke, Daphne
    Mittee. London, 1951 (n) (S. Afr.); *A Grove of Fever Trees.*
    London, 1951 (n) (S. Afr.); *Ratoons.* London, 1953 (n)
    (S. Afr.); *Wizards' Country.* London, 1957 (n) (S. Afr.);
    A Lover for Estelle. London, 1961 (n) (S. Afr.); *The Grey-*
    ling. London, 1962 (n) (S. Afr.).

Schreiner, Olive
    (first published under pseud. of Ralph Iron) *The Story of an*
    African Farm. London, 1883 (n); (first published under
    pseud. of Ralph Iron) *Dreams.* London, 1891 (s); *Dream Life*
    and Real Life. London, 1893 (s); *Trooper Peter Halket of*
    Mashonaland. London, 1897 (s); *An English-South African's*
    View of the Situation: Words in Season. London, 1899 (e);
    Stories, Dreams and Allegories, ed. S. C. Cronwright-Schreiner.
    London, 1923; *Thoughts on South Africa.* London, 1923 (e);
    Letters, 1876-1920, ed. S. C. Cronwright-Schreiner. London,
    1924; *From Man to Man.* London, 1926 (n); *Undine: A Queer*
    Little Child. London, 1929 (n).

Segal, Albert
    Johannesburg Friday. London, 1954 (n)

Sinclair, K. H. (pseud.: Brigid Knight)
    Walking the Whirlwind. London, 1940 (n); *The Sun Climbs*
    Slowly. London, 1942 (Am. edn., *Westward the Sun*) (n);
    Southern Cross. London, 1949 (n).

Smith, Pauline
    The Little Karoo. London, 1925 (s); *The Beadle.* London,
    1926 (n); *Platkops Children.* Illus. Barbara Shaw. London,
    1935 (e).

Stein, Sylvester
    Second-Class Taxi. London, 1958 (n).

Thesen, Hjalmar
    The Echoing Cliffs. Decorations Margaret Lord. New York,
    1964 (n).

Thompson, Kate
    Great House. London, 1955 (n); *Mandevilla.* Boston, 1957
    (n); *Sugar Bird.* London, 1963 (n); *Richard's Way.* London,
    1965 (n).

Van der Post, Laurens
  In a Province. London, 1934, repr. 1953 (n); *Venture to the
  Interior.* London, 1954 (m, t); *The Face beside the Fire.* Lon-
  don, 1953 (n); *Flamingo Feather.* London, 1955 (n); *The
  Dark Eye in Africa.* London, 1955, repr. New York, 1965
  (e); *The Lost World of the Kalahari.* London, 1958 (h, t, e);
  The Heart of the Hunter. London, 1962 (e).

Van Rensburg, Helen and Louwrens
  Death in a Dark Pool. London, 1954 (n); *The Man with Two
  Ties.* London, 1955 (n).

Venter, Frans
  Dark Pilgrim. London, 1959 (n) (Afrikaner life).

Young, Florence E. M.
  Laws of Chance. New York, 1918 (n); *Shadows of the Past.*
  New York, 1919 (n); *Almonds of Life.* New York, 1920 (n).

B. NON-AFRICAN WRITERS

(The same genre abbreviations are continued in this listing.
The locale of the book, if a novel and for some other works such
as short stories/memoirs, is given at the end of the entry unless
the title itself suggests the setting.)

Allen, Clifford E.
  The Underlings. London, 1952 (n) (S. Afr.).

Altman, Phyllis
  The Law of the Vultures. London, 1952 (n) (S. Afr.).

Ashley, Gerald
  Tiger Burning. London, 1954 (n) (W. Afr.).

Baily, Francis Evans
  Woman's Privilege. New York, 1936 (n) (E. Afr.).

Baker, Richard St. B.
  Kabongo: The Story of a Kikuyu Chief. London, 1955 (n);
  Kamiti. London, 1958 (n) (E. Afr.).

Baptist, R. H. (pseud.)
  Love at the Mission. Boston, 1938 (n) (S. Afr.).

Battersby, Henry F. P. (pseud.: Francis Prevost)
The Edge of Doom. London, 1919 (n) (E. Afr.).

Beadle, Charles
Witch-doctors. London, 1922 (n) (C. Afr.).

Beaver, Harold
The Confessions of Jotham Simiyu. London, 1965 (n) (Kenya);
Pardoner's Tale. London, 1966 (n) (Kenya).

Bellow, Saul
Henderson, the Rain King. New York, 1959 (n) (C. Afr.).

Berman, Ben Lucien
Rooster Crows for a Day. Illus. Alice Caddy. New York, 1945
(n) (Congo).

Berthoud, Ferdinand
Legs Parson: A Story of Up-country Africa. New York, 1924
(n).

Best, Herbert
The Mystery of the Flaming Hut. New York, 1932 (n) (Nigeria); *A Rumour of Drums.* London, 1962 (n) (W. Afr.).

Bingley, John
Mr. Khoury. London, 1952 (n) (W. Afr.).

Black, Hermina
Shadows of Roses. London, 1960 (n) (S. Afr.).

Blixen, Karen (Karen Christine Blixen Finecke, Baroness Blixen)
(pseud.: Isak Dinesen)
Out of Africa. London, 1937 (m, t, e) (Kenya); *Shadows on
the Grass.* London, 1960 (s) (Kenya).

Bradley, Kenneth C.
Africa Notwithstanding. London, 1932 (e); *Hawks Alighting.*
London, 1933 (Am. edn., *Beware the Hawks!*) (n) (E. Afr.);
The Diary of a District Officer. London, 1943, rev. 1947 (a).

Bradley, Mary H.
The Road of Desperation. New York, 1932 (n) (S. Afr.).

Brett, Rosalind
Love This Stranger. London, 1951 (n) (S. Afr.).

Brook, Ian (pseud.)
Jimmy Riddle. London, 1961 (n) (E. Afr.).

Broome, Adam
  The Porro Palaver. London, 1929 (n) (W. Afr.).

Buchan, John (Baron Tweedsmuir)
  Selective list: *Prester John.* London, 1910 (n) (S. Afr.); *The Island of Sheep.* London, 1936 (Am. edn., *The Man from the Norlands*) (n) (S. Afr.).

Buchanan-Gould, Vera
  Vast Heritage. Bellville, Cape Province, S. Afr., 1953 (n) (S. Afr.).

Buchholtz, Johannes
  The Saga of Frank Dove. Tr. (from Danish) Eugene Gay-Tifft. New York, 1938 (n) (S. Afr.).

Burgess, Anthony
  See Wilson, John Anthony Burgess

Burton, Julia, and Phyllis Louisa Garlick
  Bless This Roof. London, 1953 (n) (Nigeria).

Byron, Ronald
  Hamilton Avenue. London, 1957 (n) (S. Afr.).

Cary, Joyce
  Selective list: *Aissa Saved.* London, 1932 (n) (Nigeria); *An American Visitor.* London, 1933 (n) (Nigeria); *The African Witch.* London, 1936 (n) (Nigeria); *Castle Corner.* London, 1938 (n) (Nigeria and Ireland); *Mister Johnson.* London, 1939 (n) (Nigeria); *The Case for African Freedom.* London, 1944 (e); *Britain and West Africa.* London, 1947 (e, h); "Africa Yesterday: One Ruler's Burden," in *The Reporter* (May 15, 1951), pp. 21-24 (e); "Christmas in Africa," in *Esquire,* XL (Dec. 1953), 101, 208 (e); *Spring Song.* New York, 1960 (s).

Castle, E. B.
  Growing Up in East Africa. London, 1966 (a, e).

Catto, Max (Maxwell Jeffrey Catto)
  Gold in the Sky. London, 1957 (n) (C. Afr.).

Caute, David
  At Fever Pitch. London, 1959 (n) (W. Afr.); *The Decline of the West.* London, 1966 (n) (C. Afr.).

Chamberlain, George Agnew
Two on a Safari. Indianapolis, 1935 (n) (E. Afr.).

Charteris, Hugo
Picnic at Porokorro. London, 1958 (n) (W. Afr.).

Ching, Donald Stanley
Ivory Tales. London, 1950 (s).

Christian, Carol (pseud.)
Into Strange Country. London, 1959 (n) (Nigeria).

Clark, William
Number 10. London, 1967 (n) (E. Afr.).

Clinton, I. A.
The Clarkes Go South. Decorations Joan Chamberlain. London, 1951 (n) (S. Afr.).

Collison, W.
Congo Landing. New York, 1934 (n).

Conchon, Georges
L'état sauvage. Paris, 1957. Tr. Peter Fryer as *The Savage State.* New York, London, 1965 (n) (W. and C. Afr.).

Conrad, Joseph
Tales of Unrest. London, 1898, repr. 1925 (s); *Heart of Darkness.* London, 1902, many repr. (n) (Congo).

Cory, Desmond
See MacCarthy, John Lloyd

Coulter, Stephen
The Loved Enemy. London, 1952 (n) (W. Afr.).

Craig, Denys
See Stoll, Dennis Gray

Croft-Cooke, Rupert
Three Times for Nicholas. London, 1951 (n) (E. Afr.).

Crofts, Freeman Wills
The Groote Park Murder. London, 1924, repr. 1946 [Penguin] (n) (S. Afr.).

Davidson, Basil
The Rapids. London, 1956 (n) (W. Afr.).

Dawson, A. J.
   An African Night's Entertainment. London, 1900 (n) (Nigeria).

Deane, Norman
   Look At Murder. London, 1952 (n) (Natal).

DeCaire, E.
   Umgasi Diamonds. London, 1954 (n) (Tanganyika) .

Delius, Anthony
   A Young Traveller in South Africa. Chicago, 1959 (t); *The Last Division.* Cape Town [P. Koston] and London, 1940 (p); *The Day Natal Took Off.* London, 1963 (n).

De Polnay, Peter
   The Umbrella Thorn. London, 1946 (n) (Kenya).

Desmond, Hugh
   The Jacaranda Murders. London, 1951 (n) (Natal).

Dinesen, Isak
   See Blixen, Karen

Diolé, Philippe
   L'Okapi. Paris, 1963. Tr. Peter Green as *Okapi Fever.* New York, 1965 (n) (Congo).

Divine, Arthur (pseud.: David Divine)
   Wine of Good Hope. London, 1939 (n) (S. Afr.); *The Adventures of Juma.* London, 1949 (n) (S. Afr.); *The Golden Fool.* London, 1954 (n) (S. Afr.); *Six Great Explorers: Frobisher, Cook, Mungo Park, Burton, Livingstone, Scott.* London, 1954 (h, e).

Dobson, K. A.
   The Inescapable Wilderness. London, 1953 (n) (E. Afr.); *District Commissioner.* London, 1954 (n) (E. Afr.); *Colour Blind.* London, 1955 (n) (E. Afr.).

Driberg, Jack H.
   People of the Small Arrow. London, 1930 (n, e) (E. Afr.).

England, Jane
   See Jervis, V. N. S.

Farran, Roy
   Jungle Chase. London, 1951 (n) (Rhodesia).

Fazarkerly, George Raymond
Kongoni. London, 1955 (n) (E. Afr.).

Fielding, Ann
See Mostyn, Anita Mary

Fitzpatrick, James P.
Jock of the Bushveld. Illus. E. Caldwell. London, 1907, repr. 1949 (s).

Flaiano, E.
Short-Cut. Tr. (from Italian) Stuart Hood. New York, 1946 (n) (E. Afr.).

Fletcher, Inglis
Red Jasmine. New York, 1932 (n) (E. Afr.).

Forester, C. S.
The African Queen. London, 1935 (n) (Congo); *The Sky and the Forest*. London, 1948 (n) (C. Afr.).

Freestone, Basil
Golden Drum. London, 1954 (n) (W. Afr.).

Fuller, Blair
A Far Place. New York, 1957 (n) (E. and S. Afr.).

Fullerton, Alexander
Bury the Past. London, 1954 (n) (S. Afr.).

Gale, William Daniel
Black Sunset. London, 1954 (n) (Matabele War, S. Afr.).

Gardiner, Gordon
The Pattern of Chance. London, 1930 (n) (Cape Colony, S. Afr.).

Garnier, Christine
Fetish. Tr. (from French) Naomi Walford. New York, 1952 (n) (W. Afr.).

Gary, Romain
The Roots of Heaven. Tr. (from French) Jonathan Griffin. New York, 1958 (n) (Equatorial Afr.).

Gaunt, Mary
The Uncounted Cost. London, 1904 (n) (W. Afr.).

Gerahty, D. C. (pseud.: Robert Standish)
African Guinea Pig. London, 1958 (n) (Kenya).

Gerard, Francis
The Return of Sanders of the River. London, 1938 (n) (W. Afr.); *The Justice of Sanders.* London, 1951 (n) (W. Afr.).

Gibbs, Henry
Twilight in South Africa. London, 1950 (e); *Africa on a Tightrope.* London, 1954 (e); *Background to Bitterness: The Story of South Africa 1652-1954.* London, 1954 (h); *The Splendour and the Dust.* London, 1955 (n) (S. Afr.); *The Winds of Time.* London, 1956 (n) (S. Afr.); *Thunder at Dawn.* London, 1957 (n) (S. Afr.). See also Harvester, Simon.

Godden, Jan
Mrs. Panapoulis. London, 1959 (n) (E. Afr.).

Gordon, Gerald
Let the Day Perish. London, 1952 (n) (S. Afr.); *The Crooked Rain.* London, 1954 (n) (E. Afr.).

Gore-Brown, Robert
The Crater. New York, 1926 (n) (E. Afr.).

Green, John
A Retreat in the Sun. London, 1957 (n) (W. Afr.).

Greene, Graham
Journey Without Maps. London, 1936 (t, m) (Sierra Leone, Liberia); *The Heart of the Matter.* London, 1948 (n) (W. Afr.); *A Burnt-Out Case.* London, 1961 (n) (Congo); *In Search of a Character: Two African Journals.* New York, London, 1962 (r) (Congo, W. Afr.).

Greene, L. P.
The Major—Diamond Buyer. New York, 1924 (n) (S. Afr.).

Griffin, Gwyn
Something of an Achievement. London, 1960 (n) (S. E. Afr.); *A Scorpion on a Stone: Six Stories of Love and Betrayal in Modern Africa.* London, 1965 (s); *A Last Lamp Burning.* London, 1966 (n) (S. E. Afr.).

Griffiths, Reginald
Children of Pride. London, 1959 (n) (S. Afr.); *This Day's Madness.* London, 1960 (n) (S. Afr.).

Haggard, H. Rider
Selective list. All the undermentioned works were originally published in London. The fiction has either Southeast or South Central Africa for its locale. *Cetywayo and His White Neighbours.* 1882 (e); *King Solomon's Mines.* 1885 (n); *She.* 1887 (n); *Jess.* 1887 (n); *Allan Quatermain.* 1887 (n); *Maiwa's Revenge.* 1888 (n); *Cleopatra.* 1889 (n); *Allan's Wife.* 1889 (s); *Nada the Lily.* 1892 (n); *The History of the Transvaal.* 1889 (Am. edn., *The Last Boer War*) (h); *Black Heart and White Heart.* 1900 (s); *The New South Africa.* 1900 (e); *Ayesha: The Return of She.* 1905 (n); *Queen Sheba's Ring.* 1910 (n); *Marie.* 1912 (n) (life of Dingaan, King of the Zulus [c. 1837]; *The Holy Flower.* 1915 (Am. edn., *Allan and the Holy Flower*) (n); *The Ivory Child.* 1916 (n); *The Ancient Allan.* 1920 (n); *The Missionary and the Witch-Doctor.* 1920 (n); *Smith and the Pharaohs.* 1920 (s); *She and Allan.* 1922 (n); *Heu-Heu.* 1924 (n); *The Days of My Life.* 1926 (a).

Hahn, Emily
With Naked Foot. New York, 1934 (n) (Congo); *Africa to Me: Person to Person.* New York, 1965 (t).

Hamber, T. R.
Mine. London, 1953 (n) (W. Afr.); *Closed Area.* London, 1955 (n) (Nigeria).

Hanley, Gerald
Consul at Sunset. London, 1951 (n) (E. Afr.); *The Year of the Lion.* London, 1954 (n) (E. Afr.); *Drinkers of Darkness.* London, 1955 (n) (E. Afr.); *Gilligan's Last Elephant.* London, 1962 (n) (E. Afr.).

Hardinge, Rex
South African Cinderella: A Trek through ex-German West Africa. London, 1937 (t); *Murder on the Veld.* London, 1954 (n).

Hardy, Ronald
The Men from the Bush. New York, 1959 (n) (Tanganyika).

Hargreaves, Elisabeth
  Green Felicity. London, 1951 (n) (W. Afr.); *Handful of Silver.* London, 1954 (n) (W. Afr.).
Harman, Neal
  Peace and Peter Lamont. London, 1950 (n) (S. Afr.); *Yours Truly, Angus MacIvor.* London, 1952 (n) (S. Afr.).
Harris, John
  The Claws of Mercy. London, 1955 (n) (W. Afr.).
Harvester, Simon (pseud. of Henry Gibbs)
  Sheep May Safely Graze. London, 1948 (n) (E. Afr.); *Obols for Charon.* London, 1951 (s) (S. Afr.). See also Gibbs, Henry.
Harwood, Ronald
  George Washington September, Sir! London, 1961 (n) (S. Afr.).
Hastings, Archibald
  Gone Native. New York, 1929 (n) (Nigeria).
Head, Matthew
  The Cabinda Affair. London, 1950 (n) (C. Afr.).
Helander, Gunnar
  Black Rhapsody. Tr. (from Swedish) Margery Osberg. New York, 1956 (n) (S. Afr.).
Hemingway, Ernest
  Green Hills of Africa. New York, 1935 (a, n, t) (E. Afr.).
Hervey, Harry C.
  The Iron Widow. New York, 1931 (n) (W. Afr.); *Barracoon.* New York, 1950 (n) (W. Coast of Afr.).
Heuser, Kurt
  Journey Inward. Tr. (from German) Willa and Edwin Muir. New York, 1932 (n) (C. Afr.).
Heward, Leslie John
  If This Be Magic. London, 1955 (n) (C. Afr.).
Hinde, Thomas
  A Place Like Home. London, 1962 (n) (Kenya); *The Cage.* London, 1963 (n) (Kenya).

Hofmeyer, Hans
The Skin Is Deep. London, 1958 (n) (S. Afr.).

Holles, Robert Owen
The Bribe Scorners. London, 1956 (n) (Nigeria); *The Siege of Battersea*. London, 1962 (repr., 1964, as *Guns at Batasi*) (n) (W. Afr.).

Holtby, Winifred
Mandoa! Mandoa! London, 1933 (n) (E. Afr.).

Horn, Alfred A.
Trader Horn (Vols. 1 and 2 of *The Life and Works of Trader Horn*). Ed. Ethelreda Lewis. London, 1927 (b, s) (W. Afr.); *The Waters of Africa* (Vol. 3 of *The Life and Works of Trader Horn*). Ed. Ethelreda Lewis. London, 1929 (b, s).

Horne, Geoffrey
Land of No Escape. London, 1958 (n) (W. Afr.); *The Man Who Was Chief*. London, 1960 (n) (W. Afr.).

Hough, Henry Beetle
That Lofty Sky. New York, 1941 (n) (S. Afr.).

Hurst, Ida
A Vagabond Typist in Africa, Abyssinia, and The Gulf. Illus. London, 1937 (a, t); *African Heartbeat*. London, 1947 (n) (C. Afr.).

Hutchinson, Ray Coryton
The Answering Glory. London, 1932 (n) (W. Afr.).

Huxley, Elspeth
Note: All the undermentioned works were originally published in London and have Kenya and/or East Africa for their locale, unless otherwise notated. *Red Strangers*. 16 plates from photographs by the author. 1939 (h, n); *East Africa*. 1941 (t, e); *White Man's Country: Lord Delamere and the Making of Kenya*. 1935, 2 vols. (b); *The Sorcerer's Apprentice*. 1949 (t); *The Walled City*. 1949 (n) (W. Afr.); *A Thing to Love*. 1954 (n); *Four Guineas: A Journey through West Africa*. 1954 (t); *The Red Rock Wilderness*. 1957 (n) (C. Afr.); *The Flame Trees of Thika*. 1959 (t); *The Mottled*

Lizard. 1962 (e, t); *The Merry Hippo.* 1963 (b, d); *Back Street New World: A Look at Immigrants in Britain.* 1964 (e); *Forks and Hope: An African Notebook.* 1964 (m, a); *A Man from Nowhere.* 1964 (n).

Illsley, William
Wagon on Fire. London, 1955 (n) (Orange Free State).

Jenkins, Geoffrey
A Twist of Sand. London, 1959 (n) (S. W. Afr.); *Hunter Killer.* London, 1966 (n) (S. Afr.).

Jervis, V. N. S. (pseud.: Jane England)
Bull Whip. New York, 1929 (n) (Rhodesia); *Red Earth.* New York, 1926 (n) (Rhodesia); *Flowering Harvest.* New York, 1942 (n) (Rhodesia); *No Brighter Dawn.* New York, 1943 (n) (Rhodesia).

Johnston, Sir H(arry) H(amilton)
Selective list: *The History of a Slave.* London, 1889 (n, b); *The Negro in the New World.* London, 1910 (e); *The Man Who Did the Right Thing.* London, 1921 (n) (E. Afr.); *The Story of My Life.* 1923 (a).

Jones, Denys
Look Not Upon Me. London, 1954 (n) (Kenya).

Jordan, Humphrey
A Valley Decides. London, 1952 (n) (E. Afr.); *No One Way.* London, 1955 (n) (E. Afr.).

Kampf, Harold Bertram (pseud.: H. B. Kaye)
A Touch of the Sun. London, 1952 (n) (E. Afr.); *Death Is a Black Camel.* London, 1952 (n) (E. Afr.).

Karp, David
The Day of the Monkey. New York, 1955 (n) (E. Afr.).

Kaye, H. B.
See Kampf, Harold Bertram

Kaye, Mary Margaret
House of Shade. London, 1960 (n) (Zanzibar).

Kessel, Joseph
The Lion. Tr. (from French) Peter Green. New York, 1960 (n) (Kenya).

Kirk, Laurence
    See Simson, Eric Andrew

Krepps, Robert Wilson
    Field of Night. New York, 1948 (n) (E. Afr.); *The Courts
    of the Lion.* London, 1954 (n) (E. Afr.); *Tell It on the
    Drums.* London, 1955 (n) (E. Afr.); *Earthshaker.* London,
    1958 (n) (E. Afr.).

Laing, Nora
    The South African. London, 1952 (n).

Lait, Robert
    The Second Yoke. London, 1960 (n) (E. Afr.); *The Africans.*
    London, 1961 (Am. edn., *Honey for Tomorrow*) (n) (E.
    Afr.); *Massacre.* London, 1963 (n) (E. Afr.).

Lamptey, Jonas
    The Village in the Trees. London, 1955 (n) (W. Afr.).

Lartéguy, Jean
    Les chimères noires. Paris, 1963. Tr. Xan Fielding as *The
    Hounds of Hell.* New York, London, 1966 (n) (Katanga,
    Congo).

Latimer, Jonathan
    Dark Memory. New York, 1940 (n) (Belgian Congo).

Leavis, Ronald
    A Voice in Every Wind. London, 1953 (C. Afr.); *Hippodile.*
    London, 1961 (n) (E. Afr.).

Lee, Jonathan
    The Fate of the Grosvenor. New York, 1938 (n) (S. Afr.).

Leigh, Michael
    Cross of Fire. London, 1949 (n) (S. Afr.).

Lister, S. (pseud.)
    Everything Smelt of Kippers. London, 1957 (n) (Tangan-
    yika).

Livingstone, C. R.
    The Earth Is Red. London, 1946 (n) (E. Afr.).

Llewellyn, Richard
    A Man in a Mirror. New York, London, 1961 (n) (E. Afr.).

Lloyd, Lavender
    The Verandah Room. London, 1955 (n) (E. Afr.).

Loader, W. R.
    No Joy of Africa. London, 1955 (n) (W. Afr.); *The Guinea Stamp*. London, 1956 (n) (W. Afr.).

Lodwick, John
    Equator. London, 1957 (n).

Loe, Gladys St. John–
    Smoking Altars. New York, 1936 (n) (E. Afr.).

Lutken, Otto
    Congo Gods. Tr. from Danish. New York, 1929 (n).

Lyndon, Barrie
    Sundown. New York, 1941 (n) (Kenya).

MacArthur, David Wilson
    They Sailed for Senegal. London, 1938 (n, h).

MacCarthy, John Lloyd (pseud.: Desmond Cory)
    Height of Day. London, 1955 (n) (C. Afr.).

MacDonald, Sheila
    Sally in Rhodesia. New York, 1932 (n); *The Outsider*. New York, 1933 (n) (S. Afr.); *Mr. Crusoe's Young Woman*. New York, 1935 (n) (S. Afr.).

MacInnes, Colin
    City of Spades. London, 1957 (n) (Africans and W. Indians in England).

Mackay, Mercedes
    Shining Trouble. London, 1956 (n) (Kenya).

Mackenzie, Jean
    African Clearings. Boston, 1924 (e) (Cameroon); *A Lucky Lad*. London, 1926 (b of Rev. Robert Mackenzie); *African Adventurers*. London, 1931 (e, s); *The Trader's Wife*. London, 1930 (n) (W. Afr.); *Talking Woman*. London, 1936 (fables).

Mackenzie, Nigel
    The Dark Night. London, 1950 (n) (S. Afr.); *Murder for Two*. London, 1951 (n) (S. Afr.); *Bandit's Moon*. Lon-

don, 1952 (n) (S. Afr.); *Pyramid of Death*. London, 1953 (n) (S. Afr.).

MacVicar, Angus
Fugitive's Road. London, 1952 (n) (S. Africans in England).

Manners-Sutton, Doris
Black Gold. New York, 1934 (n) (Belgian Congo).

Mannix, Daniel Pratt
(with John A. Hunter) *African Bush Adventures*. London, 1954 (b, t).

Mathew, David
The Mango on the Mango Tree. London, 1950 (n) (C. Afr.).

Maugham, Robin (Robert Cecil Romer Maugham)
Behind the Mirror. New York, London, 1955 (n) (Tanganyika).

Meiring, Desmond
The Man with No Shadow. London, 1962 (n) (S. Afr.).

Mercer, Charles
Rachel Cade. New York, 1956 (n) (Congo); *Pilgrim Strangers*. New York, 1961 (n) (Congo); *Promise Morning*. New York, 1966 (n) (Congo).

Meredith, Peter
Floodwater. London, 1950 (n) (S. Afr.); *The Crocodile Man*. London, 1951 (n) (W. Afr.).

Miller, Wolfe
Man in the Background. London, 1958 (n) (S. Afr.).

Mills, Dorothy
The Dark Gods. London, 1925 (n) (W. Afr.).

Mitchell, Mary
Black Crusade. London, 1949 (n) (C. Afr.).

Mitchison, Naomi
When We Become Men. London, 1965 (n) (Bechuanaland).

Monsarrat, Nicholas
The Tribe That Lost Its Head. London, 1956 (n) (S. Afr.).

Moosdorf, Johanna
    Flight to Africa. Tr. (from German) Richard and Clara
    Winston. London, 1955 (n) (French Equatorial Afr.).

Moray, Helga
    Untamed. New York, 1950 (n) (S. Afr.).

Mordaunt, Evelyn (pseud.: Elinor Mordaunt)
    Pity of the World. New York, 1939 (n) (E. Afr.).

Mostyn, Anita Mary (pseud.: Ann Fielding)
    The Noxious Weed. London, 1951 (n) (W. Afr.); *Ashanti*
    Blood. London, 1952 (n) (W. Afr.).

Murray, Audrey Alison
    The Blanket. London, 1957 (n) (S. Afr.).

Murray, Marris
    The Fire Raisers. London, 1953 (n) (S. Afr.).

Muskett, Netta
    Flame of the Forest. London, 1958, repr. 1965 (n) (Sierra
    Leone).

O'Donnell, E.
    Night Cometh. New York, 1960 (n) (S. Afr.).

Olivier, Gillian
    Turn But a Stone. London, 1949 (n) (E. Afr.).

Packer, Joy
    Valley of the Vines. London, 1956 (n) (S. Afr.); *Moon by*
    Night. London, 1957 (n) (S. Afr.); *High Roof.* 1960 (n)
    (S. Afr.); *The Glass Barrier.* London, 1961 (n) (S. Afr.).

Parker, Gilbert
    The Judgment House. London, 1913 (n) (S. Afr.).

Pearson, John
    Gone to Timbuctoo. London, 1962 (n) (W. Afr.).

Perham, Margery
    Major Dane's Garden. London, 1925 (n) (E. Afr.).

Peterson, Margaret
    Dust of Desire. London, 1922 (n) (E. Afr.).

Pilotaz, Paul
    Man Alone. Tr. (from French) J. H. F. McEwen. London,
    1952 (n) (W. Afr.).

Pomeroy, Miggs
   The Janus Lovers. New York, 1966 (n) (E. Afr.).

Powys, Llewellyn
   Ebony and Ivory. With Preface by Theodore Dreiser. New York, 1923 (s) (E. Afr.); *Black Laughter*. London, 1925 (s) (E. Afr.).

Presland, J.
   See Skelton, Gladys

Prevost, Francis
   See Battersby, Henry F. P.

Prokosch, Frederick
   Storm and Echo. New York, 1948 (n) (C. Afr.).

Rand, James S.
   Run for the Trees. London, 1966 (n) (E. Afr.).

Rattray, Robert S.
   The Leopard Priestess. London, 1934 (n) (W. Afr.).

Rayner, William
   The Reapers. London, 1961 (n) (S. Afr.).

Reed, Douglas
   Reasons of Health. London, 1949 (n) (S. Africans in England).

Reid, Victor Stafford
   The Leopard. London, 1958 (n) (Kenya).

Richmond, Mary
   All That Glitters. London, 1954 (n) (S. Afr.).

Riddell, Florence
   Castles in Kenya, New York, 1929 (n); *Suspicion*. New York, 1931 (n) (Kenya); *Kismet in Kenya*. New York, 1932 (n); *Wives Win*. New York, 1932 (n) (Kenya); *Misty Pathway*. New York, 1934 (n) (Kenya).

Roberts, Esther
   The Black Spear. London, 1950 (n) (based on the life of Chaka, King of the Zulus).

Roussel, Raymond
   Impressions of Africa. Tr. (from French) Lindy Foord and Rayner Heppenstall. London, 1966 (n).

Ruark, Robert
    Something of Value. New York, 1955 (n) (Kenya); *Uhuru*.
    New York, 1962 (n) (E. Afr.).
Saint John-Loe, Gladys
    See Loe, Gladys St. John-
Scholefield, Alan
    A View of Vultures. London, 1966 (n) (S. Afr.).
Scobie, Alastair
    The Cape Town Affair. London, 1952 (n) (S. Afr.).
Severn, David
    See Unwin, David Stoor
Shaw, George Bernard
    The Adventures of the Black Girl in Her Search for God.
    London, 1932 (n).
Shaw, Robert
    The Sun Doctor. London, 1961 (n) (W. Afr.).
Shiel, Matthew Phipps
    Children of the Wind. New York, 1923 (n) (S. C. Afr.).
Simms, Katharine Louisa
    Lightning on the Veld. London, 1948 (n) (S. Afr.); *Under
    the Kopje*. London, 1950 (n) (S. Afr.).
Simson, Eric Andrew (pseud.: Laurence Kirk)
    Halfway to Paradise. London, Edinburgh, 1951 (n)
    (Kenya).
Skelton, Gladys (pseud.: J. Presland)
    Dominion. New York, 1925 (n) (S. Afr.).
Sligh, Nigel
    Copperbelt. London, 1949 (n) (Rhodesia); *The Beast with
    Two Backs*. London, 1951 (n) (S. Afr.); *The Overlords*.
    London, 1955 (n) (S. Afr.).
Smith, Anthony
    Sea Never Dry. London, 1958 (n) (W. Afr.).
Smith, Frederick E.
    Laws Be Their Enemy. London, 1955 (n) (S. Afr.).

Smith, Walton H.
    Shadow River. New York, 1927 (n) (Congo).

Southon, A. E. H.
    The Whispering Bush. London, 1924 (s); *The Laughing Ghost*. London, 1928 (s) (W. Afr.).

Sowden, Lewis
    Family Cromer. London, 1952 (n) (S. Afr.); *The Crooked Bluegum*. London, 1955 (n) (S. Afr.).

Stacey, Tom
    The Brothers M. London, 1960 (n) (E. Afr.).

Standish, Robert
    See Gerahty, D. C.

Steen, Marguerite
    The Sun Is My Undoing. London, 1941 (n) (W. Afr.); *Twilight on the Floods*. London, 1949 (n) (W. Afr.).

Stern, James
    The Heartless Land. London, 1932 (s) (Rhodesia).

Stinetorf, Louise
    White Witch Doctor. New York, 1950 (n) (C. Afr.); *Beyond the Hungry Country*. New York, 1954 (n) (C. Afr.).

Stockley, Cynthia
    Selective list: *Poppy*. London, 1910 (n) (S. Afr.); *Wild Honey*. London, 1914, repr. 1919, 1925 (n) (S. Afr.); *Perilous Women: A Story of the South African Veld*. London, 1924 (n); *Dalla, the Lion Cub*. New York, 1924 (n) (S. Afr.); *Dice of God*. New York, 1926 (n) (S. Afr.); *The Leopard in the Bush: A Sequel to Dalla, the Lion Cub*. London, New York, 1928 (n) (S. Afr.); *Tagati Magic*. London, 1928 (Am. edn., *Tagati*) (n) (S. Afr.); *Kraal Baby*. London, 1933 (n) (S. Afr.).

Stoll, Dennis Gray (pseud.: Denys Craig)
    Man in Ebony, with Introd. by Joyce Cary. London, 1950 (n) (French W. Afr.).

Stoneham, Charles T.
    The White Hunter. London, 1932 (n) (S. Afr.); *Elephant*

Brother. London, 1934 (n) (S. Afr.); *Kenya Mystery.* London, 1954 (n).

Tharaud, Jerome and Jean
Long Walk of Samba Diouf. Tr. (from French) Willis Steel. New York, 1924 (n) (Senegal).

Thomas, E. W.
Playing Poet in the South. London, 1919 (a, t) (S. Afr.); *Bushman Stories.* London, 1950 (s).

Thompson, Laurence V.
Time to Laugh. New York, 1954 (n) (Sudan).

Thorndike, Jeanie Paine
Not to the Strong. New York, 1941 (n) (Kenya).

Thornhill, O.
Mobree of the Black Coast. Nairobi, Kenya: English Press Ltd., 1955 (n) (E. Afr.).

Unwin, David Stoor (pseud.: David Severn)
The Governor's Wife. London, 1954 (n) (E. Afr.).

Viertel, Peter
White Hunter, Black Heart. New York, 1953 (n) (Congo).

Walker, Oliver
Proud Zulu. London, 1949 (n) (story of Chaka, King of the Zulus); *Wanton City.* London, 1949 (n) (S. Afr.); *Shapeless Flame.* London, 1951 (n) (S. Afr.).

Wallace, Edgar
Selective list. All the undermentioned works were originally published in London. Most of the fiction listed has West Africa for its locale. *Writ in Barracks.* 1900 (p); *Unofficial Despatches.* 1901 (e); *Sanders of the River.* 1911 (n); *The People of the River.* 1912 (s); *Bosambo of the River.* 1914 (s); *Bones.* 1915 (n); *Keeper of the King's Peace.* 1917 (n); *Lieutenant Bones.* 1918, repr. 1952 (n); *Sandi, the King-Maker.* 1922 (n); *Sanders.* 1925 (n); *Again Sanders.* 1928 (n); *Mr. Commissioner Sanders.* 1931 (n).

Walmsley, Leo
Toro of the Little People. London, 1926 (n) (C. Afr.).

Warner, Esther S(ietmann)
New Story in a Strange Land. Boston, 1948 (a); *The Silk-Cotton Tree*. London, 1958 (n) (Liberia); *Seven Days to Lomaland*. Boston, 1954 (Brit. edn., *Trial by Sasswood*, 1955) (a) (Liberia).

Waugh, Evelyn
Remote People. London, 1931 (Am. edn., *They Were Still Dancing*, 1932) (t, a); *Black Mischief*. London, 1932 (n) (E. Afr.); *Waugh in Abyssinia*. London, 1936 (t); *Scoop*. London, 1938 (n) (E. Afr.); *A Tourist in Africa*. London, 1960 (t).

Weatherby, W. J.
Out of Hiding. London, 1966 (n) (Africans in New York).

Webster, Elizabeth Cary
Ceremony of Innocence. London, 1949 (n) (S. Afr.).

Webster, F. A. M.
Black Shadow. New York, 1923 (n) (Africa, and Harlem, New York City); *Land of Forgotten Women*. London, 1950 (n) (C. Afr.).

Welman, John B.
A Thorny Wilderness. London, 1952 (n) (W. Afr.).

Wheatley, Dennis
The Fabulous Valley. London, 1934 (n) (Kalahari, S. Afr.).

White, James D.
Flamingo Lake. London, 1954 (n) (E. Afr.).

White, Jon
Build Us a Dam. London, 1955 (n) (S. Afr.).

White, Stewart Edward
Simba. New York, 1918 (n) (E. Afr.); *Back of Beyond*. New York, 1927 (n) (E. Afr.); *Lions in the Path*. New York, 1927 (t).

Wilding, Diana
Holiday Girl. London, 1955 (n) (E. Afr.).

Wiles, J.
The Moon to Play With. London, 1954 (n) (S. Afr.).

Williamson, Thames Ross (pseuds.: Edward Dragonet, Waldo Fleming, S. S. Smith, and Gregory Trent)
Talking Drums. London, 1936 (n) (W. Afr.).

Wilson, John Anthony Burgess (pseud.: Anthony Burgess)
Devil of a State. London, 1961 (n) (E. Afr.).

Wingate, Peter
Rain Doctor. London, 1958 (n) (E. Afr.).

Woodyatt, Charles Drummond
Satan's Playground. New York, 1934 (n) (W. Afr.).

Wren, P(ercival) C.
The Uniform of Glory. London, 1941 (n) (W. Afr.).

Wyllie, John
Riot. London, 1954 (n) (W. Afr.).

Young, Francis Brett
The Crescent Moon. London, 1918 (n) (C. Afr.); *Woodsmoke*. London, 1924 (n) (S. Afr.); *Sea Horses*. London, 1952 (n) (E. Afr.); *Jim Redlake*. London, 1930 (Am edn., *The Redlakes*) (n) (S. Afr.); *They Seek a Country*. London, 1937 (n) (S. Afr.); *The City of Gold*. London, 1939 (n) (S. Afr.).

III. Anthologies

Beier, Ulli, ed.
(with George Moore) *Modern Poetry from Africa*. London, 1963; *African Poetry*. Illus. Susanne Wenger. London, 1966 [tr. of poems from several African languages into Eng.]; *Introduction to African Literature*. Evanston, Ill., 1967.

Brent, P. L., ed.
Young Commonwealth Poets. London, 1965 (in association with the Cardiff Commonwealth Arts Festival).

Butler, Guy, ed.
A Book of South African Verse. London, Cape Town [Oxford Univ. Pr.], 1959.

Edwards, Paul, ed.
Modern African Narrative. London, 1966.

Grove, Alewyn, and Charles Harvey, eds.
Afrikaans Poems (with Eng. tr.). Oxford, 1964.

Hughes, Langston, ed.
An African Treasury. New York, 1960 [paperback edn., 1961];
(with Christiane Reygnault) *Anthologie Africaine et Mala-
gache*. Paris, 1962; *Poems from Black Africa*. Bloomington,
Ind., 1963.

Johnston, H. A. S., ed. and tr.
A Selection of Hausa Stories. Oxford, 1966.

Komey, E. A., and Ezekiel Mphahlele, eds.
Modern African Stories. London, 1965.

Leslan, Charlotte, and Wolf Leslan
African Folktales. New York, 1963.

Moore, George, ed.
Seven African Writers. London, 1962; (with Ulli Beier) *Modern Poetry from Africa*. London, 1963.

Morris, Henry F., ed.
The Heroic Recitations of the Bahima of Ankole. Oxford, 1964.

Mphahlele, Ezekiel, ed.
(with E. A. Komey) *Modern African Stories*. London, 1965;
New Writing in Africa. London, 1967.

Parnwell, E. C., ed.
Stories of Africa. London, 1949.

Press, John, ed.
*Commonwealth Literature: Unity and Diversity in a Common
Culture*. London, 1965.

Reed, John, and Clive Wake, eds.
A Book of African Verse. London, Ibadan [Heinemann], 1964.

Rive, Richard, ed.
*Quartet: New Voices from South Africa—Alex La Guma, James
Matthews, Alf Wanneburgh, Richard Rive*. New York, 1963;
Modern African Prose. London, 1965.

Rutherford, Peggy, ed.
  Darkness and Light. London, 1958 (Am. edn., *African Voices*, 1960).
Swanzy, Henry, ed.
  Voices of Ghana. Accra, 1958.
Tibble, Anne
  African-English Literature. New York, 1965.
Whitely, W. H., ed.
  A Selection of African Prose: Vol. I, *Traditional Oral Texts;* Vol. II, *Written Prose*. Oxford, 1964.
Wright, D., ed.
  South African Stories. London, 1966.

IV. Literary Studies and Criticism

Andrzejewski, B. W., and I. M. Lewis, eds.
  Somali Poetry. Oxford, 1964.
Balandier, Georges
  Ambiguous Africa. Tr. (from French) Helen Weaver. New York, 1966.
Baldwin, James
  Nobody Knows My Name. New York, 1961.
Beier, Ulli
  "First Fruits: A Literary Letter from Nigeria," in *New York Times Book Review* (Jan. 28, 1962), pp. 34-35.
Chadwick, H. Munro, and N. Kershaw Chadwick
  The Growth of Literature. Cambridge Univ. Pr., 1932, 3 vols. See Vol. 3.
Collins, Harold R.
  "Joyce Cary's Troublesome Africans," in *Antioch Review*, XIII (1953), 397-406.
Conrad, Joseph
  Joseph Conrad's Diary of His Journey Up the Valley of the Congo in 1890, with Introd. and Notes by Richard Curle. London, 1926.

Furay, Michael
"Négritude—a Romantic Myth?" in *The New Republic* (July 2, 1966), pp. 32-35.

Gleason, Judith Illsley
This Africa: Novels by West Africans in English and French. Evanston, Ill., 1965.

Gurrey, P., and P. Itayemi
Folk Tales and Fables. London, 1953.

Haggard, Lilian R.
The Cloak That I Left. London, 1951 (b of [Sir] H. Rider Haggard).

Hobman, D. L.
Olive Schreiner: Her Friends and Times. London, 1955.

Hollis, Christopher
Evelyn Waugh. London, 1954.

Howe, Susanne
Novels of Empire. New York, 1949.

Jabavu, D. D. T.
Bantu Literature. Johannesburg, 1921.

Jahn, Janheinz
Muntu. Dusseldorf, 1958. Tr. (from German) Marjorie Grene. New York, London, 1961.

Jahn, Janheinz, and John Ramsaran
Approaches to African Literature. Ibadan, Nigeria, 1959.

Jean-Aubry, G.
Joseph Conrad in the Congo. London, 1926; *The Sea Dreamer.* London, 1957.

Jones, Eldred
Othello's Countrymen: The African in English Renaissance Drama. London, 1965.

Kesteloot, Lilyan
Les Écrivains noires de langue française. Thèse presentée pour l'obtention du doctorat en philogie romane (Université Libre de Bruxelles, Institut de Sociologie), 1963.

Lane, Margaret
Edgar Wallace: The Biography of a Phenomenon. London, 1938, rev. 1964.

MacCarthy, Desmond
"Oom Paul and Cecil Rhodes," in *Portraits*, I, 204-209. London, 1952.

Mahood, M(olly) M.
Joyce Cary's Africa. London, 1964.

Meloné, Thomas
De la négritude dans la littérature negro-africaine. Paris: Présence Africaine, 1962.

Mesnet, M. B.
Graham Greene and "The Heart of the Matter": An Essay. London, 1954.

Mphahlele, Ezekiel
The African Image. London, 1962.

Povey, John
"Dakar: An African Rendez-vous," in *Africa Today*, XIII, No. 5 (May, 1966), 4-6.

Présence Africaine, Editions
Hommage à René Maran. Paris, 1965 (collection of essays and tributes).

Radin, Paul, and J. J. Sweeney
African Folktales and Sculpture. London, 1965.

Schmidt, Nancy Jeanne
"An Anthropological Analysis of Nigerian Fiction." Unpublished diss. submitted for Ph.D. degree at Northwestern University, Evanston, Ill.

Smith, Janet Adam
John Buchan. London, 1965 (b).

Snyman, J. F. L.
The Works of S. G. Millin. Central News Agency Ltd., S. Afr., 1955.

Stopp, F.
Evelyn Waugh: Portrait of an Artist. Boston, 1958 (b, e).

Stuart-Young, J. M.
Chits from West Africa. London, 1923 (s, e).

Wauthier, Claude
The Literature and Thought of Modern Africa. New York, London, 1966 (c).

Werner, A.
    African Mythology. London, 1925.
Wright, Andrew
    Joyce Cary: A Preface to His Novels. New York, 1957.

V. Background and Related Material

Abrahams, W. E.
    The Mind of Africa. London, 1962.
Ainslie, Rosalynde
    The Press in Africa. London, 1966.
Ajayi, J. F. Ade
    Christian Missions in Nigeria, 1841-1891. Evanston, Ill., 1965.
Ardrey, Robert
    African Genesis. New York, 1961.
Awolowo, Obafemi
    Awo, The Autobiography of Chief Obafemi Awolowo. Cambrige Univ. Pr., 1960.
Becker, Peter
    Path of Blood. London, 1962 (history of Mzilikazi, the Zulu chieftain).
Beier, Ulli
    Yemi Bisiri. Mbari, Northwestern Univ. Pr., 1964 (brass art of Ogboni secret society).
Biggers, John
    Ananse: The Web of Life in Africa. Austin, Texas: Univ. Texas Pr., 1962.
Black, Margaret
    No Room for Tourists. London, 1965 (a) (S. Afr.).
Blaxall, Arthur
    Suspended Sentence. London, 1966.
Brown, Douglas
    Against the World: A Study of White South African Attitudes. London, 1966.
Buchan, John (Baron Tweedsmuir)
    The African Colony: Studies in the Reconstruction. London,

1903; *The History of the South African Forces in France.* London, 1920.

Cameron, James
The African Revolution. London, 1961.

Carter, Gwendolen M.
Independence for Africa. New York, 1961; ed., *African One Party States.* Ithaca, N. Y., 1962.

Cary, Joyce
Britain and West Africa. London, 1946, rev. 1947; *Freedom and Other Writings on Africa.* Austin, Texas: Univ. Texas Pr., 1962.

Cope, John
South Africa. London, 1965.

Curtin, Philip D.
The Image of Africa: British Ideas and Actions, 1780-1850. Madison, Wisc.: Univ. Wisconsin Pr., 1964 (W. Afr.).

Davidson, Basil
The Lost Cities of Africa. Boston, 1959; *The African Past.* Boston, 1964; *Africa: History of a Continent.* New York, 1966.

Dia, Mamadou
The African Nations and World Solidarity. Tr. (from French) Mercer Cook. New York, 1962.

Elisofon, Eliot, ed.
Sculpture of Africa. Text by William Fagg, design by Bernard Quint. London, 1958.

Fagg, William
Nigerian Images. London, 1963 (art); *Tribes and Forms in Africa Art.* London, 1966 (c on art works).

Ferkiss, Victor C.
Africa's Search for Identity. New York, 1966.

First, Ruth (pseud.)
117 Days. New York, 1965 (a) (record of prison detention in S. Afr.).

Frobenius, Leo
African Genesis. Tr. (from German) Douglas C. Fox. New York, 1937.

Gide, André
Voyage au Congo. Paris, 1927. Tr. Dorothy Bussy as *Travels in the Congo.* New York, London, 1929, paperback repr. [Univ. California Pr.] 1962.

Grzimek, Bernhard
Doctor Jimik, I Presume. Tr. (from German) R. H. Stevens. London, 1955 (W. Afr.); (with Michael Grzimek) *Serengeti Shall Not Die.* Tr. (from German) E. L. and D. Rewald. New York, 1961 (Tanganyika).

Hallet, Jean-Pierre
Congo Kitabu. New York, 1966 (a) (C. Afr.).

Halpern, Jack
South Africa's Hostages: Basutoland, Bechuanaland and Swaziland. London, 1966 [Penguin].

Hempstone, Smith
The New Africa. London, 1961 (Am. edn., *Africa, Angry Young Giant*) (e); *Katanga Report.* London, 1962.

Herskovits, Melville J.
Dahomey, an Ancient African Kingdom. New York, 1938, 2 vols.; *The Myth of the Negro Past.* New York, 1941, repr. 1958; (with Frances Herskovits) *Dahomean Narrative.* London, 1958.

Huxley, Elspeth, and Margery Perham
Race and Politics in Kenya. London, 1954.

Ikeotunye, V. C.
Zik of New Africa. London, 1961 (b).

Italiaander, Rolf
The New Leaders of Africa. London, 1961.

Jahn, Janheinz
Through African Doors. Tr. (from German) Oliver Coburn. London, 1962 (W. Afr.).

Jahoda, Gustav
White Man. London, 1961.

Kaunda, K. D.
Zambia Shall Be Free. London, 1962.

Kitchen, Helen, ed.
Africa Report: A Handbook of African Affairs. New York, 1965.

Kopytoff, Jean Herskovits
A Preface to Modern Nigeria: The "Sierra Leonians" in Yoruba, 1830-1890. Madison, Wisc., 1965.

Kuper, Hilda
An African Aristocracy: Rank among the Swazi of Bechuanaland. London, 1947, repr. 1961; *The Uniform of Colour: A Study of White-Black Relationships in Swaziland.* Johannesburg: Witwatersrand Univ. Pr., 1947; *The Swazi.* London, 1952.

Lasky, Melvin J.
Africa for Beginners. Philadelphia, 1962.

Leakey, L. S. B.
Progress and Evolution of Man in Africa. London, 1962.

Lomax, Louis E.
The Reluctant African. New York, 1960 (a) (Americans in Africa).

Lugard, (Lord) Frederick
The Diaries. Ed. Margery Perham. Northwestern Univ. Pr., African Studies No. 3. Evanston, Ill., 1959, 3 vols.; 1 vol., 1963.

Malinowski, Bronislaw
The Dynamics of Culture. New Haven, Conn., 1961.

Mandela, Nelson
No Easy Walk to Freedom. London, 1965 (a) (S. Afr.).

Mannix, Daniel, and Malcolm Cowley
Black Cargoes. New York, 1962 (slave trade).

Martin, Bernard, and Mark Spurrell, eds.
The Journal of a Slave Trader (John Newton) 1750-1754, with Newton's "Thoughts upon the African Slave Trade." London: Epworth Pr., 1962.

Mboya, Tom
Freedom and After. Boston, 1963 (Kenya).

Merriam, Alan P.
The Anthropology of Music. Evanston, Ill., 1964.

Molnar, Thomas
Africa: A Political Travelogue. New York, 1965.

Morris, Donald R.
The Washing of the Spears: The Rise and Fall of the Zulu Nation. New York, 1965.

Newbury, C. W.
The Western Slave Coast and Its Rulers. London, 1961.

Nicol, Davidson
Africa: A Subjective View. London, 1965.

O'Callaghan, Sean
The Slave Trade Today. New York, 1962.

Parrinder, Geoffrey
West African Religion. London, 1961.

Perham, Margery, ed.
(with Jack Simmons) *African Discovery: An Anthology of Exploration.* London, 1963; *Ten Africans: A Collection of Life Stories.* Mbari, Northwestern Univ. Pr., 1963.

Présence Africaine, XIV-XV (1957). Contributions au Premier Congrès des Ecrivains et Artistes Noirs.

Quigg, Philip, ed.
Africa. New York, 1964.

Ritter, E. A.
Shaka Zulu. London, 1955 (history of Chaka, King of the Zulus).

Rittner, Peter
The Death of Africa. New York, 1960.

Robinson, Ronald, and John Gallagher (with Alice Denny)
Africa and the Victorians. New York, 1965.

Sachs, Wulf
Black Hamlet. Boston, 1947.

Schapera, I.
Married Life in an African Tribe. Evanston, Ill., 1966.

Schreiner, Olive
    A Letter on the Jew. Cape Town, S. Afr., 1906.

Smith, Anthony
    High Street Africa. London, 1961 (t, a); *Throw Out Two Hands*. London, 1963.

Stacey, Tom
    Summons to Ruwenzori. London, 1965 (Bakonjo tribe, Uganda).

Tajfel, Henri, and John L. Dawson, eds.
    Disappointed Guests. Essays by African, Asian and West Indian Students. London, 1965.

Turnbull, Colin
    The Forest People. New York, 1961 (Bambute tribe, Congo); *The Lonely African*. New York, 1963; *The Peoples of Africa*. Chicago, 1963; *Wayward Servants: The Two Worlds of the African Pygmies*. Published for American Museum of Natural History by Natural History Pr., N. Y., 1965.

Van Rensburg, Patrick
    Guilty Land. London, 1961 (S. Afr.).

Watt, Elizabeth Paris
    Febana. London, 1962 (Zulu history).

White, Stewart Edward
    Rediscovered Country. New York, 1915.

Wilson, Angus
    "The Whites in South Africa," in *Partisan Review*, XXVIII, Nos. 5-6 (1961), 612-32.

Wright, Richard
    Black Power. New York, 1954 (a, t) (Americans in Africa).

VI. Literary Journals Published in Book Form

Black Orpheus. Ed. Ulli Beier. Available from Northwestern Univ. Pr., Evanston, Ill.

The Journal of Commonwealth Literature. Ed. Arthur Ravenscroft.

Univ. of Leeds, England. Available from Heinemann Educational Books Ltd., London.

Présence Africaine. Available from Editions Présence Africaine, Paris.

Index

311